The Silent Prologue

The Silent Prologue

How Judicial Philosophies Shape Our Constitutional Rights

OFER RABAN

George Mason
University Press

Fairfax, Virginia

The Silent Prologue
How Judicial Philosophies
Shape Our Constitutional Rights

By Ofer Raban

George Mason University Press
Fairfax, Virginia

ISBN: 978-1-942695-20-2 (trade paper)

First edition.

Library of Congress Cataloging-in-Publication Data forthcoming.

Printed in the United States of America

Designed by Emily L. Cole

Acknowledgments

This book is the fruit of years of researching and teaching jurisprudence and constitutional law. Many thanks go to my diligent research assistants—Kelsie Crippen, Benjamin Farkash, Madeline Lorang, and Esther Sherman; to Aaron Mccollough and Emily Cole of GMU Press, who expertly guided this project; and to the two helpful proofreaders—the fastidious Rose Fitzpatrick and the judicious Marcella Drula-Johnston. Thank you all for helping bring this long-running project to completion!

"What rights and liberties does the Constitution protect? In this original and intriguing new book, Raban explores this doctrinal question by showing how competing judicial philosophies bear on it. He demonstrates how different judicial philosophies may produce different results, and evaluates such philosophies along two dimensions: the substantive quality of the results each one tends to produce, and the procedural legitimacy of the decision-making process each one recommends. The discussion is unusually lucid, accessible, and engaging. Raban writes in simple, unpretentious prose and uses fresh, less well-known cases to great effect, making complex constitutional doctrine, abstract philosophical claims, and the relations among them come to life. The book is an exciting new addition to constitutional scholarship. Students new to the subject and seasoned specialists alike have much to learn from it."

Nicos Stavropoulos
Faculty of Law,
University of Oxford

Table of Contents

CHAPTER 1

Introduction: The U.S. Constitution and Constitutional Interpretation

I. Constitutional Rights

The U.S. Constitution is the product of a constitutional violation. In 1781, during the War of Independence, the thirteen original American states joined forces by signing into The Articles of Confederation—the first constitution of the United States. It soon became clear, however, that the confederation they formed was too weak. The states were conducting themselves in a mutually jealous and uncooperative manner, and the American union was slowly falling apart. A convention was therefore assembled in 1787, for the explicit purpose of amending the Articles of Confederation and creating a stronger union. But instead of proposing amendments to the Articles of Confederation, the delegates opted to propose a whole new document that violated some key provisions of the Articles—including the crucial requirement that any change be approved by the unanimous consent of all thirteen states. The proposed Constitution would become effective once ratified by nine out of the thirteen states (though only in regard to the states that ratified it).

When the proposal was first presented to Congress, it produced an uproar among its members and calls for an official censure of the delegates. But supporters of the proposed new Constitution prevailed: after all, something had to be done about the crumbling American union. Before long, Congress sent the newly proposed document for ratification by the states.[1] By 1790, all thirteen states had ratified the new Constitution. A year later, ten new provisions were added to the original document. These ten amendments, which are collectively known as the Bill of Rights, contain our canonical constitutional rights and liberties, including the freedom of speech and religion, the freedom from unreasonable searches and seizures, the right to a trial by jury, and many more.

The speed with which the Bill of Rights was drafted and ratified appears remarkable: it took 142 years for the next ten amendments to be adopted and ratified. However, the original document and the Bill of Rights were, in fact, parts of a single political package. Since the new Constitution granted the federal government significant new powers that did not exist under the Articles of Confederation (including the creation of a federal presidency, a federal judiciary, and the powers to tax and to regulate the national economy), the document provoked fears of an overly powerful—and potentially tyrannical—federal government. These fears generated substantial opposition to the new Constitution, making ratification far from certain.[2] In an effort to reduce opposition and secure ratification, proponents of the Constitution agreed to a Bill of Rights that would restrict the powers of the newly created government. And so, following the Constitution's successful ratification, the first ten amendments were promptly adopted and ratified.

Accordingly, it was the federal government, and the federal government alone, that was originally restricted by the Bill of Rights.[3] The states remained free to ignore its provisions—which they surely did. For example, some states enacted laws that mandated membership in a church and were incompatible with the First Amendment's freedom of religion,[4] while others usurped private land without adequate compensation in a manner that conflicted with the Takings Clause of the Fifth Amendment.[5] But since the Bill of Rights did not apply to the states, such conduct was perfectly lawful.

This state of affairs began to change after the Civil War, following the 1868 adoption of the Fourteenth Amendment—the second of the three Civil War amendments that etched the lessons of that bloody conflict into the Federal Constitution. Unlike the Bill of Rights, the Civil War amendments limited the powers of the *states*, since slavery—which the amendments sought to end and redress—was a state institution.

The Fourteenth Amendment introduced a number of significant restrictions on the powers of the states, including the all-important Equal Protection Clause. But it did something further: in a lengthy and piecemeal process that is still in the making, the Supreme Court held that the Fourteenth Amendment also includes and embraces almost all the provisions of the Bill of Rights—thereby making these provisions binding on the states as well.[6]

Together, the Bill of Rights and the Fourteenth Amendment contain the most important collection of individual rights in the Federal Constitution; and these rights now constrain all levels of government—both federal and state (including county and municipal governments, which are subdivisions of the states). However, these rights do not apply to private individuals: people acting in private capacity are not bound by these constitutional restrictions. Your family members or your neighbors do not violate your constitutional right to free speech, or your right to the free exercise of religion, or to the equal protection of the laws—no matter how harmful or even criminally violent they are. Federal constitutional rights regulate and restrict the government's treatment of its people—not people's treatment of other people.[7] A distinctly American distrust of government power lies at the heart of our constitutional rights and liberties.

II. Constitutional Interpretation

In 2008, high school senior Abigail Fisher applied for admission to the University of Texas at Austin—the flagship of Texas' public universities. Her father and sister both graduated from the prestigious institution, and Abigail hoped to attend it as well. To her great disappointment, her application was denied. In 2009, Fisher filed a lawsuit claiming she had been denied admission because of the university's race-based affirmative action program.[8] According to the complaint, applicants with lower grades and lower SAT scores than hers were admitted to UT Austin on account of their race or ethnicity. If not for this affirmative action program, claimed Fisher, she would have been admitted. The complaint went on to allege that UT Austin's preferences in admission to members of racial and ethnic minorities violated Fisher's right to the equal protection of the laws, as guaranteed by the U.S. Constitution's Equal Protection Clause: "No state shall . . . deny to any person within its jurisdiction the equal protection of the laws."[9] The lawsuit alleged that the University was in violation of federal constitutional law.

When lawyers speak about constitutional law, they usually refer to judicial decisions interpreting the Constitution. In part, this is the result of the relative brevity of that document: together with its 27 amendments, the U.S. Constitution contains less than 8,000 words, or about 15 single-spaced pages. As such, it is one of the shortest constitutions in the world. (By way of comparison, the California Constitution or the Indian Constitution are ten times that length). This brevity in a document covering vast legal territory—from presidential powers to federalism, from police conduct to war and foreign relations, from copyright to bankruptcy to the procedures of criminal trials—necessitated the use of very vague terminology, including terms such as "freedom," "equality," "due process," "liberty," or "reasonableness."[10] Such open-ended terms obviously leave much to be worked out by judges. Judicial decisions therefore provide the concrete rules of our constitutional law.

Moreover, the Constitution of the United States is one of the World's most difficult constitutions to amend. According to Article V, constitutional amendments must first be approved by two-thirds of both houses of Congress, and then by three-quarters of the states.[11] That takes a degree of political consensus rarely achieved in regard to important political issues. Since 1787, more than 11,300 amendments were considered by Congress; of these, 33 were approved for ratification, with only 27 actually ratified (ten of those in 1791).[12] Given this state of play, judicial decisions have furnished the resolutions to almost all constitutional questions, and it should come as no surprise that they make up the bulk of our constitutional law.

But how should judges go about making these decisions? How should they decide whether UT Austin's affirmative action program violated Abigail Fisher's right to the equal protection of the laws? Should they apply the Equal Protection Clause in accordance with the intentions of its drafters? Or should they follow the Clause's text, no matter its drafters' intentions? And if the latter, should the text be read according to its meaning in 1868 (the year it was added to the Constitution), or should judges rely on what we understand by "equal protection" today?

There are, in fact, no universally accepted answers to these questions: American judges chronically disagree over whether they should prioritize the drafters' intentions or the constitutional text, whether they should refer to the original understanding of terms like "equality" and "freedom" or to their modern meaning, or whether changed circumstances should translate into changed constitutional requirements (for example, whether rapid-fire handguns should impact the scope of the right to keep and bear arms). In other words, different judges employ different judicial philosophies; and different judicial philosophies often mean different constitutional results.

Disagreements over how to interpret the Constitution are as old as the Constitution itself. In 1819, Chief Justice John Marshall—a seminal figure in the history of the Supreme Court[13]—authored an opinion that rejected a strict textual reading of the Constitutional text. The opinion declined to read the word "necessary" to mean "indispensable," reading it loosely to mean "convenient or useful" instead.[14] This linguistic elasticity was justified, according to the opinion, by the need to *adapt* the Constitution to changing times (and that barely three decades after the Constitution came into effect). "[A] Constitution," wrote Marshall, "[is] intended to endure for ages to come, and consequently to be adapted [by courts] to the various crises of human affairs." When it comes to constitutional interpretation, judges ought not be textual sticklers: "We must never forget that it is a constitution we are expounding," proclaimed the Chief Justice (not some trifling municipal code).[15]

A hundred and twenty years later, a more textualist justice took exception to Marshall's claim: "Precisely because 'it is a constitution we are expounding,'" wrote Justice Felix Frankfurter, "we ought not to take liberties with [its text]."[16]

Disagreements over the proper methodology do not stop there. Those who believe that judicial opinions may deviate from the strict constitutional text disagree as to *when* such deviations are proper; and those who insist on textual fidelity are divided over what textual fidelity means. Some think that the constitutional text must be interpreted in accordance with what it meant at the time of ratification.[17] According to this view, the Fourteenth Amendment's Equal Protection Clause secures equality under the law only as equality was understood by the people who drafted and ratified the Clause—not as we understand equality today. If we adopt this view, the Equal Protection Clause does not protect women from gender-based governmental discrimination, and does not protect homosexuals from government discrimination based on sexual orientation.[18] But other constitutional textualists maintain that the Equal Protection Clause guarantees real equality—not some outdated version of it: the Fourteenth Amendment protects the "equal protection of the laws," not "the equal protection of the laws as understood in the 19th Century."[19] Disagreements over the proper methodology occur between and within grand theories of constitutional interpretation.

And just as judges disagree over the proper methodology of interpreting the Constitution, they also disagree over the proper methodology of interpreting statutes: the debates are replicated, with some variations, at the statutory level.[20] Some argue that judges must never stray from statutory texts; others that judges must stray from statutory texts whenever the text leads to an absurd result; still others that deviations from statutory texts are justified whenever following the text would conflict with the intent of the legislature. The debates continue over how to determine the correct meaning of the text, or how to establish intent. This book also addresses disagreements over statutory interpretation, and explains how such disagreements often bleed into constitutional decisions.

III. Judicial Philosophies

The great legal philosopher Ronald Dworkin once described judicial philosophy as the "silent prologue to any discussion at law."[21] Dworkin meant that judicial philosophy was at play in every legal decision: every legal decision presumes some theory of legal interpretation. When a judge decides whether an affirmative action policy violates the Equal Protection Clause, her decision necessarily assumes some methodology of interpreting the Equal Protection Clause: does the opinion follow the intention of the drafters of the Fourteenth Amendment? Does it follow the 19th century understanding of the word "equality"? Does it take into account the vast political and social changes that took place since 1868? Does it appeal to moral or political values? Unless the case is entirely governed by precedent, these questions and others like them must be answered before the case can be decided. Some methodology of constitutional interpretation necessarily stands as the basis of—and is therefore a prologue to—any constitutional decision.

That prologue is usually silent because judges seldom articulate the judicial philosophy underlying their legal conclusions. Most judicial opinions proceed directly to the business at hand without any methodological introduction. Their judicial philosophies are never explicitly explained; they are evident only implicitly. Indeed, it would be quite impracticable to begin every legal opinion with an essay in judicial philosophy.

But sometimes the reason for the silence is deeper—and disturbing. Some judges simply take no interest in judicial philosophy. In other words, some judges decide legal cases without bothering to articulate, even for themselves, a coherent judicial methodology. Unfortunately, such judges can be found at all levels of our judicial practice. Supreme Court Justices Sandra Day O'Connor and Anthony Kennedy, for example—who acted as the Court's ideological swing-votes for decades—have been described by numerous scholars as having no consistent theory of constitutional interpretation.[22] Of course, some methodology was necessarily presumed by each of Justices O'Connor and Kennedy's decisions, but they seemed uninterested in identifying those methodologies, or in consistency. For such judges, judicial philosophy is silent not merely because it is not explained or defended in their legal opinions, but because it is not explained or defended even in their own minds—and that is a problem. In a practice committed to rationality and impartiality, methodological ignorance is an invitation to rashness and inconsistency, to careless decisions, and to unprincipled methodological switches.

Fortunately, lack of interest in judicial philosophy is not the norm among American judges—as the criticism directed at O'Connor and Kennedy implies. Many American judges take avid interest in legal philosophy, and even include it in their legal opinions. Some judges have been leading exponents of certain judicial philosophies. Supreme Court Justice William Brennan was renowned for his advocacy of living constitutionalism; Justice Antonin Scalia was famous for his writings on originalism and textualism; and Seventh Circuit Judge Richard Posner was a prominent champion of legal pragmatism. In fact, skilled American lawyers research the judicial philosophies of those deciding their cases, and craft their arguments to suit those philosophies.

IV. Choosing a Judicial Philosophy

How do judges choose a judicial philosophy? How do they pick between living constitutionalism and originalism, or between textualism and legal pragmatism? In other words, what makes for a good judicial philosophy, and what makes for a bad one?

Two concerns loom large in choosing a judicial philosophy: the merit of the results that it generates, and the legitimacy of the process it employs.

Meritorious results. A good judicial philosophy must have a tendency to produce good constitutional results—results that are sensible, ethical, and reasonably stable. A judicial philosophy that tends to produce impractical or unfair constitutional results does not deserve anybody's allegiance. Of course, people disagree about what counts as sensible or ethical results—which is partly why people disagree about the correct judicial philosophy. In fact, different judicial philosophies may tend to favor—or disfavor—different constitutional rights. Some judicial philosophies may produce greater protections for property rights or gun rights, whereas others may result in greater equality rights or greater rights for criminal defendants. Disagreements over the proper judicial philosophy are therefore, at least in part, struggles for different visions of constitutional law.

Legitimate process. The second major concern in evaluating a judicial philosophy is the legitimacy of the decision-making process that it mandates. Good judicial philosophies guide judicial power, and keep it constrained to its proper role in a separation-of-powers democracy. They do not allow judges to simply impose their own policy preferences, since, in a democracy, policy choices are supposed to be made by elected representatives, not by unelected judges. A proper judicial philosophy should therefore impede judges from usurping the power of the elected branches of government. In other words, judicial philosophies function as *separation of powers* theories—theories that define the proper role of the judiciary in a constitutional democracy. Of course, jurists disagree about how to draw the line between legitimate legal interpretation and improper policy-making— between the proper roles of the judge vis-à-vis the executive and the legislature. Some see shades and subtleties where others adhere to clear and unambiguous lines. Thus, this complex question of political theory is another source for disagreements over the correct judicial philosophy.

In the following chapters, we will evaluate various judicial philosophies along these two important axes—their ability to generate good constitutional results, and their ability to constrain judicial power. As we will soon discover, that evaluation is made difficult by the fact that the two axes often pull in opposite directions: the ability to produce sensible, moral, and stable results may necessitate the exercise of considerable judicial judgment, whereas a legitimate process seeks to constrain that judgment. A good judicial philosophy must therefore successfully navigate these opposing pulls. A philosophy that calls on judges to interpret legal texts by simply following the first entry in the Oxford English Dictionary may greatly restrict the influence of judges' own policy preferences—but it might also produce many unreasonable results. Conversely, a philosophy might produce sensible results but may insufficiently constrain judicial policy-making. The legal philosophy known as legal pragmatism, for example, has been described by its leading expositor, Richard A. Posner, as follows:

> The ultimate criterion of pragmatic adjudication is reasonableness . . . . [T]here isn't too much more to say to the pragmatic judge than make the most reasonable decision you can, all things considered.[23]

A philosophy that instructs judges to reach legal conclusions by simply reaching for the most reasonable result would, by definition, produce reasonable results (assuming the appointment of reasonable judges); but it would fail to keep judicial power sufficiently controlled and constrained—as critics of legal pragmatism routinely charge.[24]

In short, a good judicial philosophy must walk a fine line between delivering judicious, practical, and enduring conclusions, and constraining judicial power. And given rife disagreements about what counts as a judicious result, rife disagreements about what counts as a legitimate process, and rife disagreements about how best to balance these two concerns, it is no surprise that jurists are greatly divided over the correct judicial philosophy.

V. Judicial Review

Good judicial results and a legitimate judicial process are important for all legal decisions; but they are particularly important for constitutional decisions, given the power of judicial review. The power of judicial review is the power of judges to have the final say over what the Constitution requires, and have their say take precedence over the decisions of other branches of government. It allows judges to invalidate statutes enacted by a democratically elected legislature, and to order executive officials—from police officers to military commanders to the President—to cease and desist. That is momentous judicial power, and it is enormously difficult to modify its results. While simple legislative majorities can nullify judicial decisions interpreting statutes, by simply amending these statutes, it may take a constitutional amendment to nullify a constitutional decision—and we already know the great difficulty of achieving those.

The great difficulty of amending the Federal Constitution is, of course, intentional: one of the principal reasons for having a constitution in the first place is to make some legal requirements difficult to amend or repeal. But the difficulty underscores the importance of picking a proper methodology for constitutional interpretation. The very legitimacy of the power of judicial review depends on the judicial philosophy that judges employ when they use it. If judges employ judicial philosophies that result in superb constitutional decisions while respecting the powers of the elected branches of government, judicial review would be perfectly justified. By contrast, if judges employ judicial philosophies that usurp the powers of other government officials, or that routinely result in bad constitutional decisions, judicial review would lose much of its justification.

Some scholars believe that judges should not possess the power of judicial review: courts' authority to invalidate statutes or forbid executive actions, they say, is both unnecessary and unwarranted.[25] The power of judicial review is not explicitly granted to the courts by the U.S. Constitution,[26] and is not a necessary corollary of having a constitution: a number of well-functioning constitutional democracies do not grant such powers to their judiciaries.[27] These critics charge that the American judiciary regularly reaches bad constitutional decisions, and that it regularly usurps the power of the elected branches of government. Unelected federal judges, say these critics, should not have the power to veto the decisions of elected legislative or executive officials.

In 2015, Erwin Chemerinsky—one of America's leading constitutional scholars—published a book questioning the power of judicial review on account of the consistently bad constitutional decisions reached by the Supreme Court. Chemerinsky's indictment includes dozens of landmark cases on issues ranging from race relations to police brutality to gender equality to consumer protection laws. "For more than thirty years," he wrote, "I have taught these cases and been outraged by them."

> I have wanted to believe that they are the exceptions to the Supreme Court's overall successful enforcement of the Constitution. But as the years went by . . . I came to realize that it is time for me to reexamine the Supreme Court. It is important to ask directly the question, [h]as the Supreme Court been a success or a failure? My conclusion is the thesis of this book: The Court has frequently failed, throughout American history, at its most important task [—i.e., enforcing the U.S. Constitution].[28]

At the end of his long and fiery critique, Chemerinsky concluded that judicial review was, after all, worth saving; but others are less charitable.[29]

The second perennial critique of judicial review claims that judges usurp the power of elected officials. The critique alleges that constitutional rulings are essentially policy decisions, which therefore belong to elected representatives—not to unelected and unaccountable judges appointed for life. The conservative justice Antonin Scalia (who passed away in 2016) sat on the federal bench for thirty-four years; his colleague Justice John Paul Stevens (who retired in 2010) sat on the bench for 40 years. Few elected officials survive that long in office. Stevens was nominated to the federal judiciary by the conservative president Richard Nixon, then elevated to the Supreme Court by the conservative president Gerald Ford. Yet by the time he retired, Stevens was the most reliably liberal vote on the Court.[30]

Having never been elected for office, and acting against the political creeds of those who had given him his job, Stevens occupied a seat at the heart of American political power for four full decades. Much of that power came from the Court's authority of judicial review. This—say the critics of judicial review—is an offense to democracy.

The belief that constitutional decisions are in essence political has taken hold in many respectable circles, and is often proclaimed by leading politicians (as in the publicized squabble between Chief Justice John Roberts and President Donald Trump over "Obama judges and Clinton judges"[31]). It is also the view implicit in much of the coverage of constitutional decisions by the media, where Supreme Court decisions are often presented as mere functions of the justices' political affiliations. This perspective also has its supporters among distinguished academics—both in legal academia,[32] and, even more commonly, among political scientists: the so-called "attitudinal model," which views constitutional decisions as the function of judges' political affiliations, is the most popular theory of constitutional adjudication in American political science departments. To be sure, that model enjoys substantial empirical support: studies demonstrate a statistically significant correlation between judges' political preferences and their constitutional decisions.[33]

However, correlation is not causation, and this particular correlation is in any case far from perfect. After all, judges regularly reach decisions that are incompatible with their political beliefs (from Chief Justice Roberts' opinion that saved the Affordable Care Act, to Justice Ruth Ginsburg's decision to invalidate a buffer zone protecting the access to abortion clinics).[34] Moreover, even if constitutional decisions *were* essentially political, there may still be good justifications for judicial review.[35] And yet, the allegation that constitutional interpreters are politicians dressed in judicial robes is a forceful reminder of the stakes involved: a judicial philosophy producing desirable results and employing a legitimate process is particularly important when it comes to constitutional decisions.

VI. The Road Ahead

To sum up: The Federal Constitution contains a series of rights and liberties operating as restrictions on the powers of government, and courts have the final authority to determine what these often-nebulous restrictions require. But judges are deeply divided over the correct methodology with which to make these determinations: different judges employ different judicial philosophies—which often entail different constitutional results. Understanding these methodological disagreements is therefore crucial for anyone wishing to attain a full understanding of our constitutional law, or to appraise the legitimacy of our institutional arrangements—including that of judicial review.

The following chapters examine the leading judicial philosophies vying for dominance in our Constitutional landscape, and show how these judicial philosophies shape it. We will therefore deal with two subject matters and the close relations between them: judicial philosophy and constitutional doctrine. And while judicial philosophy is our main focus, the reader should also expect to learn constitutional law—specifically, the law of our constitutional rights and liberties. Indeed, the cases for this book were chosen not only for their exemplification of various judicial philosophies, but also for their constitutional subject matter. Moreover, an effort was made to stray away from the beaten track of canonical constitutional cases, and to provide a fresh and interesting perspective on constitutional doctrine also for those who are versed in the subject.

As the reader will soon perceive, I am no agnostic about the subject matter of this book. I have written extensively and enthusiastically in favor of what has been named, for lack of a better term, "dynamic legal interpretation"—a methodology that requires judges to consider all pertinent factors, including pertinent moral and political values, and that shuns attempts to restrict judicial deliberations to fact-like considerations like a dictionary definition or the original understanding of a constitutional term. Notwithstanding my strong personal opinions, the book strives to provide all judicial philosophies with a fair shake: I have searched for the strongest points in support of all the discussed judicial philosophies—and for the strongest points of their critics. My aim has been first and foremost to inform, only secondarily to convince.

CHAPTER 2

The Rise and Fall of Natural Law: The Controversy Surrounding Incorporation Doctrine, and the Right to a Trial by Jury

Natural law theory has been around for millennia. Its basic ideas are implicit in humanity's earliest legal codes, and its intellectual remnants are still with us today. The theory's thesis, in a nutshell, is that some laws are "natural" in that they are God-given and form part of the natural world. These laws—which are often moral in character (i.e., they constitute God's moral order)—take precedence over laws that are purely man-made: whenever there is a conflict between a positive law (from "posited," meaning they are a human creation) and a natural law, the natural law takes precedence and makes the positive law null and void.

Many of humanity's historical legal luminaries championed the theory of natural law—figures such as Cicero, Ancient Rome's most famous lawyer; Thomas Aquinas, the famed 14th century Christian theologian; or Sir William Blackstone, the renowned 18th century commentator on the English common law. But the theory did not survive long into modernity: for reasons explained below, natural law theory became increasingly incompatible with modern ideas of the proper judicial role. By the 19th century, the theory was giving its last gasps as a practical judicial philosophy; by the 20th century it was dead. Today, natural law theory is taken seriously only by a handful of jurists, almost all of them devout Catholics—a testament to the theory's enduring religious affinity. For most contemporary jurists, natural law theory is a remnant of a past long gone. *Sic Transit Gloria Mundi*.[1]

But the demise of natural law theory also implied a broader, and far more controversial, principle: namely, the delegitimization of moral considerations in legal interpretation. Since natural law championed moral judicial deliberations (moral laws were often taken to be natural laws), many saw in its demise the repudiation of judicial appeals to morality or justice. Today, judicial opinions that rely on a judge's sense of justice often draw the accusation that they hark back to the discredited natural law theory.

The most memorable instances where such accusations were made against the Supreme Court came in the Court's "incorporation" cases—the series of constitutional decisions that applied the Bill of Rights to the states. The doctrine of incorporation, especially in its earliest version, determined whether a Bill of Rights protection applied to the states by asking whether it represented a "fundamental principle of justice." If it did, the states were subjected to it; if it did not, the states did not have to comply with it. But this unabashedly moral test produced an outcry from opponents of the doctrine, many of whom wanted the entire Bill of Rights to be binding on the states—not just selected portions of it. They claimed that incorporation doctrine was a throwback to natural law theory.

The harsh accusation resulted in a revision to incorporation doctrine, making the doctrine far less dependent on explicit moral evaluation; and that revision brought radically different results: many Bill of Rights provisions that were previously held inapplicable to the states have now become applicable in a quick succession. One of those rights was the right to a trial by jury—whose interesting historical evolution is the subject of our last section.

I. Incorporation Doctrine

The Bill of Rights—with its various constitutional protections for the freedoms of speech and religion, the freedom from unreasonable searches and arrests, the right to counsel and to a trial by jury, and more—originally applied only to the federal government.[2] State governments (and their subdivisions—county and city governments) did not have to comply with its constitutional guarantees. All this changed with the ratification of the Fourteenth Amendment, but the change was very slow and gradual. In 1873, five years after the Fourteenth Amendment was added to the U.S. Constitution, the Supreme Court decided that—contrary to the beliefs of many at the time—the Amendment did not make the Bill of Rights binding on the states.[3] It took a while, but the Court ultimately revised its opinion on this enormously significant matter: in a series of decisions beginning in the 20th century and stretching to this day, the Supreme Court held that practically all the protections of the Bill of Rights were also binding on the states through the Fourteenth Amendment's Due Process Clause.[4]

This change of heart was prompted, in no small part, by the egregious conduct of some state governments—often directed (unsurprisingly) at their most vulnerable citizens. Consider, for example, a death penalty case from 1936 titled *Brown v. Mississippi*. A white man had been murdered, and three African Americans were rumored to have committed the crime. The three were immediately arrested, and were then badly tortured (one was hanged by the neck from a tree, the others had their backs cut to pieces with a leather strap with buckles on it)—until they confessed to the crime in all the manner of detail dictated to them by the police. "Further details of the brutal treatment to which these helpless prisoners were subjected need not be pursued," wrote the U.S. Supreme Court when it finally reversed their conviction, "[It is] sufficient to say that . . . the transcript reads more like pages torn from some medieval account than a record made within the confines of a modern civilization . . . ."[5]

The actions of the Mississippi police had their counterparts in the actions of the Mississippi courts. The torture-induced confessions were the only evidence presented at the trial. It was perfectly known to all concerned—prosecutors, grand jurors, petit jurors, and judges—that these confessions were extracted by the most brutal of means. The officers involved openly recounted their interrogation methods in open court. In fact, "the signs of the rope on [one defendant's] neck were plainly visible during the so-called trial," wrote the Supreme Court. When asked how severely he whipped another defendant, the deputy sheriff—who happened to act as the courthouse officer during the trial—responded, "Not too much for a Negro . . . ." Regardless, the grand jurors indicted the defendants, and a judge found the indictments legal; a jury convicted the defendants, and a judge found the convictions legal; and when the defendants were sentenced to death, the Supreme Court of Mississippi affirmed the convictions and sentences.

The interrogations and the trial conflicted with a number of Bill of Rights guarantees—including the Fifth Amendment right against self-incrimination, and the Sixth Amendment right to counsel (the defendants' attorney was appointed to the case less than 24 hours before the trial). Nevertheless, in 1936 these Bill of Rights protections did not yet apply to the states,[6] and the Supreme Court was reluctant to make them apply. Indeed, the Court ended up reversing the *Brown v. Mississippi* convictions on different grounds.[7] Still, cases like *Brown v. Mississippi* ultimately made the Supreme Court overcome its reluctance: in the following decades, the Court subjected the states to practically all the protections of the Bill of Rights. It did so through the doctrine of incorporation.

Incorporation doctrine operates by way of incorporating, or assimilating, the protections of the Bill of Rights into the Fourteenth Amendment's Due Process Clause.

The Due Process Clause prohibits "any state" from "depriv[ing] any person of life, liberty, or property, without due process of law . . ." —that is to say, without providing a robust legal process (which includes things like the right to be heard before an impartial adjudicator, or the right to examine witnesses). But in its incorporation decisions, the Supreme Court went further and held that the words "due process of law" also encompass "principle[s] of justice so rooted in the traditions and conscience of our people as to be ranked as fundamental."[8] In other words, the Due Process Clause also imposed on the states a general obligation to comply with fundamental moral principles. The Court then found that many of the protections of the Bill of Rights embodied fundamental moral principles—and were therefore binding on the states by virtue of the Due Process Clause.

But the Court progressed slowly and gradually with this theory, and at first rejected the incorporation of some important constitutional protections. For example, in 1937 the Court declared that the Double Jeopardy Clause of the Fifth Amendment was not a "principle of justice so rooted in the traditions and conscience of our people as to be ranked as fundamental"; thus, it was not binding on the states.[9] The same was true, said the Court, about the Sixth Amendment's right to a trial by jury.[10] And even those provisions that did qualify did not necessarily apply to the states with the same force with which they applied to the federal government. In short, incorporation doctrine was difficult to satisfy, piecemeal and messy, and it quickly became the subject of some harsh criticism.

Some critics, including Justice Hugo Black, wished to see the Bill of Rights applied to the states wholesale, and they charged that incorporation doctrine—with its judicial morality-based picking and choosing (and usually rejecting)—was a manifestation of the discredited natural law theory. In 1947, when the Court found that the Fifth Amendment's guarantee against self-incrimination ("No person... shall be compelled in any criminal case to be a witness against himself"[11]) did not embody a fundamental principle of justice—and was therefore inapplicable to the states—Black accused the opinion of employing natural law:

> [Incorporation doctrine] reasserts a constitutional theory . . . that this Court is endowed . . . with boundless power under 'natural law' periodically to expand and contract constitutional standards to conform to the Court's conception of . . . 'fundamental principles of liberty and justice.' . . . [This] 'natural law' theory . . . appropriate[s] for this Court a broad power which we are not authorized by the Constitution to exercise.[12]

Justice Black contended that incorporation doctrine, which asked judges to determine whether a Bill of Rights provision was a "principle of justice so rooted in the traditions and conscience of our people as to be ranked as fundamental," was no different than the question of fundamental and divine justice under natural law theory.

That was a serious charge: by 1947, natural law theory was supposed to have long vanished from American courtrooms.

II. The Rise and Fall of Natural Law Theory

Natural law theory has a simple premise: the fundamental rules governing human conduct are fixed, eternal, and originate from a divine power. According to natural law theory, these fundamental rules are superior to, and have priority over, any man-made law. They are "natural" because they form part of the natural world—just as scientific laws form part of the natural world. Neither scientific laws nor natural laws can be changed or abolished by humans.

Natural laws have their origin in religious authority, and natural law theory has always remained connected with religious belief. Natural laws were the laws of divine morality and justice. Cicero, writing in the First century B.C., described the Romans' understanding of natural law as follows:

> There is a true law, a right reason, conformable to nature, universal, unchanging, eternal. . . . It is not one thing at Rome and another at Athens; one thing today and another tomorrow; but in all times and nations this universal law must forever reign, eternal and imperishable. It is the sovereign master and emperor of all beings. God himself is its author—its promulgator—its enforcer.[13]

When Rome turned Christian, so did natural law theory. Like their Roman predecessors, Christian jurists identified natural law with moral precepts, and declared the supremacy of natural laws over man-made laws: "An unjust law is no law at all," declared Augustine of Hippo, the renowned fourth century Christian theologian.[14] His claim was echoed a millennium later by St. Thomas Aquinas, the eminent 13th century Catholic theologian and jurist: "If in any point [human law] deflects from the law of nature," wrote Aquinas, "it is no longer a law but a perversion of law."[15] If a man-made rule failed to comply with natural law, that rule carried no legal authority.

This concept was carried into the English common law—the collection of mostly judge-made legal rules later inherited by the United States. William Blackstone, the leading 18th century commentator on the common law (and a man still quoted regularly by American courts) explained what are natural laws in his celebrated *Commentaries on the Laws of England*:

> These are the eternal, immutable laws of good and evil, to which the Creator Himself in all his dispensations conforms; and which He has enabled human reason to discover, so far as they are necessary for the conduct of human actions. . . . This law of nature, being coeval with mankind and dictated by God Himself, is of course superior in obligation to any other. It is binding over all the globe in all countries, and at all times: no human laws are of any validity, if contrary to this . . . .[16]

Seventeen centuries separated Blackstone and Cicero, but on the issue of natural laws, their jurisprudential views were essentially the same.

Natural law theory made a significant early appearance in the United States. The American Declaration of Independence appealed to natural law to justify the break from Great Britain:

> When in the Course of human events, it becomes necessary for one people . . . to assume . . . the separate and equal station to which the Laws of Nature and of

Nature's God entitle them . . . they should declare the causes which impel them to the separation.[17]

The Declaration proceeds to refer to the rights to "Life, Liberty and the pursuit of Happiness" as "self-evident truths"—another staple of natural law theory, which regarded many natural laws as universally recognizable.[18]

Early American courts made regular references to natural law.[19] A 1798 Supreme Court opinion relied on natural law in denying "the omnipotence of a State Legislature, or that it is absolute and without control; although its authority should not be expressly restrained by the Constitution."[20] In other words, statutes may be legally invalid if they conflict with natural law. The opinion gave some examples: "A law that punished a citizen for an . . . act, which, when done, was in violation of no existing law; a law that destroys, or impairs, the lawful private contracts of citizens; a law that makes a man a Judge in his own cause; or a law that takes property from A and gives it to B . . . ." Such laws conflicted with the natural order of things, and were therefore—in the eyes of the court—without legal force.

But even as the Court was making this statement, dark clouds were gathering on the horizon of natural law theory. They were given voice in the concurring opinion filed by Justice James Iredell:

> It is true that some speculative jurists have held that a legislative act against natural justice must, in itself, be void; but I cannot think that . . . any Court of Justice would possess a power to declare it so.[21]

The problem, as Iredell saw it, was that "[t]he ideas of natural justice are regulated by no fixed standard: the ablest and the purest men have differed upon the subject." This understanding of the problem with natural law theory would soon become widely accepted. By the 20th century, natural law theory came to stand for an illegitimate method of legal decision-making, and soon disappeared as a viable judicial philosophy.

The causes for the theory's decline are multiple and interrelated. The onset of modernity undermined many of the theory's underlying assumptions. The spectacular rise of scientific thought caused a corresponding depreciation in the prestige of theological discourse. Europe's growing religious pluralism further fueled a decline in the authority of its religious establishment—and growing skepticism of its purported guardianship of moral truths. Western Enlightenment, with its focus on reason and rationality, brought new boldness to man's attempt to shape his own destiny. And natural law—always identified with religious morality and religious authority—began to be seen as a thing of the past, a theory steeped in the backwater of a subjective, unknowable, and non-scientific theology. By the 18th century—the same century that saw William Blackstone and the American Declaration of Independence proclaiming the self-evident truth of natural laws—the process of dismantling the theory was already under way. British philosopher Jeremy Bentham, born in 1748 (one of the fathers of utilitarianism—itself an effort to rationalize both morality and the law), wrote scathing critiques that ridiculed the idea of natural laws—and its derivative, natural rights:

> Right . . . is the child of law: from real laws come real rights; but from imaginary laws, from laws of nature, fancied and invented by poets, rhetoricians, and dealers in moral and intellectual poisons, come imaginary rights, a bastard brood of monsters . . . .[22]

John Austin, the famed 19th century English jurist, concurred: "[T]o say that human laws that conflict with the divine Law are not binding, that is to say, are not laws, is to talk stark nonsense."[23] Natural law theory, wrote Austin, was in fact pure wishful thinking:

> The most pernicious laws have been and are continually enforced as laws by judicial tribunals. . . . Supposed an act innocuous, or positively beneficial, be prohibited by the sovereign under the penalty of

death; if I commit this act, I shall be tried and condemned, and if I object to the sentence, that it is contrary to the law of God . . . the Court of Justice will demonstrate the inconclusiveness of my reasoning by hanging me . . . .[24]

Moreover, since people profoundly disagreed about the content of God's natural laws, the theory was dangerous: "[T]o proclaim generally that all laws which are pernicious or contrary to the will of God are void and not to be tolerated," claimed Austin, "is to preach anarchy . . . ."

According to its ever-expanding circle of critics, natural law theory misunderstood the nature of law, and was actually harmful to its cause. And as a judicial philosophy, it came with a potentially fatal problem: "[the idea] that a judge is to enforce morality enables the judge to enforce just whatever he pleases," wrote Austin.[25] Such judicial powers conflicted with basic ideas of the Rule of Law.

Finally, the rise of the idea of democracy has also proven problematic for natural law theory. In a democracy, questions of morality and good public policy seem to belong to elected representatives—not to unelected judges. But natural law theory allowed—indeed required—judges to impose their own moral or ideological convictions on the law. Such judicial powers were arguably incompatible with proper democratic principles. By the 20th century, this argument took center stage in the opposition to natural law. It was, indeed, the heart of Justice Black's complaint against incorporation doctrine:

[T]he "natural law" formula which the Court uses to reach its conclusion in this case should be abandoned as an incongruous excrescence on our Constitution. I believe that formula to be itself a violation of our Constitution, in that it subtly conveys to courts, at the expense of legislatures, ultimate power over public policies in fields where no specific provision of the Constitution limits legislative power.[26]

Growing sensitivity to the requirements of democracy was the final nail in the coffin of natural law theory. Its theoretical assumptions questioned and its practical implications condemned, by the 19th Century natural law was a quickly fading judicial philosophy; by the 20th century it was dead. "Natural law, which was for many centuries the basis of the predominant Western political thought," wrote one prominent political theorist, "is rejected in our time by almost all students of society who are not Roman Catholics. . . . [N]atural law is today primarily not more than a historical subject."[27]

Still, it takes a long time for a theory as old and deeply entrenched as natural law theory to vanish. Even as it remains wholly discredited as a practical judicial philosophy, its ideas remain in circulation. Supreme Court Justice Clarence Thomas, for example, who is a devout Roman Catholic, had spoken favorably about the theory. This came to light in the buildup to Thomas' confirmation hearing in 1991, and some commentators sounded the alarm.[28] But when he was asked about it during the hearing, Thomas—wisely—walked away from the theory as fast as he could: "I don't see a role for the use of natural law in . . . adjudication," he said. "My interest in exploring natural law and natural rights was purely in the context of political theory."[29] The response appeared to have satisfied the senators (although, as mentioned in the Introduction, judicial philosophy *is* a political theory). Natural law theory came up again in the run-up to the 2017 confirmation of Justice Neil Gorsuch. Gorsuch, who was raised a Roman Catholic, wrote a doctoral thesis in legal theory under the supervision of a famed Catholic legal scholar, who still champions natural law theory as a viable judicial philosophy.[30] Some media outlets featured headlines like "Does Donald Trump's Supreme Court Nominee Believe the Constitution Is God's Law?"[31] But in the end, natural law theory was not mentioned during the proceedings—if only because Gorsuch's confirmation was consumed by a different controversy.[32]

These anecdotes show that the ideas animating natural law theory are still in circulation, but they also demonstrate the unacceptability of the theory as a modern judicial philosophy. This unacceptability was well in place when the Supreme Court's incorporation doctrine was accused of dabbling in natural law.

III. Incorporation Revisited

As mentioned above, Justice Black's attack against incorporation doctrine was motivated by his belief that the entire Bill of Rights was binding on the states by virtue of the Fourteenth Amendment. Black urged the Court to do away with incorporation doctrine, overrule its 1873 precedent that held that the Fourteenth Amendment did not make the entirety of the Bill of Rights applicable on the states,[33] and make all the protections of the Bill of Rights applicable in one fell swoop—through the Fourteenth Amendment's Privileges or Immunities Clause.[34] The majority of the Court never adopted Black's proposal: the Court never overruled its 1873 case and never declared the Bill of Rights applicable to the states through the Privileges or Immunities Clause. But Black's proposal had been adopted in practice, if not in name. Over time, the Supreme Court revised its incorporation doctrine and—overruling many of its own incorporation precedents—made practically the entire Bill of Rights binding on the states.

The Supreme Court addressed the allegation of natural law in its incorporation doctrine by de-emphasizing the question of justice and shifting the focus to a question of history—namely, whether the right in question was fundamental *as judged by American history and tradition.* Here is how the Court explained its newfound approach to incorporation:

> [R]ecent cases . . . represent a new approach to the "incorporation" debate. Earlier the Court can be seen as having asked . . . if a civilized system could be imagined that would not accord the particular protection . . . . The recent cases, on the other hand, [ask whether a right] is necessary *to an Anglo-American regime*

of ordered liberty. When the inquiry is approached in this way the question . . . appears quite different from the way it appeared in the older cases . . . .[35]

This new emphasis on history—claimed the Court—reduced the need for moral judgments (thereby distancing the doctrine from natural law theory):

In determining which rights are fundamental, judges are not left at large to decide cases in light of their personal and private notions. Rather, they must look to the traditions and [collective] conscience of our people to determine whether a principle is so rooted [there] . . . as to be ranked as fundamental.[36]

This methodological shift was followed by a rapid change in incorporation results. Before long the Court held that practically all the protections of the Bill of Rights were in fact fundamental, and therefore enforceable against the states.[37]

In 1937, when the Court was first called to decide whether the right to a trial by jury applied to the states, it answered in the negative: "Few would be so narrow or provincial as to maintain that a fair and enlightened system of justice would be impossible without [the right to a trial by jury]."[38] The Court added: "The right to trial by jury . . . may have value and importance, [but it is] not of the very essence of a scheme of ordered liberty . . . ." But the shift to a historical test led the Court to reverse that earlier decision. In 1968 the Court declared:

Because we believe that trial by jury in criminal cases is fundamental to the *American scheme of justice*, we hold that the Fourteenth Amendment guarantees [the] right of jury trial . . . A criminal process which was fair and equitable but used no juries is easy to imagine. . . . Yet no American State has undertaken to construct such a system. . . . In every State [we find] reliance upon jury trial.[39]

The right to a trial by jury may not have been essential for a just and orderly criminal justice system, but it was an essential part of the *American* criminal justice system: that is to say, it was an essential part of American history and traditions.

The development of the right to a trial by jury in Anglo-American history is a fascinating tale: the last segment of this chapter takes us on a detour into that interesting story, and its present constitutional ramifications. We begin with a joke.

IV. The Sixth Amendment

Two old friends, a monkey and a lion, were desperately looking for entertainment in the African savannah.

"I have a suggestion," said the monkey, "let's go beat up the rabbit."

"Great idea," answered the lion, stirring up, "On what pretext?"

"If he wears a hat," said the monkey, "we will beat him up because he wears a hat; if he doesn't, we'll beat him up because he doesn't."

"Brilliant!" exclaimed the lion.

The two friends went searching for the rabbit. "Hey rabbit," said the monkey to the rabbit when they found him, "where the heck is your hat?"—and the two laid into him.

The next day, finding themselves equally bored, the monkey again suggested that they go beat up the rabbit. "Great idea," said the lion, stirring up; "On what pretext?"

"We'll ask him for a drink," said the monkey. "If he offers us water, we'll beat him up because he doesn't offer us soda; if he offers us soda, we'll beat him up because he doesn't offer us water."

"Brilliant!" exclaimed the lion.

Some compassionate birds overheard the conversation and forewarned the rabbit. When the two bullies showed up, the rabbit pulled out water and soda and asked for their choice.

A moment of silence ensued. "Hey rabbit," said the monkey, "where the heck is your hat?"—and the two laid into him.

This story of realpolitik is reminiscent of a real episode in the annals of the right to a trial by jury. In 1670, William Penn (who later founded Pennsylvania) was arrested in London for preaching the Quaker doctrine in public—a violation of the English Conventicle Act that limited public worship exclusively to the services of the Anglican Church. The facts were not in dispute, but the jury refused to convict Penn. When the jury foreman announced the "not guilty" verdict, the infuriated judge told the jurors to get back to their room and deliberate again. When the jurors returned with the same verdict a second and then a third time, the judge ordered them locked up "without meat, drink, fire and tobacco" until they came back with a guilty verdict; else, said the judge, they can "starve for it."[40]

Punishing juries for their verdicts was a practice inherited from ancient times. Historically, jurors were chosen for the job because of their personal knowledge of the case, and they swore to the facts that were known to them. Accordingly, jurors could be punished for perjury, like witnesses. Over time, jurors stopped being selected for their personal knowledge of the events, but the ability to punish juries persisted. It was said to be justified by the need to deter "corrupt judgments"—understood as judgments contrary to the facts.

But by 1670, the time of Penn's trial, new sensibilities were emerging about the institution of juries, and about the importance of their independence. So when the judge in the case locked up the jurors in an attempt to force a guilty verdict, the headstrong jury foreman arranged for papers to be filed with a higher court—the Court of Common Pleas—challenging the imprisonment. In its famous *Bushell's Case* decision (named after the willful foreman) the Court of Common Pleas sided with the jurors:

> [Is there] any thing . . . more common, than for two men students, barristers, or judges, to deduce contrary and opposite conclusions out of the same case in law? . . . Must therefore one of these merit fine and imprisonment, because he doth that which he cannot otherwise do, preserving his oath and integrity? This often is the case of the judge and jury.[41]

Indeed, the ability to disagree with the judge was not only legitimate, it was also the entire point of having a jury! If a judge could force his opinion on jurors, what was the point of a jury trial? The Court of Common Pleas ordered the jurors' immediate release and the entry of a verdict of acquittal.

But that was not the end of Penn's legal travails: Penn was soon convicted and jailed for Contempt of Court—a criminal conviction for which there was, and still is, no right to a trial by jury. The basis for the charge: Penn entered the courtroom for his criminal trial with his hat on. Although Quakers were known for refusing to take off their hats before English magistrates—claiming to reserve that honor to God alone when in church—Penn did take off his hat when he entered the courtroom. But he was then told by the bailiff—acting surreptitiously on the instruction of the judge—to re-cover his head. He did and was then prosecuted for it—after his acquittal on the charge that brought him to the courtroom in the first place. Such is life: when the King of England (the complaint against Penn charged that his public prayer was "against the peace of the said lord the king") or the King of the Jungle are out to get you, you are in trouble whether or not you are wearing your hat. This is why the American colonists rid themselves of their king and adopted a written constitution—which included a right to a trial by jury.

i. Jury Acquittals

One of the principles that emerged from *Bushell's Case* was the right of juries to acquit in contradiction with the facts and the law—an act known as "jury nullification." Jury nullification has a checkered history in the United States. It was commonly used by northern juries to acquit defendants charged with helping fugitive slaves, but also by southern juries who acquitted defendants charged with lynching. In more recent times jury nullifications have been observed, *inter alia*, in prosecutions of marijuana possession and gambling. They used to be common in prosecutions of drunk driving, but no more.

Many commentators believe that jury nullifications are a bad idea—a violation of the rule of law and an offense to the democratic legislative process. They say it should not be up to twelve individuals to determine what the law should or should not forbid. American courts generally prohibit attorneys from arguing for jury nullification to the jury,[42] and civic organizations dedicated to informing jurors of that prerogative have been banned from the vicinity of courthouses. On occasion, their members were even prosecuted for jury tampering.[43] As one judge once put it, informing jurors of their right to jury nullification is like telling children not to put beans up their noses: it's a bad idea, and they wouldn't have come up with it on their own.[44]

But the claim that jury nullification is as desirable as pushing beans up one's nose was certainly not shared by the framers of the U.S. Constitution.[45] Many of the framers believed that jury nullification was sometimes not only proper, but mandatory—a sentiment echoed by the first Vice President and second President of the United States, John Adams (also a practicing attorney), who stated that "It is not only [the juror's] right but his duty . . . to find the verdict according to his own best understanding, judgment, and conscience, though in direct opposition to the direction of the court."[46] Indeed, criminal prosecutions are a common method by which governments suppresses dissent, and judges—let us never forget—are government officials, hired, trained, and paid by the government. Granting criminal defendants the right to have their guilt or innocence determined by their peers rather than by government employees provides an important check on the government's ability to misuse the criminal justice system. In the United States, accordingly, jury nullification was and remains a constitutionally protected privilege of the jury.

ii. Jury Convictions

But while jury acquittals in contradiction with the facts and the law are constitutionally protected, that is certainly not the case with jury convictions. To the contrary: generally speaking, judges are under a positive obligation to reverse jury convictions that are not supported by the facts or the law.[47] There may be good reasons to allow a jury to acquit in such circumstances; it makes far less sense to allow them to convict.

Nevertheless, as a general matter, courts are reluctant to reverse jury convictions, even when there seem to be sound reasons for doing so. That reluctance was on full display in a Supreme Court case involving a prosecution under a federal corruption statute.[48] The defendants in the case—who were involved in an allegedly corrupt bidding process involving a federally guaranteed loan—were tried twice: the first prosecution resulted in a hung jury (the jury failed to reach the required unanimity), but a second attempt produced convictions.[49] After the convictions, and one day before the date set for sentencing, the defendants' lawyers filed papers with the court arguing that their clients' jury convictions violated the Sixth Amendment right to an *impartial jury*, and demanded a new trial. ("In all criminal prosecutions, the accused shall enjoy the right to a speedy and public trial, by an impartial jury," reads the Sixth Amendment to the U.S. Constitution).

The claim was based on sworn affidavits by two of the jurors, who had felt remorse for what had transpired during the trial and decided to come clean. The trial—stated one of those affidavits—"was one big party."[50] During every lunch recess, four of the twelve jurors shared between them three pitchers of beer. A fifth—the foreperson—

drank a liter of wine. Two others consumed cocktails. Four of the jurors smoked marijuana "[j]ust about every day"—which put them in a "giggly mood," according to the testimony of one of the attorneys. The weed was apparently first rate: one of the jurors bought a quarter-pound of it from another during the trial. Two other jurors regularly snorted cocaine in the courthouse's bathroom. Some jurors were high on all three substances—alcohol, marijuana, and cocaine—while hearing trial testimony. "[W]e were 'flying,'" testified a juror. And when they landed, they often took a nap: according to eyewitness testimony, some jurors were "falling asleep all the time during the trial." In short, expressed in the somber language of a Supreme Court justice, "the jurors' senses were significantly dulled . . . ."[51]

It may seem obvious that the constitutional right to an impartial jury should include the right to mentally competent jurors: jurors collected from the local asylum would make a mockery of that constitutional right. And highly intoxicated jurors seemed to be no different. But the Supreme Court, in a 5–4 decision, rejected the claim: "however severe their effect and improper their use," wrote the Court, "drugs or alcohol voluntarily ingested by a juror seems not [much different] than a virus, poorly prepared food, or a lack of sleep." And a virus, poorly prepared food, or a lack of sleep do not justify reversing a jury verdict.

The Court referred approvingly to a decision of the Second Circuit Court of Appeals, which rejected a similar request for a retrial based on mental incompetence. In that case, a man convicted of criminal fraud received an unsolicited letter from one of his jurors soon after the guilty verdict. The letter read—or rather rambled—as follows:

> Dear Mr. Dioguardi,
> Under the situation and such circumstance I hope that I have made the right decision. . . . One word appear before me repent. . . . Before I continue I must explain something to you. I have eyes and ears that I can see

things before it happen. I can tell you about other and what they are thinking and doing. If I am wrong about this it is the first time. I would like to visit you. I would like to talk to you about what appear before me. I would like to do so when my eyes fully open. They are only partly open. I don't know at the present when they will open. Unfortunate, a curse was put upon them some years ago. I have some people working on them. Everything is being done that can be done. So we will have to wait.[52]

Armed with the affidavits of seven psychiatrists opining that the author was crazy, Mr. Dioguardi asked for a new trial. One juror, mind you, could have made all the difference, since conviction required jurors' unanimity. But the Second Circuit Court of Appeals denied his request: the allegation did not justify a reversal of the jury verdict, said the court. An impassioned dissent objected that since the juror "believe[d] she was clairvoyant, is it really necessary to spell out why she could not fairly try the guilt or innocence of any man? It seems obvious to me that a 'clairvoyant' juror might honestly 'see' a defendant's guilt despite the lack of evidence because she can see into the defendant's mind."[53]

These refusals to reverse the jury convictions are stark demonstrations of today's courts' deference to jury verdicts. We have come a long way since the days of *Bushell's Case*. Both the Supreme Court and the Second Circuit were concerned that reversing these verdicts would encourage unsubstantiated claims of jurors' incompetence—made worse by the difficulty of evaluating psychological competence. They were also concerned that jurors would be harassed: emissaries of convicted defendants might hunt for evidence of jurors' incompetence by approaching jurors and the people close to them. "[F]ull and frank discussion in the jury room, . . . and the community's trust in a system that relies on the decisions of laypeople, would all be undermined by a barrage of post-verdict scrutiny of juror conduct," admonished the Supreme Court's opinion: "It is not at all clear . . .

36

that the jury system could survive such efforts to perfect it." To which the dissenters responded that, under the majority's decision "the jury system may survive, but the constitutional guarantee on which it is based [may] become meaningless."

V. Review

To sum up: natural law theory, which dominated legal philosophy for millennia, stood for judicial enforcement of God-given morality. But the decline in the authority and prestige of theological discourse, the growing acceptance of moral pluralism, and increasing sensitivity to the principles of democracy, have combined to delegitimize the theory as a judicial philosophy. By the 20th century, natural law theory has become synonymous with judicial usurpation of power. Judicial appeals to a higher moral law—and even to morality itself—have become discredited.

Critics of incorporation doctrine—which asked courts to determine whether a Bill of Rights provision protected a "fundamental principle of justice"—argued that the doctrine dabbled in natural law theory. In response, the Supreme Court revised the doctrine by making it less dependent on moral evaluation and more dependent on American history and tradition. The result had been the rapid incorporation of Bill of Rights provisions that were previously declared inapplicable to the states.

But the question raised by the critique of incorporation doctrine remains far from settled. Chapter 3 delves deeper into this important issue of judicial philosophy: should courts consult morality or justice when deciding what the Constitution requires?

CHAPTER 3

The Debate Over Unenumerated Constitutional Rights: The Ninth Amendment, Substantive Due Process, and the Right to Not Be Executed if Innocent

The previous chapter dealt with the claim that incorporation doctrine harked back to natural law theory on account of its explicit moral evaluation. But while the controversy surrounding incorporation doctrine soon died out—if only because the application of the Bill of Rights to the states was soon a *fait accompli*—the role of moral evaluation in Due Process doctrine continues to be debated. That is so because the constitutional protections of the Fourteenth Amendment's Due Process Clause are not exhausted by the incorporated protections of the Bill of Rights: the Clause contains a host of other constitutional protections that courts have identified and enforced.

Moreover, here the debate over the role of morality is even starker, because unlike the incorporated protections of the Bill of Rights, these other substantive due process protections are nowhere mentioned in the Constitution. The freedom of speech or the right to counsel or the right to a trial by jury—which are incorporated into the Fourteenth Amendment's Due Process Clause—are explicitly listed in the constitutional text; but due process rights like the right to be free from police brutality, or the right to marry, or the right to refuse life-saving medical treatment, are nowhere mentioned in the Constitution. These constitutional rights are known as "unenumerated rights." Their very existence (not merely their applicability to the states) is a result of some judicial moral determination. Thus, the controversy surrounding the role of morality in constitutional interpretation is here thrown into even sharper relief: unenumerated rights implicate the difficulties that plagued natural law theory far more than incorporation doctrine ever did. Indeed, unwritten constitutional rights may seem perfectly natural if you subscribe to natural law theory; but in a legal order that rejects natural law—either because it doubts that universal principles of justice actually exist, or because it rejects the idea that such principles should be identified and enforced by judges—unenumerated constitutional rights can be highly objectionable.

This chapter examines an attempt to create a new unenumerated constitutional right: a substantive due process right to not be executed if innocent. This right may sound obvious, but it ran head-on into the debate over the legitimacy of unenumerated constitutional rights. When the question landed at the Supreme Court, the justices were bitterly divided over it. The majority refused to grant recognition to such alleged constitutional protection. Their decision was soon used to resolve a case dealing with the constitutionality of the death penalty.

I. Substantive Due Process

The Federal Constitution contains two Due Process clauses: the first, which is part of the Fifth Amendment, is binding on the federal government; the second, which is part of the Fourteenth Amendment (and added to the Constitution 77 years after the first), is binding on the states.[1] "No person shall be . . . deprived of life, liberty, or property, without due process of law," reads the Fifth Amendment, and the Fourteenth employs similar language. Literally speaking, the Due Process clauses protect rights pertaining to the judicial process. The government cannot deprive people of their lives, their liberty, or their property, without proper judicial process that allows them to defend themselves against such deprivations. Examples of such procedural rights include the right to an impartial adjudicator, the right to testify on one's own behalf, the right to present evidence, the right to have sufficient time to prepare for trial, or the right to have one's criminal guilt proven beyond a reasonable doubt.

But the phrase "due process of law" has been read to include some non-procedural rights as well: the Supreme Court has long interpreted the Due Process Clause as protecting rights that have nothing to do with the legal process. These are *substantive* due process rights. And while some Supreme Court justices dubbed such rights "an oxymoron"[2]—a contradiction in terms that confusedly fuses procedure and substance—scholars have traced such substantive due process rights all the way back to the 14th century, when the phrase "due process of law" appeared for the first time in a statutory codification of the Magna Carta.[3]

The U.S. Supreme Court has interpreted the Due Process Clause as providing substantive protections at least since the 19th century.[4] The reason for this interpretation of the Clause was explained in an often-quoted 1961 concurring opinion:

> Were due process merely a procedural safeguard, it would fail to reach those situations where the deprivation of life, liberty or property was accomplished by legislation which . . . could, given even the fairest possible procedure . . . nevertheless destroy the enjoyment of all three.[5]

Thus, although the constitution says not a thing about police brutality or about involuntary medical treatment, American courts held that such government actions were so deeply in conflict with American values that they were unconstitutional. Put differently, some rights, although not explicitly mentioned in the Constitution, are so much a part of our moral and political fabric that the question for courts was not so much whether the Constitution protected them, but what constitutional provision did. The choice fell on the Due Process Clause—partly because some more textually-appropriate provisions were ruled out by long-standing precedents.[6]

Here's an example of such a constitutional decision. In 1923, the Supreme Court reviewed a Nebraska statute that made it a crime to teach foreign languages to young children. The statute—which was passed in 1919, a time of high jingoism following the First World War—was purportedly aimed at facilitating the assimilation of immigrants into American life. But the Supreme Court agreed with a teacher, who was convicted under the statute, and held that the statute violated the Due Process Clause. The Court explained its decision as follows:

> [The Greek philosopher] Plato suggested a law which should provide: "That the wives of our guardians[7] are to be common, and their children are to be common, and no parent is to know his own child, nor any child his parent." . . . In order to submerge the individual and develop ideal citizens, Sparta assembled the males at seven into barracks and entrusted their subsequent education and training to official guardians. Although such measures have been deliberately approved by men of great genius, their ideas touching the relation between individual and state were wholly different from those upon which our institutions rest; and it hardly will be affirmed that any Legislature could impose such restrictions upon the people of a state without doing violence to both letter and spirit of the Constitution.[8]

Successful societies and celebrated geniuses have deemed it beneficial for the government to tightly control the education of children; but the idea is wholly foreign to American political values. So even though the Constitution did not forbid such actions explicitly, it did forbid them implicitly. And the same goes for extracting criminal confessions by torture,[9] or forcing adults to undergo surgery they don't want,[10] or making it a crime to use contraceptives,[11] or making it impossible for a grandmother to live with her grandchildren[12]— all examples of government actions that violated substantive due process rights. Whether explicitly or implicitly, the Constitution enshrines and protects our most fundamental values.

But not all substantive due process rights are as uncontroversial as those mentioned above. Some of our most contested constitutional rights are substantive due process rights—including the right to have an abortion,[13] the right to engage in homosexual sodomy,[14] and the right to same-sex marriage.[15] And so, substantive due process doctrine has attracted considerable fire—much of it concentrated on the fact that substantive due process rights were "unenumerated." "[G]uideposts for responsible decisionmaking in this unchartered area are scarce and open-ended," declared a majority of justices in 1997.[16] Some justices go further: substantive due process doctrine, wrote Justices Thomas and Scalia in 2015, "distorts the constitutional text . . . [and] invites judges to . . . roam at large in the constitutional field guided only by their personal views as to the fundamental rights protected by that document.[17] "[T]reating the Due Process Clause as a font of substantive rights," they added, is a "dangerous fiction."

In other words, some jurists, including some who sit on the U.S. Supreme Court, would like to do away with substantive due process doctrine—the source for some of the most cherished rights presently protected by the Federal Constitution. Much is at stake in the struggle between proponents and opponents of unenumerated constitutional rights.

II. The Ninth Amendment and the Defense of Unenumerated Rights

Often, the first line of defense of unenumerated constitutional rights is the Ninth Amendment to the U.S. Constitution: "The enumeration in the Constitution, of certain rights," reads the Ninth Amendment, "shall not be construed to deny or disparage others retained by the people." The Amendment was written to quiet concerns that the adoption of a Bill of Rights meant that Americans possessed only those rights appearing in it—but nothing more. As a legal maxim has it, *expressio unius est exclusio alterius*—the explicit mention of one means the exclusion of others. But according to the Ninth Amendment, the fact that some rights are enumerated shall not be read to deny the existence of other, unenumerated rights.

This constitutional endorsement of unenumerated rights soon ran into a formidable difficulty. It is generally understood that the drafters of the Ninth Amendment understood those unenumerated rights to be "natural rights"—a form of natural laws.[18] But as mentioned previously, natural law theory has since been discredited and repudiated. This produced a serious predicament for modern constitutional interpreters: what to do with a constitutional provision that appeared to incorporate into the Constitution a wholly discredited theory of law? If natural rights were—as Jeremy Bentham once put it—"nonsense upon stilts," what are we to do with a constitutional provision that endorses such nonsense?[19] The answer was: do nothing.

Present constitutional doctrine regards the Ninth Amendment as unenforceable.[20] And while some jurists explain this unenforceability through sophisticated doctrinal arguments,[21] a cruder but clearer explanation was provided by Robert Bork, Ronald Reagan's 1987 Supreme Court nominee, in his testimony during his failed Supreme Court confirmation hearing:

> [I]f you had an amendment that says 'Congress shall make no' and then there is an ink blot and you cannot read the rest of it and that is the only copy you have, I do not think the court can make up what might be under the ink blot if you cannot read it.[22]

The same was true, said Bork, about the Ninth Amendment. Natural laws and natural rights are arguably no different than an ink blot: a Rorschach test that means whatever a person decides that it means. Allowing judges to identify such natural rights—say those who want to keep the Ninth Amendment unenforceable—would allow judges to invent constitutional rights out of whole cloth. The Ninth Amendment is unenforceable essentially for the same reason that natural law theory is no longer enforced.

Still, there is something paradoxical in the refusal to enforce the Ninth Amendment in the name of limiting judicial power. After all, picking and choosing what constitutional provisions to enforce is itself a far-reaching exercise of judicial power.[23] Moreover, as supporters of unenumerated rights are quick to point out, constitutional doctrine is replete with "unenumerated" requirements—that is to say, with requirements that do not appear explicitly in the constitution. Our constitutional law strays often and sometimes far from the literal constitutional text (from the constitutional prohibition on state laws that restrict interstate commerce, to state constitutional immunity from certain federal lawsuits, to the constitutional right of a President to refuse to disclose certain information).[24] Why, then, single out unenumerated individual rights?

The unenforceability of the Ninth Amendment remains under constant protest—from legal scholarship, and from actual lawsuits alleging the infringement of Ninth Amendment rights. Recent examples include an alleged Ninth Amendment right to experiment with mind-altering drugs,[25] a right to clone oneself,[26] and the alleged right of minors not to be bequeathed a world devastated by carbon emissions.[27]

The Ninth Amendment remains unenforceable as a source of constitutional rights. But the Amendment was used to provide support for unenumerated rights located in other constitutional provisions—including the Due Process Clause.[28] For example, the federal district court that first decided *Roe v. Wade*, recognized the right of women to procure an abortion under the Ninth Amendment.[29] The Supreme Court subsequently disagreed and located that right in the Fourteenth Amendment's Due Process Clause;[30] but in doing so the Supreme Court also relied, in part, on the Ninth Amendment.[31] Supreme Court Justice Arthur Goldberg made a similar point in regard to the right to use contraceptives:

> [T]hough [substantive due process rights are] not mentioned explicitly in the Constitution . . . [they

are] supported . . . by the language and history of the Ninth Amendment. [The] Ninth Amendment . . . was proffered to quiet expressed fears that a bill of specifically enumerated rights could not be sufficiently broad to cover all essential rights and that the specific mention of certain rights would be interpreted as a denial that others were protected.[32]

In short, today's Ninth Amendment is not itself a source for unenumerated constitutional rights, but it is a source of support for unenumerated rights that are located in other constitutional provisions—particularly in the Due Process Clause.

III. The Right to Not Be Executed if Innocent

Substantive due process rights experienced a great revival under the liberal Warren Court in the 1960s. However, in subsequent years the Supreme Court has become ever more conservative, and hostility to substantive due process grew within the Court. By the late 1980s, four justices opined that "the Court should be extremely reluctant to breathe still further substantive content into the Due Process Clause."[33] And yet, merely four years after that skeptical declaration, the Supreme Court agreed to review the claim of Leonel Torres Herrera, a death row inmate convicted of the murder of two Texas police officers, that his execution would violate a novel, hitherto unrecognized and unenumerated substantive due process right: the right to not be executed if innocent.

In 1981, on a late September evening near Los Fresnos, Texas, a police officer was murdered by a shot to the head.[34] A few minutes later, a second officer was shot and killed when (unaware of the earlier murder) he pulled over the murderer's car for speeding. Within days the Texas police arrested Leonel Torres Herrera—a local roofer suspected to be an enforcer for a drug smuggling operation. In 1982, Herrera was convicted of the two murders and sentenced to death. As with most death sentences, there began a long series of appeals in both state and federal courts. In 1992, more than a decade after he was first tried and convicted, the Supreme Court accepted review of the claim that Herrera's impending execution would violate the Federal Constitution's Due Process Clause.[35]

The Federal Constitution provides numerous protections for criminal defendants: the right to a trial by jury,[36] a right to an appointed attorney if a defendant cannot afford one,[37] a right to remain silent,[38] to confront one's accusers,[39] to be presumed innocent,[40] to be informed of any exculpating evidence,[41] and many more. All these rights were duly respected in Herrera's trial. Moreover, the prosecution presented substantial evidence supporting Herrera's guilt: among other things, his photo was identified by the second police officer before he died at the hospital; Herrera's social security card was found near the first officer's body; the officer's blood was found on Herrera's clothing and wallet; and when he was arrested, five days after the shooting, Herrera was carrying a note explaining the killings.

But Herrera's appeal was not based on any of his rights to a fair trial, or on the sufficiency of the evidence against him. Instead, the claim advanced by Herrera's attorneys went straight to the heart of their client's case: the right threatened by Herrera's conviction, they wrote, was the right of an innocent person to not be executed.

The allegation of Herrera's innocence was supported by newly discovered evidence that emerged after the trial. The evidence included an affidavit from an attorney and former state judge who represented Herrera's brother, who stated that the brother had confessed to him that he committed the murders; and an affidavit from Herrera's brother's son—nine years old at the time of the murders—who swore that he was alone in the car with his father on that fateful day in September 1981, and had witnessed his father murder the two officers. Given this new evidence, said the attorneys, it would be a violation of the Due Process Clause to execute Herrera. By the time these allegations were made, Herrera's brother was already dead.

At the Supreme Court, there was some obvious hostility to Herrera's claims. Many of the justices did not believe in Herrera's alleged innocence, and they also looked askance at his novel constitutional argument. For these justices, Herrera's newly concocted unenumerated right was a sore loser's attempt to circumvent the criminal justice system: after going through the carefully orchestrated motions of a criminal trial, with its layer upon layer of constitutional protections (the right to competent counsel, the right to remain silent, the right to confront one's accusers, the right to have guilt proven beyond reasonable doubt, the right to a jury trial, etc.), and having been found guilty, Herrera pulled out of a hat some easy-to-fabricate evidence and demanded a new trial under a novel unenumerated right. "The Constitution," said the Supreme Court's eventual opinion, "makes no mention of new trials."[42]

By contrast, a dissenting opinion by Justice Harry Blackmun, joined by two other justices, argued that the Court must recognize Herrera's alleged constitutional right. What could be more basic, more fundamental, and more self-evident—they argued—than the right of an innocent man not to be executed? This, after all, was what all constitutional protections for criminal defendants were ultimately about: making sure that only the guilty get punished. But

> These protections sometimes fail. We really are being asked to decide whether the Constitution forbids the execution of a person who has been validly convicted and sentenced but who, nonetheless, can prove his innocence with newly discovered evidence. Despite the State of Texas' astonishing protestation to the contrary, I do not see how the answer can be anything but "yes."[43]

It is of course possible, said the dissent, that Herrera was in fact the murderer, and that his conviction and sentence should be reaffirmed; but whatever the ultimate fate of Herrera's own case, a convicted person in possession of new exculpatory evidence should have a constitutional right to have his case reopened.

Underlying this disagreement were starkly different visions of the Federal Constitution and the proper methodology of interpreting it. The dissenting justices thought it absurd to deny a constitutional right to not be executed if innocent, even if that right did not appear explicitly in the Constitution. For them—and for those who support unenumerated constitutional rights more generally—the Constitution protected the nation's fundamental moral and political values, and could not be reduced to its literal text: "The full scope of the liberty guaranteed by the Due Process Clause," quoted the dissented an earlier opinion, "cannot be found in or limited by the precise terms of the specific guarantees . . . provided in the Constitution."[44]

But for their ideological opponents the Constitution was a set of fixed rules that contained only those rights that were explicitly mentioned. Rights that were not explicitly written into the document were simply not protected: "I can understand," wrote Justice Scalia in *Herrera*, "or at least am accustomed to, the reluctance of the present Court to admit publicly that Our Perfect Constitution lets stand any injustice, much less the execution of an innocent man . . . . [However,] not every problem was meant to be solved by the United States Constitution . . . ."[45] Many injustices were simply not addressed in the constitutional text, and were therefore not addressed by the Federal Constitution. The injustice of executing the wrongly convicted happened to be one of them.

Still, even the justices of the majority realized the difficulty of an outright rejection of Herrera's constitutional claim. Imagine next day's newspapers headlines were the Court to adopt such an approach. "Supreme Court Holds It Constitutional to Execute an Innocent Man" was only one such possible caption. No, an outright rejection was ill advised: the reputation of the Court could be harmed—and for no good reason. After all, the Court could reject Herrera's constitutional claim without completely rejecting his constitutional argument. In other words, the Court could decide the case without deciding the issue—which is precisely what the Court proceeded to do:

We may assume, for the sake of argument in deciding this case, that in a capital case a truly persuasive
demonstration of "actual innocence" made after trial
would render the execution of a defendant unconstitutional . . . . But . . . the threshold showing for such
an assumed right would necessarily be extraordinari-
ly high. The showing made by petitioner in this case
falls far short of any such threshold.[46]

Herrera's claim was rejected whether there was or wasn't a constitutional right to not be executed if innocent. That question was left for
another day.[47] As two concurring justices noted with apparent satis-
faction: "Nowhere does the Court state that the Constitution permits
the execution of an actually innocent person."[48] But then again, nowhere did the Court state that it didn't.

Justice Harry Blackmun ended his *Herrera* dissent with a *cris
de cœur*: "The execution of a person who can show that he is innocent," wrote Blackmun, "comes perilously close to simple murder."[49]
Justices John Paul Stevens and David Souter joined all of Blackmun's
opinion except for the short paragraph containing that sentence: apparently, they found it a little too intense.

Leonel Torres Herrera refused a last meal and was executed by
lethal injection on May 12, 1993—four months after the Supreme
Court refused to reopen his case. His five last words were "I am innocent, innocent, innocent."[50] To be sure, such statements have been
made by perfectly guilty death row inmates. But statistically speaking, sometimes such statements must be true: according to the Innocence Project, 21 people who served time on death row were exonerated with the help of DNA evidence since 1989.[51] A federal district
court examining the available data concluded, in 2002, that at least
20 additional death row inmates were exonerated for reasons unrelated to DNA since 1989.[52] Between 1989 and 2002, 716 executions
were carried out.[53] Relying on such statistics, the federal district court
held, in a rather surprising decision, that the death penalty was un-

constitutional. But the Supreme Court's *Herrera* opinion became the basis for reversing the decision.

IV. *Herrera*, the Death Penalty, and Alito's Confirmation Hearing

In 2002, a federal district court judge declared the death penalty unconstitutional based on an innovative legal argument: according to the opinion, capital punishment was unconstitutional because death row inmates had a constitutional right to prove themselves innocent, no matter how much time had elapsed since their conviction; and the death penalty effectively extinguished that important right. The district court wrote:

> [Recent] evidence has emerged that clearly indicates that . . . innocent people—mostly of color—are convicted of capital crimes they never committed . . . with a frequency far greater than previously supposed. . . . [I]n just the past decade, at least 20 additional defendants who had been duly convicted of capital crimes and were facing execution have been exonerated and released. . . . [T]he inference is unmistakable that numerous innocent people have been executed whose innocence might otherwise have been similarly established, whether by newly-developed scientific techniques, newly-discovered evidence, or simply renewed attention to their cases. Just as there is typically no statute of limitations for first-degree murder—for the obvious reason that it would be intolerable to let a cold-blooded murderer escape justice through the mere passage of time—so too one may ask whether it is tolerable to put a time limit on when someone wrongly convicted of murder must prove his innocence or face extinction. In constitutional terms, the

issue is whether—now that we know the fallibility of our system in capital cases—capital punishment is unconstitutional because it creates an undue risk that a meaningful number of innocent persons, by being put to death before the emergence of the techniques or evidence that will establish their innocence, are thereby effectively deprived of the opportunity to prove their innocence—and thus deprived of the process that is reasonably due them in these circumstances under the Fifth Amendment . . . .[54]

The decision was soon reversed by a federal court of appeals, which relied on the Supreme Court's *Herrera* decision:

[In *Herrera v. Collins*, the Supreme Court] declined to hold that execution of a person who is innocent of the crime . . . amounts to a [constitutional] violation . . . . [W]hile the Court assumed, only for the sake of its analysis, that capital punishment of a person who is able to demonstrate his innocence prior to execution violates the Constitution, it made no such holding. . . . *Herrera* prevents us from finding capital punishment unconstitutional [under the reasoning of the district court] . . . .[55]

The coyness of the *Herrera* opinion has proven successful: it prevented damaging media reports, while making clear to the lower courts that Herrera's claim to this alleged right remained unrecognized.

And yet, notwithstanding that appeals court decision, since the Supreme Court declined to declare outright that a right not to be executed if innocent did not exist, litigants continue to press such claims at the lower courts. In 2006, the Supreme Court again accepted review of a case alleging such a substantive due process right. As it happened, the case was argued at the Supreme Court on the same day that Justice Samuel Alito was testifying before the Senate in his tense confirmation hearing (during which Alito's wife burst into tears over the rough questioning of her husband). One of the testy exchanges between Alito and democratic members of the judiciary committee included the following question from Senator Russ Feingold (a senator from Wisconsin and a graduate of Harvard Law School):

> Let's say that the trial was procedurally perfect and there were no legal or constitutional errors, but later evidence proves that the person convicted was unquestionably innocent. Does that person have a constitutional right not to be executed?[56]

Feingold had in mind the case that was argued that morning across the street at the Supreme Court. Alito, a conservative whose sympathies lay with the *Herrera* majority, responded with plenty of "ehs" and "ums" but refused to concede the existence of such a constitutional right.[57] Feingold, unhappy with Alito's answer—or (like the *Herrera* opinion itself) its lack thereof—cited it when voting against Alito's confirmation. "I was particularly troubled," he said,

> by his refusal to say that an individual who went through a procedurally perfect trial, but was later proven innocent, had a constitutional right not to be executed. . . . I pressed Judge Alito on this topic, but rather than answering the question directly or acknowledging how horrific the idea of executing an innocent person is, or even pointing to the . . . case currently pending in the Supreme Court . . . , Judge Alito mechanically laid out the procedures a person would have to follow in state and federal court to raise an innocence claim . . . . Judge Alito's record and response suggest that he analyzes death penalty appeals as a series of procedural hurdles that inmates must overcome, rather than as a critical backstop to prevent grave miscarriages of justice.[58]

Here was another articulation of the fundamental clash between proponents and opponents of unenumerated constitutional rights: between those who believe that the Constitution protects our most fundamental values even in circumstances that are not explicitly addressed by the constitutional text, and those who believe that the Constitution is a small set of explicit and specific constitutional rules that do not extend beyond its text.

Six months after Alito's confirmation, the Supreme Court issued its decision in that 2006 case—again declining to recognize a constitutional right to not be executed if innocent.[59]

V. Review

To sum up: constitutional decisions have long recognized that the Due Process Clause protects some substantive unenumerated constitutional rights. These decisions see the Constitution as a depository of our nation's most cherished moral and political values: they reject the idea that constitutional rights are limited only to those appearing explicitly in the constitutional text, and the related claim that judges ought to abstain from moral judgments in determining the content and scope of constitutional rights. Thus, although natural law theory is long dead, the debate over the role of morality and justice in constitutional interpretation continues. For many jurists, the error of natural law theory did not consist in its appeal to morality, but in its appeal to a God-given and universal morality, and to the notion that that morality was self-evident (leaving little room for deliberative argumentation and theory construction).[60] Notwithstanding the present illegitimacy of natural law theory, the attempt to wash legal interpretation of all moral judgments—say these jurists—is a grave and harmful error, and it often serves only to push such considerations under the rug: it is not for nothing that our legal institutions are called our "justice system."

In contrast, others see in substantive due process rights all the pitfalls of natural law theory and consider them a judicial usurpation of power. This latter view has been gaining acceptance in an increasingly conservative Supreme Court, and it has led the Court to deny the seemingly obvious right to not be executed if innocent.

The effort to separate moral evaluation from constitutional decisions necessitated the development of interpretive strategies that prevented judges from making value judgments. One of the most common of these strategies is the turn to history and tradition: determining the scope and content of constitutional rights by relying on historical facts. This strategy—an example of which we met in the previous chapter in the revised incorporation doctrine—raises two fundamental questions: is the turn to history and tradition likely to produce an obsolete and outdated body of constitutional law? And can it in fact eliminate judicial moral evaluations? These two issues are explored in the following chapter.

CHAPTER 4

The Role of History in Constitutional Interpretation: The First Amendment and Unprotected Speech

The fall of natural law theory gave rise to judicial philosophies that sought to curtail moral judicial judgments. One such common strategy was—and still is—the appeal to history: judges establish the content and scope of constitutional rights by referring to some historical example. This strategy reaches its most comprehensive and ambitious form in the theory of originalism, which is the subject of the next two chapters. This chapter examines judicial reliance on history and tradition in localized constitutional doctrines.

Localized historical tests are sprinkled throughout our constitutional landscape. We already saw a historical test introduced into incorporation doctrine to address the charge that the doctrine dabbled in natural law. More recently, a historical test was introduced into the supremely important decision of whether a particular category of speech is protected by the First Amendment. The Supreme Court used to approach that question through a pragmatic inquiry that balanced the value of the speech in question against its potential harms. But in 2010, the Court called that pragmatic inquiry "highly manipulable," and replaced it with a historical test: historical precedents became the touchstone for determining whether a category of speech is or is not constitutionally protected.[1] The new approach therefore replaced an open-ended and potentially moral inquiry with one based on an objective historical assessment—or so it seemed. As this chapter will discuss, critics argue that the historical test is not only insufficiently attuned to current values and needs, but also that it is no less manipulable—or moral—than the test it supplanted. We will examine that critique through two relatively recent cases that deal with the First Amendment's freedom of speech; but we begin with a historical test deployed in the context of an alleged substantive due process right.

I. Historical Tests and Their Critics

In 1986, the Supreme Court refused to recognize the constitutional right of a biological father for visitation rights with his young daughter—who was moved by her mother from the father's home to the mother's marital household. A plurality opinion explained that in order to establish visitation rights under the Constitution, the father had to demonstrate that such visitation rights were respected as a matter of American history and traditions: "Our cases reflect continual insistence upon respect for the teachings of history," said the opinion.[2] "This insistence that the asserted [constitutional right] be rooted in history and tradition" doomed the father's constitutional claim because, according to the opinion, the father had failed to establish such historical precedent.

The principal dissent was authored by the liberal giant William Brennan, who sat on the Court from 1956 to 1990. Justice Brennan, who favored acceptance of the father's constitutional argument, criticized the plurality's excessive reliance on history:

> The document that the plurality construes today is unfamiliar to me. It is not the living charter that I have taken to be our Constitution; it is instead a stagnant, archaic, hidebound document steeped in the prejudices and superstitions of a time long past. *This* Constitution does not recognize that times change, does not see that sometimes a practice or rule outlives its foundations. I cannot accept an interpretive method that does such violence to the charter that I am bound by oath to uphold.[3]

We know the response of the advocates of historical tests: historical tests may tie constitutional doctrine to the past, but they prevent constitutional decisions from being based on judges' personal value judgments. But Justice Brennan took issue with that claim as well: "[I]t would be comforting to believe," he wrote,

> that a search for 'tradition' involves nothing more idiosyncratic or complicated than poring through dusty volumes on American history. Yet, . . . [b]ecause reasonable people can disagree about the content of particular traditions, and because they can disagree even about which traditions are relevant . . . [historical tests cannot provide] the objective boundary that [the plurality] seeks.[4]

Brennan's critique can be examined in light of a pair of constitutional decisions, handed down more than two decades later, which introduced a historical test into the heart of the First Amendment. We start with a fundamental feature of First Amendment doctrine: the distinction between protected and unprotected categories of speech.

II. Unprotected Categories of Speech

The First Amendment speaks of the freedom of speech in absolutist terms: "Congress shall make *no law* . . . abridging the freedom of speech . . ." (emphasis added). But the freedom of speech cannot be absolute: the government should and does abridge lots of speech. Saying "I will pay you to kill my wife" is solicitation for murder punishable by decades behind bars; saying "I will kill you" is a criminal threat. Blackmail, harassment, fraud, perjury, or espionage—like numerous other crimes—can all be committed solely through speech. In short, notwithstanding the First Amendment's peremptory language, not all types of speech are protected by the First Amendment. It fell to the courts to detect the principles separating protected from unprotected speech.

One such principle draws the distinction by reference to the proximity of the speech in question to harmful action: proximity to harmful action can remove First Amendment protections. This limitation on the freedom of speech has an illustrious history. John Stuart Mill explained it in his canonical essay, *On Liberty* (1859):

> [E]ven opinions lose their immunity when the circumstances in which they are expressed are such as to [make] their expression a positive instigation to some mischievous act. An opinion that corn dealers are starvers of the poor, or that private property is robbery, ought to be unmolested when simply circulated through the press, but may justly incur punishment when delivered orally to an excited mob assembled before the house of a corn dealer.[5]

Justice Oliver Wendell Holmes made a similar—and similarly famous—point in a 1919 Supreme Court opinion: "The most stringent protection of free speech," wrote Justice Holmes, "would not protect a man in falsely shouting fire in a theatre and causing a panic."[6]

The Supreme Court followed that principle when it declared, in 1969, that speech "directed to inciting or producing imminent lawless action [that] is likely to incite or produce such action" was not protected by the First Amendment.[7] This unprotected category of speech is titled "incitement." (The flip side of the Court's pronouncement is that even explicit calls for violence—like the advocacy of violence against abortion clinics, or the advocacy of terrorism—remain constitutionally protected unless they are likely to produce imminent lawless action.[8])

Another category of speech that has no First Amendment protection because of its proximity to unlawful action is child pornography. (Visual representations—like photographs or paintings or films—are considered "speech" for First Amendment purposes.)

Child pornography is unprotected because it is created through the criminal sexual exploitation of children—i.e., because it is linked to harmful and criminal actions.[9] Accordingly, child pornography that is *not* produced through sexual crimes—like merely *written* child pornography, or virtual images of child pornography, or adults pretending to be minors—remains constitutionally protected.[10] (The Supreme Court rejected the argument that such materials should be unprotected as well because they may "whet the appetites" of pedophiles, and therefore produce sexual assaults on children. In fact, some evidence points to the opposite conclusion—namely, that such materials may provide sexual outlet for potential predators and may therefore reduce actual crime).

Yet another category that is unprotected because of its proximity to unlawful action is "fighting words"—defined as "personally abusive epithets which, when addressed to the ordinary citizen, are . . . inherently likely to provoke violent reaction."[11] People who address such personally abusive insults to others ("Son of a B . . . ," "F . . . moron") can be constitutionally convicted of offenses like disorderly conduct or disturbing the peace, because of their potential link to actual violence.

Proximity to unlawful action is not the only ground for removing speech from First Amendment protections. Threats of violence, for example, are unprotected speech irrespective of whether they are closely related to actual violence—since even empty threats can produce harms like fear and anxiety. Sexually obscene materials (which today essentially means extreme or hardcore porn) are also unprotected, irrespective of their association with any unlawful action.[12] Still, proximity to unlawful and harmful action is a leading principle distinguishing protected from unprotected speech.

In 2010, the Supreme Court reviewed a case that argued for a new unprotected category of speech based on that speech's proximity to unlawful and harmful action: depictions of animal cruelty produced for financial gain.

III. Crush Videos

In the 1990s, so-called "crush videos" began proliferating on the Internet. The following depiction of a crush video is taken from the Supreme Court opinion examining the constitutionality of banning these vile films. It is a difficult read, but it is important for understanding the stakes in the case:

> [A] kitten, secured to the ground, watches and shrieks in pain as a woman thrusts her high-heeled shoe into its body, slams her heel into the kitten's eye socket and mouth loudly fracturing its skull, and stomps repeatedly on the animal's head. The kitten hemorrhages blood, screams blindly in pain, and is ultimately left dead in a moist pile of blood-soaked hair and bone.[13]

Thousands of such sickening films were sold online. In 1999, Congress took action: it enacted the Depictions of Animal Cruelty Act, which made it a crime to create, sell, or possess depictions of unlawful animal torture produced for commercial purposes. The statute included exemptions for depictions having serious religious, political, scientific, educational, journalistic, historical, or artistic value.[14] Within months, the market in crush videos had dried out.

A decade later, the Supreme Court declared the statute an unconstitutional restriction on the freedom of speech.

As it happened, the first prosecution under the Depictions of Animal Cruelty Act did not concern crush videos but videos of dog fights. Robert J. Stevens was prosecuted and convicted for selling gruesome videos of pit bulls tearing into each other and into terrified farm animals. Stevens appealed his criminal conviction by claiming that the statute violated his First Amendment right to free speech.

The prosecution's principal argument was that commercially sold depictions of animal torture were not protected by the First Amendment because of their necessary connection to unlawful and harmful action. Like child pornography—argued the government—

these prohibited materials were produced by inflicting illegal and terrible harm on defenseless creatures (the gratuitous infliction of cruelty on animals is a crime in all fifty states). And also like child pornography, these prohibited materials serve no cognizable social value, especially given the statute's exemptions for depictions having serious religious, political, scientific, educational, journalistic, historical, or artistic value. The courts—argued the government's lawyers—should uphold the statute by recognizing that depictions of animal cruelty made for commercial purposes were an unprotected category of speech.

The Supreme Court rejected the argument by rejecting the constitutional methodology upon which it was based. The prosecution's argument, explained the Court, was based on "a simple cost-benefit analysis": "The Government . . . proposes that a claim of categorical exclusion [from First Amendment protections] should be considered under a simple balancing test: 'Whether . . . the value of the speech [outweighs] its societal costs.'"[15] Such a test, said the Court, was unacceptable:

> As a free-floating test for First Amendment coverage, that [test] is startling and dangerous. The First Amendment's guarantee of free speech does not extend only to categories of speech that survive an ad hoc balancing of relative social costs and benefits. The First Amendment itself reflects a judgment by the American people that the benefits of its restrictions on the Government outweigh the costs. Our Constitution forecloses any attempt to revise that judgment simply on the basis that some speech is not worth it.[16]

The cost/benefit analysis, said the Court, constituted a "highly manipulable balancing test" that gave judges too much leeway when deciding what speech was protected and what speech wasn't. It allowed judges to extend constitutional protections to speech they favored and remove those protections from speech they disliked—based on their personal value judgments.

The all-important determination of whether a category of speech was protected should not be decided with such a manipulable methodology, said the Court. Instead, the determinative test should be a historical one: unprotected categories of speech, announced the Stevens opinion, were only those categories of speech "that have been historically unprotected." If a category of speech had not been historically unprotected, it must remain protected. And since there was no evidence that commercial depictions of animal cruelty were historically unprotected, they were protected—and the federal statute was unconstitutional.[17]

United States v. Stevens is a good example of why the Court turns to historical tests. It is also a good example of what Brennan had in mind when he accused such tests of turning the Constitution into a "stagnant, archaic, hidebound document steeped in the prejudices and superstitions of a time long past." Although care for the well-being of animals, or "ahimsa," have ancient roots, widespread concern for animal welfare in the United States is mostly a 20th century phenomenon. It is therefore unsurprising that prohibitions on representations of animal cruelty have played no role in American history and tradition. But why shouldn't new moral insights and sensitivities be taken into account in deciding whether a category of speech is unprotected? Why shouldn't the government be able to suppress such vile materials based on our new sensibilities to the sufferings of animals? And why delegate constitutional decisions to a tradition that has been dreadfully wrong on so many occasions? As Brennan put it, "*This* Constitution does not recognize that times change," and that what seemed acceptable once may now seem utterly repugnant.

To its credit, Congress promptly returned to the drawing board after the Supreme Court invalidated its statute. Within months, the invalidated statute was replaced with a new one: The Animal Crush Video Prohibition Act. The new act, however, was far narrower than its predecessor. The Animal Crush Video Prohibition Act made it a federal felony to create, sell, or distribute animal crush videos, which it defined as follows:

> Definition: the term 'animal crush video' means any photograph, motion-picture film, video or digital recording, or electronic image that—(1) depicts actual conduct in which 1 or more living non-human mammals, birds, reptiles, or amphibians is intentionally crushed, burned, drowned, suffocated, impaled, or otherwise subjected to serious bodily injury . . . ; and (2) is obscene.[18]

Thus, Congress sought to assure the constitutionality of its new statute by fitting the prohibited materials into an already existing category of unprotected speech: i.e., sexually obscene materials. In other words, the lawmakers gambled that judges and juries would find crush videos to be a form of sexual perversion. The possession and sale of sadistic videos devoid of sexual implications—like the videos of the deadly dog fights sold by Robert J. Stevens—remained legal.

IV. Military Valor, Military Medals, and Factual Lies

United States v. Stevens exemplified the historical test's potential to keep constitutional doctrine stagnant, archaic, and hidebound. A case decided two years later exemplified Brennan's second critique: that the historical test may not provide the objective, ideology-free evaluation that its proponents proclaim.

In 2005 Congress enacted the Stolen Valor Act, which made it a federal crime, punishable by one year of imprisonment, to fraudulently claim to be a recipient of a U.S. military decoration or medal.[19] As enacted, the Act could be violated in the privacy of one's home. ("It is a pleasure to have you over! You look stunning. Cheers! No no, that's not takeout food, it's my own cooking. By the way, did I ever mention I'm a recipient of the Navy Cross?"). The FBI took this threat to national security seriously: a special FBI task force was dedicated to enforcing the statute, and it investigated approximately 200 cases a year—filing criminal charges in about a quarter of those. One of those prosecutions involved Xavier Alvarez, a habitual liar who previously claimed, among other things, that he played hockey for the Detroit Red Wings, and that he was married to a well-known Mexican actress. When Alvarez claimed he was awarded the Congressional Medal of Honor, he was prosecuted and convicted under the Stolen Valor Act.[20] Alvarez appealed his conviction by claiming that the statute violated his constitutionally protected freedom of speech. The Ninth Circuit Court of Appeals agreed that the statute was unconstitutional, and the government appealed the decision to the Supreme Court.

The government's main argument was that "factual lies" were an unprotected category of speech. The Supreme Court rejected the claim by relying on the historical test announced two years earlier in *Stevens*: a four-Justice plurality found that since factual lies were not historically unprotected, they were protected. The Stolen Valor Act was an unconstitutional restriction on the freedom of speech.

But as Justice Brennan predicted, the deployment of the historical test failed to eliminate the ideological divisions on the Court: although seven of the nine justices employed the historical test, the three most conservative justices disagreed with the rest that factual lies were not historically unprotected. There was—wrote the conservative dissenters—a rich history of removing factual lies from First Amendment protections, including criminal prohibitions on fraud, perjury, making false statements to government officials, and false defamatory speech. And since factual lies were historically unprotected, the Stolen Valor Act was constitutional.

The plurality rejected the argument by drawing a distinction between the factual lies in the dissent's historical precedents, and the sort of factual lies prohibited by the Stolen Valor Act: fraud, perjury, or defamation—they wrote—involved factual lies that caused demonstrable harm to identifiable victims, or were employed to obtain some tangible value (money in the case of fraud, a favorable legal disposition in the case of perjury). But the factual lies prohibited by the Stolen Valor Act were mere lies, nothing more: they did not necessarily involve gaining any tangible advantage. And such bare factual lies were not historically unprotected.

Whether the plurality's argument was or was not convincing, one thing was made clear: deciding whether a category of speech was historically protected was not as straightforward as the Stevens majority may have thought. As Justice Brennan had cautioned, "because reasonable people can disagree about the content of particular traditions, and because they can disagree even about which traditions are relevant," historical tests may not provide the certainty and objectivity that its proponents proclaim. Historical inquiries can quickly become as complicated, as open-ended, and as ideological as the "balancing of costs and benefits" that the Stevens opinion decried.[21]

V. Cost/Benefit Analysis

Unlike the plurality and the dissent, the two remaining justices employed a different methodology: "I agree with the plurality that the Stolen Valor Act of 2005 violates the First Amendment," read Justice Breyer's concurrence, "But I . . . base that conclusion upon the fact that the statute works First Amendment harm, while the Government can achieve its legitimate objectives in less restrictive ways." The concurrence explains its methodology as follows:

> In determining whether a statute violates the First Amendment, this Court has often found it appropriate to examine . . . speech-related harms, justifications, and potential alternatives. In particular, it has taken account of the seriousness of the speech-related harm the provision will likely cause, the nature and importance of the provision's countervailing objectives, the extent to which the provision will tend to achieve those objectives, and whether there are other,

less restrictive ways of doing so. Ultimately the Court has had to determine whether the statute works speech-related harm that is out of proportion to its justifications . . . .[22]

This was the precise methodology that the Court abandoned in *Stevens* after calling it "highly manipulable"—in an opinion joined by Justice Breyer himself. (I will touch on methodological opportunism in Chapter 6.) Breyer's concurrence listed some of the potential benefits of factual lies:

> False factual statements can serve useful human objectives, for example: in social contexts, where they may prevent embarrassment, protect privacy, shield a person from prejudice, provide the sick with comfort, or preserve a child's innocence; in public contexts, where they may stop a panic or otherwise preserve calm in the face of danger; and even in technical, philosophical, and scientific contexts, where (as Socrates' methods suggest) examination of a false statement (even if made deliberately to mislead) can promote a form of thought that ultimately helps realize the truth.[23]

On the other hand, allowing the government to suppress factual lies came with substantial potential costs:

> [T]he pervasiveness of false statements . . . provides a weapon to a government broadly empowered to prosecute falsity without more. And those who are unpopular may fear that the government will use that weapon selectively, say by prosecuting a pacifist who supports his cause by (falsely) claiming to have been a war hero, while ignoring members of other political groups who might make similar false claims.[24]

The Ninth Circuit Court of Appeals, whose opinion was affirmed by the Supreme Court, featured its own concurring opinion that listed the potential benefits of factual lies:

> Saints may always tell the truth, but for mortals living means lying. We lie to protect our privacy ("No, I don't live around here"); to avoid hurt feelings ("Friday is my study night"); to make others feel better ("Gee you've gotten skinny"); . . . to avoid social stigma ("I just haven't met the right woman"); for career advancement ("I'm sooo lucky to have a smart boss like you"); to avoid being lonely ("I love opera"); to eliminate a rival ("He has a boyfriend"); to achieve an objective ("But I love you so much"); to defeat an objective ("I'm allergic to latex"); to make an exit ("It's not you, it's me"); . . . to get someone off your back ("I'll call you about lunch"); . . . to get a clerkship ("You're the greatest living jurist") . . . . And we don't just talk the talk, we walk the walk, as reflected by the popularity of . . . elevator shoes, wood veneer paneling, cubic zirconia, toupees, artificial turf and cross-dressing. Last year, Americans spent $40 billion on cosmetics—an industry devoted almost entirely to helping people deceive each other about their appearance.[25]

If mere factual lies were an unprotected category of speech—said the opinion—the government could make it a crime to lie about one's height or weight or age on Match.com or on Facebook. But "the right to shape one's public and private persona by choosing when to tell the truth about oneself, when to conceal and when to deceive" is "[an] important aspect of personal autonomy."[26]

These cost/benefit analyses reached the same conclusion that the Supreme Court plurality reached through the historical test—but with one important difference: unlike the historical test, they did so by considering what was actually at stake in the case. Thus, unlike the historical test, the cost/benefit analyses laid bare the value judgments that led the concurring judges and justices to invalidate the Stolen Valor Act: telling factual lies was constitutionally protected because factual lies were beneficial and common, and allowing the government to ban them would create a substantial risk of selective enforcement, and could endanger people's legitimate ability to manipulate public perceptions of themselves.

Justice Breyer ended his concurrence with advice for Congress:

> [I]t should be possible significantly to diminish or eliminate these . . . risks by enacting a similar but more finely tailored statute. [A] more finely tailored statute might . . . insist upon a showing that the false statement caused specific harm . . . .[27]

Congress took the advice. As with the Depictions of Animal Cruelty Act, within a year Congress amended the Stolen Valor Act in accordance with the Court's constitutional pronouncement:

> Whoever, with intent to obtain money, property, or other tangible benefit, fraudulently holds oneself out to be a recipient of a decoration or medal described in subsection (c)(2) or (d) shall be fined under this title, imprisoned not more than one year, or both.[28]

There is an important lesson here about separation of powers: even when courts invalidate statutes, their decisions often result only in the partial frustration of legislative policies, since legislatures can salvage their statutes by tweaking them to make them conform to courts' constitutional pronouncements.

VI. Review

To sum up: the Supreme Court has turned to historical tests in various constitutional context, substituting seemingly open-ended and potentially ideological determinations with interpretations based on historical determinations. But critics claim that historical tests unduly freeze constitutional protections, and attach them to a past that is often outdated—or, worse, positively pernicious. And while such tests purport to make constitutional decisions more objective and less ideological, critics allege that in fact they are no different than the tests they replace: historical interpretation involves substantial judgment that can be no less subjective or ideological or manipulable than, say, a cost/benefit analysis. But while cost/benefit analyses lay bare the value judgments of courts, the value judgments' underlying historical analyses remain hidden beneath the marshalled historical facts.

CHAPTER 5

The Rationality of History and Tradition: The Equal Protection Clause and The Right to Same-Sex Marriage

In the previous chapter we saw how the Supreme Court turned to history and tradition in search of a more objective and less ideological constitutional methodology. But curbing judicial discretion is not the only reason for turning to history and tradition: for conservatives, history and tradition are authoritative in their own rights. Deference to history is a matter of first principles for conservatives, who believe that traditions represent the slowly accumulated and painstakingly acquired wisdom of humanity, and that historical perseverance is a testament to a practice's utility and justifiability—even if its precise utility and justifiability are obscured from view.

Critics respond that tradition may represent humanity's wisdom or humanity's stupidity, as the case may be, and that they often outlast their potential utility. Baseball players continue to spit obsessively even though they have long stopped chewing tobacco. Historical traditions should enjoy no special constitutional deference simply because they are historical traditions.

That division of opinions was on full display in 2015, when the Supreme Court reviewed the constitutionality of denying recognition to same-sex marriages. One major constitutional question in the case concerned the rationality (or irrationality) of that denial—rationality being a mandatory constitutional requirement under several constitutional guarantees. But since denying recognition to same-sex marriages had been a long-held historical tradition, some of the justices argued that it should be considered *ipso facto* rational—i.e., rational simply by virtue of its long historical endurance. A bare majority disagreed.

This chapter examines the constitutional question of rationality surrounding the same-sex marriage controversy. We will also look at the claim that rationality is an illegitimate constitutional requirement—a claim that borrows from work in political theory about the democratic legislative process. We start with some equal protection basics.

I. Equal Protection Doctrine and Same-Sex Marriage

The Fourteenth Amendment's Equal Protection Clause reads: "No state shall . . . deny to any person within its jurisdiction the equal protection of the laws." That does not mean, of course, that the law must treat all people equally. The law treats different people differently all the time: only those who are 18 and above can vote; those with large incomes pay a larger percentage of their income in taxes; undocumented immigrants are denied welfare payments that are given to lawful immigrants—and so on. These laws do not violate the Equal Protection Clause because the Clause does not require equal treatment for all; it only requires that any unequal treatment be justified. So, while a law that denies driving privileges to those under 16 is perfectly constitutional, a law that denies driving privileges to blonds is unconstitutional—because it lacks the justification that the Equal Protection Clause demands.

In 2015, the Supreme Court agreed to decide whether laws that denied marriage privileges to same-sex couples possessed a proper justification. The Equal Protection Clause requires compelling justifications in some cases, less strong justifications in others. In principle, strong justifications are required when a law singles out a group that is especially susceptible to unjustified discrimination—for example, members of a racial minority or of a single gender. However, if the law does not target a particularly susceptible group, it is enough if the law is merely "rational"—that is, if it constitutes a rational means of achieving a legitimate purpose.[1] Thus, one central question in the same-sex marriage case was whether homosexuals constituted a group that is particularly susceptible to unjustified discrimination. If they were, the prohibition on homosexual marriage would be constitutional only if the government had a compelling reason for the prohibition; but if homosexuals were not particularly susceptible to unjustified discrimination, the prohibition could be constitutionally validated with relative ease.

The opinion for the Court was written by Justice Anthony Kennedy, a usually conservative justice with a history of joining the liberal wing of the Court in invalidating discrimination against homosexuals. Indeed, the same-sex marriage decision was the culmination of several previous Supreme Court opinions extending constitutional anti-discrimination protections to homosexuals—including the landmark *Lawrence v. Texas* (2003), which invalidated a Texas statute making homosexual sodomy a criminal offense.[2] Significantly, the *Lawrence* decision held that mere moral disapproval of homosexuality could not justify treating homosexuals worse than anyone else. Justice Kennedy was the author of that *Lawrence* opinion, and also of practically all other Supreme Court decisions invalidating discrimination against homosexuals (authorship he was in a position to demand, being the linchpin between the four conservative opponents and the four liberal proponents of most these decisions), securing for himself a place of honor in American constitutional history.

The 2015 5–4 decision, *Obergefell v. Hodges,* held that the prohibition on same-sex marriage violated both the Due Process Clause and the Equal Protection Clause. Homosexuals, said the Court, were constitutionally entitled to enjoy the significant benefits of marriage—which included tax benefits, immigration benefits, inheritance and property rights, hospital visitation privileges, medical decision-making authority, custody adoption rights, and many more.[3] Homosexuals were also entitled to enjoy the intangible benefits of marital unions. "Marriage is a wonderful institution," observed Groucho Marx, "but who wants to live in an institution?" The Obergefells did, along with hundreds of thousands of other homosexual couples.

The Supreme Court supported their choice with effusive praise for marital unions:

> The lifelong union of a man and a woman always has promised nobility and dignity to all persons, without regard to their station in life. Marriage is sacred to those who live by their religions and offers unique fulfillment to those who find meaning in the secular realm. . . . [M]arriage is essential to our most profound hopes and aspirations.[4]

"Marriage," added the Court in a surprisingly candid comment, "responds to the universal fear that a lonely person might call out, only to find no one there." According to the U.S. Supreme Court, marriage is founded on the fear of being alone.

But like his previous opinions involving discrimination against homosexuals, Kennedy's *Obergefell* opinion was remarkably cavalier in its approach to constitutional doctrine. Significantly, the opinion failed to specify whether homosexuals were susceptible to unjustified discrimination—a crucial doctrinal question that divided the lower courts. Some lower courts had little difficulty to conclude that homosexuals were historically, chronically, and unfairly discriminated against, and were particularly vulnerable to unjustified discrimination;[5] but other courts demurred. The *Obergefell* opinion dodged this potentially decisive question: it simply never addressed it.

II. Non-Moral Justification for Prohibiting Same-Sex Marriage?

The recognition of a constitutional right to same-sex marriage—together with the murky legal reasoning and the soaring moral rhetoric—infuriated the four dissenters in the case, who filed four apoplectic opinions. Chief Justice John Roberts labeled the decision "an act of will, not legal judgment" and claimed that:

Those who founded our country would not recognize the majority's conception of the judicial role. . . . They after all risked their lives and fortunes for the precious right to govern themselves. They would never have imagined yielding that right on a question of social policy to unaccountable and unelected judges.[6]

"Just who do we think we are?" added Roberts—meaning, of course, just who do *they* think *they* are? Justice Antonin Scalia called the decision a "threat to American democracy" and claimed that "[a] system of government that makes the People subordinate to a committee of nine unelected lawyers does not deserve to be called a democracy."[7] "[W]hat really astounds is the hubris reflected in today's judicial Putsch," wrote Scalia, who went on to describe the decision as "a naked judicial claim to legislative—indeed, super-legislative—power; a claim fundamentally at odds with our system of government." He added that "The Supreme Court of the United States has descended from . . . disciplined legal reasoning . . . to the mystical aphorisms of the fortune cookie," and concluded: "If . . . I ever joined [such] an opinion . . . I would hide my head in a bag." Justice Thomas wrote that the decision evidenced "disdain for the understandings of liberty and dignity upon which this Nation was founded" and that it "undermin[ed] the political processes that protect our liberty."[8]

All these apocalyptic dissents took issue with the majority's constitutional methodology—in the words of Justice Alito, with the "deep and perhaps irremediable corruption of our legal culture's conception of constitutional interpretation."[9] For the dissenters, the decision was not merely mistaken—it was utterly illegitimate.

One of the clashes between the justices in the majority and the dissents revolved around the rationality of prohibiting same-sex marriages. Since the majority opinion refused to decide whether homosexuals deserved special protections under the Equal Protection Clause, the prohibition on same-sex marriage could have been constitutional if it were a rational means to achieving a legitimate end—a test that is easily satisfied. But was it?

The most obvious purpose of the reluctance to recognize same-sex marriage pertained to moral disapproval of homosexual relationships (which was, of course, the actual motivation for these statutes). But as already mentioned, in 2003 the Court declared that moral disapproval of homosexuality was not a legitimate end, and could not justify treating homosexuals worse than anyone else.[10] Since moral disapproval was out, the states of Michigan, Kentucky, Ohio, and Tennessee—the respondents in *Obergefell* (which was a consolidation of several cases)—had to come up with another purpose that was legitimate and rationally advanced by the prohibition on same-sex marriages.

The states argued that the prohibition served to maximize children's chances of being raised in marital households. If same-sex couples were allowed to marry—argued the four states—fewer heterosexual couples would opt for marriage, and more children would find themselves in non-marital homes.

The Supreme Court called the claim "unrealistic" and "counterintuitive," and noted that there was no evidence to support it. Indeed, why would marriage become less popular if same-sex couples could marry? If anything, marriage would become *more* popular (by adding homosexuals to the rosters), and more children would be raised in marital households—since homosexual couples were raising hundreds of thousands of children in the United States.

The difficulty of coming up with a legitimate purpose once the moral purpose was out became transparently clear long before *Obergefell* reached the Supreme Court. Since 2003, the year *Lawrence* was decided and moral disapproval rejected as a legitimate justification for discriminating against homosexuals, states resorted to a variety of ever-more convoluted attempts to justify their prohibition on same-sex marriage. In 2014, the states of Indiana and Wisconsin argued that the purpose of marriage was to increase the number of children born of *unintentional pregnancies* who were raised by two parents.[11] Since homosexual sex could not result in unintentional pregnancies—argued the states—the refusal to recognize same-sex marriages was justified. The Seventh Circuit said of the argument that it was "so full of holes that it cannot be taken seriously." "[I]f channeling procreative sex into marriage were the only reason that Indiana recognizes marriage," wrote the court, "the state would not allow an infertile person to marry."[12] But not only could infertile heterosexual couples marry, Indiana even carved an exception to its prohibition of marriage between first-cousins for those 65 years old or older—presumably because there was no longer a risk of birth defects resulting from that marriage. Neither same-sex couples nor infertile first cousins could produce unintentional pregnancies, but only the latter could marry.

Moreover, even if "accidental births are indeed the state's sole reason for giving marriage a legal status," said the court, there was still no good reason to deny marriage licenses to same-sex couples— and a good reason to grant it: "Unintentional offspring are the children most likely to be put up for adoption, and if not adopted, to end up in a foster home", and American same-sex couples adopted and provided foster care for two hundred thousand children (including 3,000 in Indiana itself). "If the fact that a child's parents are married enhances the child's prospects for a happy and successful life, as Indiana believes not without reason, this should be true whether the child's parents are natural or adoptive," said the Seventh Circuit Court of Appeals. "The discrimination against same-sex couples is irrational, and therefore unconstitutional," concluded the court.

III. Rationality and Tradition

In *Obergefell*, arguing before the Supreme Court, the states offered one last argument for the rationality of the refusal to recognize same-sex marriage: it was rational, they said, because it was traditional; the recognition of marriage as only between a man and a woman is a long held and near universal tradition, and it is rational and constitutional for that reason. The argument has proven successful with the Sixth Circuit Court of Appeals. In 2014, that court held that the preservation of the traditional definition of marriage was a "rational explanation" for refusing to recognize same-sex marriages:

> [A] State might wish to wait and see before changing a norm that our society (like all others) has accepted for centuries. . . . How can we say that [the State] acted irrationally for sticking with the seen benefits of thousands of years of adherence to the traditional definition of marriage . . . ? A State still assessing how this has worked . . . is not showing irrationality, just a sense of stability and an interest in seeing how the new definition has worked elsewhere. . . . [T]he only thing anyone knows *for sure* about the long-term impact of redefining marriage is that they do not know. A Burkean sense of caution does not violate the Fourteenth Amendment, least of all when measured by a timeline less than a dozen years long and when assessed by a system of government designed to foster step-by-step, not sudden winner-take-all, innovations to policy problems.[13]

But the Supreme Court rejected the argument—as did the Seventh Circuit before it, when it was faced with a similar claim. "The state's argument from tradition," stated the Seventh Circuit, "runs head on into *Loving v. Virginia*, 388 U.S. 1 (1967)"—the famous Supreme Court decision that invalidated the prohibition on interracial marriages—since "[l]aws forbidding black-white marriage dated back to colonial times and were found in northern as well as southern colonies and states."[14] The Seventh Circuit added:

> Wisconsin points out that many venerable customs appear to rest on nothing more than tradition—one might even say on mindless tradition. Why do men wear ties? Why do people shake hands (thus spreading germs) or give a peck on the cheek (ditto) when

greeting a friend? Why does the President at Thanksgiving spare a brace of turkeys (two out of the more than 40 million turkeys killed for Thanksgiving dinners) from the butcher's knife? But these traditions . . . are at least harmless. . . . Tradition per se has no positive or negative significance. There are good traditions, [and] bad traditions . . . such as cannibalism, foot-binding, and suttee, and traditions that from a public-policy standpoint are neither good nor bad (such as trick-or-treating on Halloween). Tradition per se therefore cannot be a lawful ground for discrimination—regardless of the age of the tradition. . . . If no social benefit is conferred by a tradition *and* it is written into law *and* it discriminates against a number of people and does them harm beyond just offending them, it is not just a harmless anachronism; it is a violation of the equal protection clause.[15]

In 1897, Justice Oliver Wendell Holmes made a similar point at a speech at Harvard University: "It is revolting to have no better reason for a rule of law than that it was laid down in the time of Henry IV," said Holmes.[16] And—we might add—if that rule of law discriminates unjustifiably, it is not only revolting, it is also unconstitutional.

The *Obergefell* dissenters disagreed with all that: they thought that the prohibition on same-sex marriage was rational and hence constitutional simply by virtue of it being a long and venerated tradition. One dissenter proclaimed:

It is far beyond the outer reaches of this Court's authority to say that a State may not adhere to the understanding of marriage that has long prevailed, not just in this country and others with similar cultural roots, but also in a great variety of countries and cultures all around the globe.[17]

Another asserted that "a State's decision to maintain the meaning of marriage that has persisted in every culture throughout human history can hardly be called irrational."[18]

The four dissenters in *Obergefell* were all conservatives; and conservatism derives its very name from its veneration of tradition. Conservatives believe that traditions represent potentially optimal social or political solutions, since they developed organically over a long period, and have survived the test of time—as opposed to concocted instant solutions that emerge, fully formed, from the wishful thinking of armchair intellectuals. As the Sixth Circuit put it, we cannot always fully fathom the function performed by a tradition: its utility may be opaque; but its mere emergence and survival are strong indications of its utility—and hence of its rationality. That is why impugning the rationality of this long-held and near-universal tradition seemed the height of intellectual hubris to the four conservative justices: for them, the rationality of a social practice can be measured against its time-tested endurance.

IV. The Rationality of Statutes and Public Choice Theory

Some jurists have gone further and have questioned the very idea that statutes ought to be rational. Their argument is based on the claim that the rough and tumble of the democratic legislative process often produces statutes that simply lack rationality; and that respect for democracy means that judges should not invalidate such legislation.[19]

The claim borrows from Public Choice Theory, an influential theory in political science. According to public choice theory, even if people's policy preferences are coherent and rational, when we aggregate their policy preferences into government policies—as we do in democracies—we often reach public choices that are neither coherent nor rational.[20] That is so because people have different and potentially conflicting interests and values, so that legislative negotiations often result in modifications and accommodations that do not cohere with the original proposal. Political logrolling, or manipulation of the legislative voting agenda, also contribute to less consistent and less rational legislative results.[21] In short, democratic law-making may produce statutes that do not represent any rational or coherent policy determination. It is a mistake, wrote one legal scholar, to conceive of the legislative process "as if a reasonable person were framing coherent legislative policy."[22] To the contrary: a process that aggregates multiple antagonistic and irreconcilable choices should be expected to result in some inconsistencies and incoherence. As Justice Antonin Scalia once put it: "Laws promulgated by the legislative branch can be inconsistent, illogical, and ad hoc . . . ."[23] That is the price of democratic politics. And so—and this is an additional step in the argument—incoherence or irrationality are not proper bases for invalidating statutes. Again, Justice Scalia:

> There are pretty absurd statutes out there. That is what you get from legislative compromise. . . . [T]he deals brokered during a committee markup, on the floor of the two Houses, during a joint House and Senate Conference, or in negotiations with the President . . . are not for us to judge or second-guess.[24]

The democratic legislative process is a dirty sausage factory, and judges must eat that sausage—or, more accurately, dish it out to litigants—however irrational or incoherent that sausage might be.[25]

Criticism of constitutional rationality requirements is not new.[26] The requirement "makes of our courts lunacy commissions sitting in judgment upon the mental capacity of legislators . . . ." wrote one scholar in the 1930s.[27] But the recent critique, with its reliance on public choice theory, summons a more radical idea: unlike the old criticism, the new skepticism is not grounded in doubt over judicial capacity to be more rational than the legislature, but in the assertion of legislative authority to enact potentially irrational, incoherent, and even absurd legal requirements.[28]

Proponents of constitutional rationality requirements disagree that the democratic process tends to produce irrational statutes; but even if it does—they say—it is an entirely different question whether the judiciary should be able to insist on rationality when examining the constitutionality of statutes.

Since rationality requirements are found under various constitutional provisions, the debate over the legitimacy of requiring that statutes be rational—and judicial capacity to enforce that requirement—can have far reaching consequences for constitutional law.[29]

V. Review

To sum up: equal protection doctrine requires that statutes serve a legitimate purpose in a rational manner. Statutes that fail to serve a legitimate purpose, or else fail to rationally advance that purpose, are unconstitutional. But some jurists argue that long-lasting historical traditions ought to be automatically considered rational, simply by virtue of their historical longevity. Other jurists challenge the very idea that statutes ought to be rational. They support their position with public choice theory—a theory that describes and examines the democratic legislative process. Rationality, coherence, or reasonableness, argue these critics, should not be expected of statutes in pluralistic democracies.

Their position has serious ramifications for constitutional interpretation, but also for how judges ought to interpret *statutes*. A rational and coherent statutory purpose has been a working assumption of many judicial philosophies, so the claim that legitimate statutes may be irrational is also a critique of these methodologies. We will examine the controversy surrounding statutory purpose in the chapters dealing with statutory interpretation. The next chapter, however, deals with the most famous of all constitutional philosophies: originalism.

CHAPTER 6

Classic Originalism: The Second Amendment, 18th Century Dictionaries, and Semiautomatic Glocks

History often plays an important role in constitutional interpretation. However, the judicial philosophy called originalism takes that role to a whole new level. According to originalism, constitutional provisions require what they were understood to require at the time of their ratification. If in 1791—the year the Bill of Rights was ratified—it was understood that the First Amendment required X and did not require Y, then the First Amendment, today, requires X and does not require Y. End of story. To be sure, some constitutional questions have no relevant original understanding, and these questions remain unresolved by an originalist approach. But originalists maintain that if there is an original understanding on a given matter, courts must adopt it as the governing constitutional doctrine. In fact, if there is an identifiable original understanding in regard to a constitutional question, that original understanding is the *only relevant factor* in deciding that constitutional question. In other words, the original understanding is both the beginning and the end of the judicial inquiry.

Originalism may appear surprising and even counterintuitive: why is the original understanding necessarily the correct understanding of the Constitution? And why must our constitutional law follow the opinions and beliefs of people who lived in a world that was often very different from ours? This chapter examines these questions, evaluates the persuasiveness of the answers, and concludes by re-evaluating originalism in light of that discussion.

I. *District of Columbia v. Heller* and the Second Amendment

"A well regulated militia being necessary to the security of a free state," reads the Second Amendment, "the right of the people to keep and bear arms shall not be infringed." In 2008, the Supreme Court decided *District of Columbia v. Heller*, and revolutionized Second Amendment doctrine. The plaintiff in the case was Dick Heller, a Washington D.C. resident and a security guard who carried a gun for work. Under the restrictive gun control measures in Washington D.C., Heller needed a special license to keep his gun at home, and was forced to keep it there "unloaded and dissembled or bound by a trigger lock or similar device."[1] *District of Columbia v. Heller* was a test case—a case that was devised from the get-go with the purpose of changing Second Amendment doctrine. Dick Heller was recruited as a plaintiff by a group of conservative jurists who prepared and financed the case. Test cases are common practice in the United States, and a number of landmark Supreme Court cases were test cases.[2]

District of Columbia v. Heller achieved what it set out to do: the lawsuit radically changed the Supreme Court's interpretation of the Second Amendment. Prior to 2008, Second Amendment doctrine was guided by the Amendment's purpose—namely, preserving the states' militias as a force against a potentially tyrannical federal government. As we know, the Bill of Rights was adopted to quiet concerns over the increased powers of the federal government under the U.S. Constitution. The Second Amendment fulfilled that purpose by assuring the states that they could keep their military forces—their militias—in case the federal government turned belligerent and threatened their freedom. Accordingly, in accordance with the Second Amendment's purpose and text, "the right of the people to keep and bear arms" was understood as a right of those serving in state militias—not as a right of the general public.

District of Columbia v. Heller changed all that. "[T]he Second Amendment's prefatory clause," declared the *Heller* decision, "announces the purpose for which the right was codified: to prevent elimination of the militia."[3] But that purpose did not govern the Amendment's constitutional requirements. The Amendment's constitutional requirements was determined solely by reference to the original understanding of the Second Amendment. And that original understanding—said the Supreme Court—was violated by Washington D.C.'s gun restrictions.

District of Columbia v. Heller was therefore a landmark decision for two reasons: first, for holding that the Second Amendment granted individuals who were not serving in a state militia the right to carry a gun; and second, for its originalist judicial philosophy. Indeed, *Heller* was not only a decision that fulfilled the long-held dreams of many gun rights activists, it was also the most originalist Supreme Court opinion in modern constitutional history.

II. Originalism and Judicial Power

Stripped to its essence, originalism is a simple methodology. As the *Heller* opinion put it, "Constitutional rights are enshrined with the scope they were understood to have when the people adopted them."[4] What the Second Amendment requires is simply what it was understood to require in 1791—the date of its ratification. If in 1791 the Second Amendment was understood to confer a right to possess handguns at home, then a 21st century law that forbids the possession of handguns at home is unconstitutional. In fact, if in 1791 the Second Amendment was understood to confer a right to possess bombs at home, then, per originalism, a law that forbids the possession of bombs at home is also unconstitutional.

Having stated its constitutional methodology, the *Heller* decision set out to determine what 18th century Americans understood by the Second Amendment. The evidence included 18th century dictionaries and newspaper articles, some writings by James Madison, Alexander Hamilton, and Thomas Jefferson, and even some 18th century debates in the English House of Lords (since the constitutional right to keep and bear arms had its origin in English law). These and other historical sources led the Court to conclude that 18th century Americans understood the Second Amendment to encompass a right to possess readily operable handguns at home, for all individuals (not only those serving in state militias).

The opinion paid no heed to the enormous differences between 1791 and 2008—differences which included the contemporary pervasiveness of gun-related crime, the large number of accidental shootings, the high rate of gun suicides, and the incomparable fire-power of modern handguns. The Court deemed these differences irrelevant to its constitutional conclusion: "modern developments . . . cannot change our interpretation of the right," said the Court. The justices simply refused to consider the enormous changes in circumstance over the past 200 years, or the purpose for which the Second Amendment was drafted and ratified, or even the practical consequences of recognizing a constitutional right to possess operative handguns at home.

One might wonder: why ask judges to ignore the practical consequences of their anticipated decisions, or the purposes for which constitutional provisions were ratified, when they apply these provisions? Most Americans might find it surprising to realize, for example, that the Supreme Court revolutionized Second Amendment doctrine without giving a thought to mass shootings. And why, in the 21st century, take as authoritative the opinions of some 18th century men, who lived in a world very different from ours, who held to some values that were at odds with our own, and who (in the case of the Second Amendment) had handguns that could barely shoot? Moreover, the 18th century people whose understanding of the Constitution is determinative to originalism—i.e., those who held the franchise and could therefore participate in the constitution-making process—were a small, non-representative minority: they did not include non-whites, they did not include women, and they did not even include the overwhelming majority of adult white males—who lacked the requisite property qualifications for the franchise. In other words, judged by today's standards, the people who drafted, adopted, and ratified the Constitution and the Bill of Rights did not even possess proper democratic legitimacy.

So why delegate complete control over our current constitutional requirements to these long-dead individuals? Why regard their opinions about the right to bear arms—or about the freedoms of speech or religion—as dispositive for our constitutional law today? To put things bluntly, the originalist methodology sounds a little nuts: nobody doubts that the original understanding of the Constitution is a thing to consider when interpreting the Constitution, but why must it be the only thing?

According to classic originalism, the answer to this question is this: originalism prevents judges from making constitutional decisions that are based on their personal values.

Although courts have long referred to original constitutional understandings, originalism emerged as a self-contained judicial philosophy only in the 1980s—partly as a result of simmering conservative resentment over decades of liberal Supreme Court decisions (particularly those of the Warren Court of the late 1950s and 1960s). Conservative jurists believed that liberal justices were shaping constitutional law in the image of their political ideology. Their solution was a method of constitutional interpretation that purported to minimize judges' opportunities to inject their own ideological preferences into constitutional decisions. Originalism therefore purports to transform constitutional interpretation into a fact-based and objective historical inquiry. According to originalism, the requirements of the Equal Protection Clause or the First Amendment's freedom of speech are the function of sheer historical facts: i.e., what these provisions were understood to require at the time they were ratified.

In short, proponents of originalism claim that it provides a fixed and objective methodology with which to establish constitutional requirements. Most originalists adopt originalism for this reason.[5] The point of classic originalism—its very *raison d'être*—is that it constrains judicial power by taking away judges' ability to impose their value judgments on constitutional interpretation. But some serious questions surround the philosophy: can originalism really deliver on its promise of a fact-based inquiry—and if it can, at what price?

III. Can Originalism Deliver?

When evaluating originalism, we must ask whether the benefits of originalism are worth its price: whether preventing judges from using speculative and potentially ideological considerations can justify preventing them from considering the practical realities surrounding their decisions, or the purposes of constitutional provisions, or their expected consequences.[6] After all, asking judges to consider the expected consequences of constitutional purposes or changed conditions appears essential for wise and practical constitutional solutions, and may be worth the drawbacks of broad judicial power.

But even before we inquire whether originalism comes at too high a price, we must first ask whether originalism can actually curb judicial power: is originalism the factual, non-ideological method of constitutional interpretation that it purports to be? There are good reasons to believe it is not. Some possible obstacles for originalism's aspiration for objectivity and ideological neutrality follow.

i. One Original Understanding?

One difficulty involves originalism's assumption of a single original understanding. In reality, the drafters and ratifiers of the U.S. Constitution may have had several different understandings of the constitutional text. Scholars point to examples like the Sedition Act of 1798. Enacted a mere seven years after the ratification of the First Amendment, the Act made it a criminal offense:

> To write, print, utter or publish ... any false, scandalous, and malicious writing against the government of the United States, or either House of Congress, or the

President, with intent to defame, or bring either into contempt or disrepute . . . .[7]

Editors and journalists were prosecuted and imprisoned for up to five years under this Act, although its constitutionality was rigorously protested by its opponents.

The constitutional validity of the Sedition Act involved the most basic principles of the First Amendment's freedom of speech. And yet, the very people who drafted and adopted the First Amendment were bitterly split over the constitutionality of the Act. Here were two irreconcilable original understandings of the First Amendment. In fact, such divergent understandings were instrumental in allowing the fledgling nation to coalesce around a new Constitution and a Bill of Rights, for each faction saw in the vague constitutional text a promise for its own vision of America. Without this haziness, conflicting factions may have never been able to agree on a constitutional text. And if this is the case, then originalist interpretation simply allows judges to choose, from among several available options, the original understanding that best fits their own personal or ideological preferences.

ii. Historical Interpretation

Even if there was a single original understanding, the process of unearthing it could be riddled with error and abuse. The historical record surrounding the drafting and ratification of the U.S. Constitution is notoriously incomplete and deficient. For example, the official record of the 1787 Constitutional Convention fails to include all the resolutions and votes, contains obvious mistakes, neglects to mention the dates of some proceedings, and had entire sections that were deliberately destroyed.[8] "Careless" is how a leading constitutional historian described that record keeping.[9]

It is unsurprising, therefore, that disagreements about the purported original understanding are rife. One scholar tells us that "In equal protection jurisprudence, for example, originalist analysis has run virtually the entire gamut of possible [results], from . . . [rejecting] virtually all the major developments from the time of the Warren Court to the present, to . . . [embracing] almost all of these developments . . . ."[10] In fact, many of today's originalists are divided into reliably conservative originalists and reliably liberal ones—with each camp marshaling its own historical support to reach its favorite ideological results.[11]

Heller is a good example of the phenomenon. Although they were not originalists, the dissenters in *Heller* filed a forty-six-page opinion arguing that the original understanding of the Second Amendment granted the right to bear arms only to those serving in state militias. Like the majority, they cited the writings of the Founding Fathers, records of Congress, statements made in the ratifying conventions, 18th century dictionaries, and newspaper articles from the time—all in order to reach the opposite conclusion from the majority's. The majority responded by claiming that the dissent "flatly misreads the historical record . . . ."[12] But that was precisely what the dissent said about the majority. A Pulitzer Prize–winning historian wrote that "neither of the two main opinions in *Heller* would pass muster as serious historical writing."[13]

Historical interpretation, it turns out, is no less controversial—and no less ideological—than alternative methodologies of constitutional interpretation. The historical record—sometimes sparse, often vague, frequently ambiguous—does not speak for itself. The record requires interpretation, and that interpretation may be as contestable as any non-historical one.

iii. Precedents

There are yet more opportunities for originalist judges to inject their ideological preferences. It is indisputable that current constitutional doctrine is, by and large, the result of non-originalist interpretation, and is therefore replete with allegedly non-originalist conclusions.

Notable examples include the extensive power of the federal government under the Commerce Clause (which grants Congress the power to "To regulate Commerce with foreign Nations, and among the several States. . . ."[14]), the prohibition on gender discrimination under the Equal Protection Clause, free speech protections for defamatory or profane speech under the First Amendment, or the Eighth Amendment's ban on corporal punishment.

Realizing that a purely originalist jurisprudence would amount to a veritable revolution in constitutional doctrine (since so much would need to be overruled), originalists agree that many non-originalist interpretations should be left to stand: "almost every originalist," wrote the originalist Justice Scalia, "would adulterate [originalism] with the doctrine of *stare decisis* . . . ."[15]—i.e., the principle that, barring special circumstances, courts should stand by their previous decisions.[16] In other words, originalist judges reserve for themselves the prerogative to decide whether a non-originalist precedent should be overruled or left intact; and that decision, the standards for which are extremely vague, introduces another layer of potentially ideological discretion into the originalist decision. If an originalist judge dislikes a non-originalist decision, she may decide to overrule it; if she likes it, she may opt to comply with the doctrine of *stare decisis*.

iv. Bitter Pills

Additionally, most originalists concede that some originalist positions are flat-out unacceptable. For example, it seems that the original understanding of the Equal Protection Clause did not forbid racially segregated public schools. The Thirty-Ninth Congress that passed the Fourteenth Amendment, and most of the states that ratified it, maintained segregated school systems at the time that the Amendment was added to the Constitution, and there was no indication that they understood the Amendment to outlaw the practice.[17] The same is true of the prohibition on interracial marriages, and—in regard to the Eighth Amendment—of mutilation and branding as criminal punishments. But as Justice Scalia put it: "I cannot imagine myself, any more than any other federal judge, upholding a statute that imposes the punishment of flogging."[18] In other words, originalist judges also reserve the right to decide whether the originalist understanding should be followed, or whether it should be bypassed for being too unpalatable. Such decisions inject yet another layer of potential influences of judges' moral or political sensibilities.

v. Modern Times

Even if there was one original understanding, and even if we correctly identified it, even if we put aside any contrary precedent, and even if the originalist solution was palatable, there is still the question of whether the original understanding actually applied to the situation at hand. Does the original understanding of the Fourth Amendment apply to GPS tracking devices? Does the original understanding of the Second Amendment apply to automatic assault rifles, given that the arms in existence when the Second Amendment was ratified resemble the AR-15 as much as a horse resembles a car, or an abacus a modern computer? At what point do these enormous differences in technology and capacity make the original understanding irrelevant and therefore inapplicable to modern cases? At what point does the analogy between the original understanding and the question before the Court becomes too attenuated? Originalists have no coherent theory for making these fraught determinations. These determinations, it seems, may simply depend on a judge's own ideological preferences.

In short, the difficulties of historical analysis, and the many layers of discretionary judgments placed on top of it, appear to belie the claim that originalism is merely a fact-based inquiry that precludes judicial value judgments.

IV. Reevaluating Originalism

Some have argued that originalism cannot be right because originalism was not the original understanding of proper constitutional interpretation. At the time that the Constitution was drafted and ratified, it was generally understood that constitutional interpretation did not consist in adherence to some original understanding.[19] But although there is some delicious irony here, this fact cannot prove originalism wrong: like all judicial philosophies, originalism is a political theory about the best judicial practices, and its propriety depends on its ability to produce a beneficial body of constitutional results, and to guide and constrain judicial power. If it can deliver on those two fronts, it is a good judicial philosophy—regardless of the judicial philosophies of the Founding Fathers. But does it deliver?

As for beneficial results, originalism ties our constitutional law to the often-obsolete opinions of people who had lived under markedly different conditions, and who held to some social and political values we now find objectionable. Earlier in this chapter, we examined a host of alleged originalist results that most modern Americans would consider unacceptable. They include the constitutionality of racially segregated public schools, the constitutionality of the prohibition on interracial marriages, the constitutionality of barring women from jury duty or from dangerous occupations, or the constitutionality of criminalizing homosexuality. Most modern Americans would also object to having no constitutional protections for speech defaming public officials, no free speech protections for profanities, no constitutional entitlement to government-paid counsel for those who cannot afford one in criminal trials, and the permissibility of corporal punishments like branding and ear cropping. The parade of originalist horrors is long.

Originalism also insists that judges must shut their eyes to the real-life circumstances and consequences of their constitutional decisions. But as one of the two dissenting opinions in *Heller* put it, courts should not make important constitutional decisions while ignoring the realities on the ground:

[T]o see whether the statute is unconstitutional . . . requires us to focus on practicalities, the statute's rationale, the problems that called it into being . . . . [Should we assume that the Framers] would not have cared about the children who might pick up a loaded gun on their parents' bedside table? That they . . . would have lacked concern for the risk of accidental deaths or suicides that readily accessible loaded handguns in urban areas might bring? . . . How can the Court assess the strength of the government's regulatory interests without addressing issues of empirical fact? How can the Court determine if a regulation is appropriately tailored without considering its impact?[20]

The originalist methodology binds our constitutional law to obsolete and outdated positions, while forbidding consideration of many seemingly important and relevant factors. Such an approach, claimed the *Heller* dissent, is a recipe for irrational and harmful constitutional decisions. Originalism is a judicial philosophy that so distrusts judicial power that it is willing to curb it at the steep price of less rational and less practical constitutional laws.

Moreover, while originalism proclaims itself a fact-based, objective inquiry that leaves little room for judges' own political beliefs, it does not appear to live up to that promise. In practice, originalism involves extensive judicial discretion that appears to be no different than the judicial philosophies that its proponents decry, with an added disadvantage: the judicial discretion involved in originalist interpretation lacks the transparency that many of its philosophical competitors have. In *Heller*, the majority accused Justice Breyer's dissent of proposing an illegitimate "judge-empowering interest-balancing inquiry" for determining the scope of the Second Amendment. Breyer responded:

The majority derides my approach as "judge-empowering." I take this criticism seriously, but I do not think it accurate . . . . Application of such an approach, of course, requires judgment, but the very nature of the approach—requiring careful identification of the relevant interests and evaluating the law's effect upon them—limits the judge's choices; and the method's necessary transparency lays bare the judge's reasoning for all to see and to criticize.[21]

Taking into account the expected impact of a constitutional decision surely involves some judicial value judgment; but that judgment lays the cards on the table, so to speak: it shows to the world the reasons, and the values, that led the judge to the conclusion. Originalism, by contrast, involves no less discretion, but (as with the historical test we previously examined) its value judgments are masked and obscured as historical fact-finding. As one scholar put it:

Scalia argued that originalism supplies a fixed ascertainable meaning of the constitutional text . . . . In fact, nearly the opposite is true. . . . [O]riginalism involves the courts in policy disputes and value judgments no less than the currently prevalent nonoriginalist approach. But at least the nonoriginalist approach allows them to do so openly, and thus (one hopes) to approach the choices involved more clearly and honestly.[22]

Transparency in decision making is an important check on judicial power: it allows us to examine whether constitutional decisions are based on sound and convincing reasoning—or on prejudices and unsound conjectures—and to evaluate the moral or political judgments that may lie at the base of constitutional decisions. It is crucial for the public assessment of the work of our courts.

In short, originalism's doubtful ability to fulfill its methodological promise, and its potential to produce impractical or even harmful results, raise serious doubts about its merit as a leading constitutional philosophy. That is one reason why a substantial number of constitutional scholars broke rank with classic originalism, and proposed radical revisions to the philosophy. We will examine their proposals in the following chapter. But first, let's look at another possible consequence of the methodological difficulties of classic originalism: its habitual betrayal by people who purport to adhere to it.

V. Methodological Opportunism?

The 2008 *Heller* decision signaled that a majority of Supreme Court justices endorse originalism. Many commentators believed that the decision heralded a new, more dominant era for originalism in our highest court. However, it soon became clear that *Heller* did not mark any significant change in the Court's constitutional philosophy. In fact, in the years following *Heller*, some of the very justices who joined that opinion expressed open skepticism of originalism.

In 2010, the Supreme Court heard oral arguments in *Brown v. Entertainment Merchants Association*, a First Amendment challenge to a California statute that limited the sale of violent video games to minors.[23] At one point, Justice Scalia expressed doubt about the constitutionality of the statute by telling the California Deputy Attorney General: "You are asking us to create a whole new prohibition [on speech] which the American people never ratified when they ratified the First Amendment."[24] That was textbook originalism: everything depended on how the people who ratified the First Amendment understood it. But before the Deputy could respond, Justice Samuel Alito chimed in: "I think what Justice Scalia wants to know is what James Madison thought about video games." Alito added, to general laughter, "Did he enjoy them?"[25] Justice Scalia was not amused. But amusement value aside, Alito's comment alluded to a fundamental difficulty of originalism—and that, merely two years after he joined, without qualification, Justice Scalia's opinion in *Heller*. Indeed, the potential absurdity of applying 18th century understandings to 21st century issues is a perennial problem for originalism. And the *Heller* opinion itself may have been guilty of such absurdity, by treating the original understanding regarding flintlock pistols as dispositive to rapid fire handguns (and who knows what Madison thought about semiautomatic Glocks, or if he enjoyed them).

Two years after *Brown v. Entertainment Merchants Association*, Alito again derided originalism. *United States v. Jones* (2012) was about whether the police had to obtain a search warrant in order to place a GPS device on a vehicle.[26] Justice Scalia's opinion for the Court relied on an originalist methodology in holding that a warrant was required. Justice Alito, joined by three other justices, agreed with the result but criticized the opinion's originalist methodology: "It is almost impossible to think of late-18th-century situations that are analogous to what took place in this case," he wrote.

> Is it possible to imagine a case in which a constable secreted himself somewhere in a coach and remained there for [a month] in order to monitor the movements of the coach's owner? . . . [T]his would have required either a gigantic coach, a very tiny constable, or both—not to mention a constable with incredible fortitude and patience.[27]

Once again, Alito raised a fundamental objection to originalism—four years after casting the fifth and decisive vote in the most originalist Supreme Court opinion in modern history.

Judges are supposed to be consistent in their choice of judicial philosophy—not cherry-pick the philosophy that happens to produce their desired result. Judicial philosophies are expected to constrain judicial power and make sure it is properly used; but such constraint cannot work if judges switch judicial philosophies from one case to the other.

VI. Review

To sum up: originalism's principal justification is its purported ability to provide an objective and factual methodology for constitutional interpretation. But critics argue that originalism fails to fulfill that promise. The reasons for the alleged failure include the potential existence of numerous original understandings; the difficult and open-ended nature of historical interpretation; the originalists' vague standard for overruling non-originalist precedents; their vague standard for *stare decisis*; and finally, the difficulty of determining the relevance of originalist understandings to modern circumstances. All these produce substantial judicial discretion in originalist constitutional interpretation. At the same time, as with other historical tests, originalist interpretation lacks the transparency possessed by some of its competing philosophies. Finally, originalism tethers constitutional interpretation to potentially obsolete and outdated positions, and may thus tend to produce obsolete and impractical results.

In short, judged against the twin criteria of legitimate process and desirable results, originalism appears to fare only moderately in regard to the former, and in all likelihood poorly in regard to the latter.

Partly as a response to persistent critiques, a new form of originalism has emerged recently, one that is radically different than the classic originalism presented above. That new originalism is the subject of the next chapter.

CHAPTER 7

New Originalism and Moral Truths: The Cruel and Unusual Punishment Clause, and Ear Cropping for Overtime Parking.

This chapter examines the emergence of a new form of originalism—the "new originalism"—which constitutes a radical break from the classic originalism surveyed in the previous chapter. Classic originalism—promoted in the 1980s by jurists like Judge Robert Bork, Attorney General Edwin Meese, and Justice Antonin Scalia[1]—was propounded as a restraint on judicial value judgments. But the new originalism disclaims any such interest. The new originalists agree with the old originalists that the original understanding of the constitutional text is the authoritative measure of constitutional requirements. But from this cardinal principle the new originalists derive a methodology that is radically different than the one proclaimed by their predecessors.

The new originalists believe that judges must establish the originalist meanings of vague and moral constitutional terms like "liberty," "cruelty," or "equality," and must then apply those meanings to the question before the court. Needless to say, such an interpretive methodology leaves plenty of room for judicial value judgments—indeed, it calls for them.

The chapter surveys this divide among originalists, and also examines one of the more philosophically complex questions implicated in judicial philosophy: whether moral determinations have a truth value (i.e., can be true or false) or are merely matters of personal preference or subjective opinion.

I. Ear Cropping for Overtime Parking

In the early morning hours of May 12, 1986, Ronald Harmelin ran a red light in Oak Park, Michigan. It proved to be a fatal mistake. Two officers seated in an unmarked car saw the traffic violation, gave chase, pulled over Harmelin, and discovered 672 grams of cocaine (about 1.5 pounds) in the trunk of his old Ford. Harmelin had an honorable discharge from the US Air Force and no criminal record. But, under Michigan law at the time, he was sentenced to a mandatory life in prison without the possibility of parole.[2] In 1990, four years after Harmelin's initial arrest, the U.S. Supreme Court agreed to review his claim that his sentence violated the Eighth Amendment's prohibition on cruel and unusual punishment.

According to standing constitutional doctrine, the Cruel and Unusual Punishment Clause prohibits punishments that are disproportionate to the crime—i.e., punishments that are too severe in relation to the gravity of the offense.[3] That understanding of the Cruel and Unusual Punishment Clause led the Supreme Court to hold, for example, that it was unconstitutional to impose the death penalty for rape.[4] The Court also declared unconstitutional the imposition of life imprisonment without the possibility of parole on a repeat offender who forged a $100 check.[5]

Like the forger whose sentence was vacated, Harmelin was also sentenced to life imprisonment without the possibility of parole for a non-violent offense (drug possession). Moreover, unlike the forger, Harmelin had no previous record. But the Supreme Court rejected Harmelin's appeal: in a divided decision that produced five judicial opinions and was decided on the strength of a single vote, the Supreme Court held that Harmelin could be made to serve the rest of his life in prison, without the possibility of parole, for a single violation of drug possession.[6]

Seven of the justices agreed—in accordance with precedent—that the Eighth Amendment prohibited disproportionate punishments: if a statute punished overtime parking with life imprisonment (wrote Justice White in his dissenting opinion), wouldn't that be both "cruel" and "unusual"?[7] But the seven justices were divided over the application of the test to Harmelin. Whereas four thought that Harmelin's punishment was disproportionate to his crime, three believed that it wasn't: "Possession, use, and distribution of illegal drugs," they wrote, "represent one of the greatest problems affecting the health and welfare of our population."[8] Harmelin, they noted, was convicted of possessing between 32,500 and 65,000 doses of cocaine: "Petitioner's suggestion that his crime was nonviolent and victimless . . . is false to the point of absurdity. To the contrary, petitioner's crime threatened to cause grave harm to society."[9] The three voted to affirm Harmelin's sentence.

The case was therefore decided by the two remaining justices—Justice Scalia and Chief Justice Rehnquist—who rejected the very idea that the Eighth Amendment required proportionality between punishment and crime. Their rejection began with an argument we have met before:

> [The dissent] argues that the Eighth Amendment
> must contain a proportionality principle, because
> otherwise legislatures could make overtime parking
> a felony punishable by life imprisonment. . . . [The]
> argument has force only for those who believe that
> the Constitution prohibited everything that is intense-
> ly undesirable—which is an obvious fallacy, *see* Art. I,
> § 9 (implicitly permitting slavery).[10]

The Constitution did not require perfection: it used to permit slavery, and it still permitted disproportionate punishments.

The justification for this conclusion was twofold. First, a proportionality requirement contradicted the original understanding of the Cruel and Unusual Punishment Clause. Second, proportionality determinations were too subjective.

II. The Old and the New Originalism

"[T]he ultimate question," wrote Justice Scalia in a part of the opinion joined only by Chief Justice Rehnquist, "is . . . what 'cruel and unusual punishments' meant . . . to the Americans who adopted the Eighth Amendment."[11] To establish that meaning, the opinion turned to the usual sources of originalist interpretation—including the Federalist Papers, an 1828 edition of Webster's American Dictionary, records of debates at the state ratifying conventions, the actions of the First Congress, and early commentary on the Eighth Amendment. The justices summed up their findings:

> The Eighth Amendment received little attention during the proposal and adoption of the Federal Bill of Rights. However, what evidence exists from debates at the state ratifying conventions that prompted the Bill of Rights, as well as the floor debates in the First Congress which proposed it, confirm the view that the cruel and unusual punishments clause was [only] directed at prohibiting certain *methods* of punishment.[12]

According to this originalist interpretation, at the time of its ratification the Eighth Amendment was understood to forbid only certain gruesome punishments—not to forbid punishments that were grossly disproportionate to their crimes.

The reasoning was classic originalism. But classic originalism is no longer the only game in town: recent decades saw the remarkable rise of a new version of originalism.[13] That new version—which began to emerge back in the 1990s—is a fundamentally different judicial philosophy. While it agrees with the classic originalist view that the Constitution requires simply what its original understanding requires, the approach of the new originalism to constitutional decision-making is remarkably different.

In explaining that difference, new originalists often resort to a distinction between constitutional "interpretation" and constitutional "construction."[14] Originalist decisions, they say, require a two-step process. The first, called "interpretation," consists in establishing the original linguistic meaning of a constitutional provision—for example, the original meaning of the term "commerce" in the Commerce Clause, or the original meaning of the phrase "freedom of speech" in the First Amendment. Once the original meaning has been established, a second step—which they call "construction"—consists in applying that meaning to the case at hand. Since the linguistic meaning of many constitutional terms is quite vague and abstract, the process of construction is often (though not always) both evaluative and deeply controversial. Think, for example, of constitutional phrases like "freedom," "liberty," "equal protection," "unreasonable searches," and many more: their linguistic meanings are highly philosophical and value-laden, and may allow for radically different applications (Is this a reasonable police search, given the original meaning of "reasonable"? Is that a violation of equality, given the original meaning of "equality"?).

Needless to say, classic originalists would have none of that: for them, the whole point of originalism is to prevent judges from engaging in moral or other potentially ideological evaluations; that is originalism's *raison d'être*. The original meaning that old originalists are after is therefore always specific and concrete, never abstract: they refer to concrete statements, concrete practices, and specific understandings of the original meaning. Unlike the new originalists, when the old originalists apply the Eighth Amendment's Cruel and Unusual Punishment Clause, they do not first establish the abstract linguistic meaning of "cruelty" in 1791, and then apply that abstract meaning to the case before them. Instead, they seek specific historical statements or facts that provide ready-made answers to the constitutional questions they face. For example, if the death penalty had been imposed continuously and without protest throughout the 18th century, both before and after the ratification of the Cruel and Unusual Punishment Clause, that would provide conclusive evidence for the classic originalists that capital punishment is constitutional under the original understanding of the Eighth Amendment.[15] For classic originalists, originalist interpretation must revolve around historical statements or practices that demonstrate concrete and specific constitutional requirements. Allowing judges to plumb the depths of 18th century moral concepts would defeat the whole point of originalist theory.

Thus, unlike classic originalism, the new originalism openly asks judges to make evaluative judgments, including moral judgments, when they make constitutional decisions: new originalism does not even pretend to be a sheer fact-based philosophy. "It is true that when originalism became revived in the 1980s, one of the reasons for reviving it was to constrain judges because the idea was that judges were unconstrained," wrote one leading new originalist; but the new originalism "is not an enterprise in constraining judges. . . . Sometimes [originalism] will constrain judges and sometimes [it] will empower judges."[16] This crucial distinction between classic originalism and new originalism explains the different ideological orientation of their followers: while the classic originalists are overwhelmingly conservative jurists, many of the new originalists are liberals—and many of their conclusions are liberal too. (The division between conservatives and liberals in the choice of judicial philosophy will be considered in the last chapter.)

In truth, were it not for the earnestness with which the new originalists press their claims, one might have thought the theory was a cynical ploy—a Trojan horse bent on making originalism less conservative and more liberal—which is precisely how some classic originalists view the theory. But the new originalism may also be viewed as an unavoidable correction of classic originalism.

III. Old Originalism v. New Originalism

Many scholars believe that classic originalism is intellectually unsound. It is true that concrete statements and concrete practices may provide *indications* as to the original understanding of a constitutional provision, but surely they are not necessarily *dispositive* as to that original understanding (as the old originalists would have it). After all, both historical statements and historical practices may fail to comply with the correct original understanding of a constitutional provision. Here are three such probable examples.

In 1983, the Supreme Court held that the Nebraska Legislature's practice of opening its sessions with prayers led by a government-paid chaplain did not violate the Establishment Clause, which forbids certain intermingling between church and state. In doing so, the Court relied exclusively on the fact that the Congress of 1789—which drafted and adopted the Establishment Clause—itself held legislative prayers both before and after the 1791 ratification of the Establishment Clause, as did subsequent Congresses.[17] For classic originalism, that fact suffices to conclude that legislative prayers do not violate the original understanding of the Establishment Clause.

And yet it seems perfectly plausible that the Establishment Clause, as originally understood, was actually violated by the practice: Congress may have intentionally flouted its own understanding of the Establishment Clause, or may have done so in error. (To be sure, politicians are not immune to hypocrisy nor to error of judgment.) And if this were so, 18th century legislative prayers could not be taken as irrefutable proof of the original understanding of the Establishment Clause regarding legislative prayers. In fact, no less an authority than James Madison—the most important of the constitutional drafters—actually believed that Congress' legislative prayers were unconstitutional (after initially supporting the practice).[18]

Here is another example: The Congress that drafted and adopted the Fourteenth Amendment's Equal Protection Clause, and the state legislatures that ratified it, did not think that the Clause would be violated by racial segregation in public schools. At the time that the Amendment was drafted and ratified (and for a long time thereafter), Washington, D.C. and most of the states that ratified it maintained racially segregated school systems.[19] Federal and state representatives did not think they were making their segregation unlawful.

They also did not understand the Equal Protection Clause to prohibit gender-based discrimination. Still, both racially segregated schools and gender-based government discrimination may be in violation of the original meaning of "equal protection of the laws." The drafters and ratifiers of the Fourteenth Amendment may have failed to take their own concepts to their logical conclusion: they may have failed to realize the full implications of their own constitutional requirement or were unwilling to comply with it. Indeed, this is precisely what some new originalists now claim: the original meaning of the Equal Protection Clause—argue a number of new originalists—in fact prohibits segregated schools and protects against sex discrimination.[20]

Finally, consider the federal Sedition Act of 1798, which was mentioned in the previous chapter. The very people who gave us the constitutional protection for the freedom of speech also adopted a statute that criminalized criticism of the federal government. Isn't it possible that this controversial Act evidenced a profound misunderstanding—or worse, a conscious betrayal—of what the constitutionally-protected freedom of speech actually meant, even in the 18th century?

In short, concrete statements and concrete practices may fail to capture the real original understanding of a constitutional provision.

Unlike classic originalists, the new originalists do take seriously the possible gap between statements and practices at the time of ratification and the correct original meaning of the constitutional text. And this means that proper originalist interpretation may require the hard work of exploring and applying some abstract moral terms like "equality" or "cruelty" or "reasonableness" or "freedom"—as the new originalists argue.

It also means—as previously mentioned—that the new originalism cannot even pretend to constrain judicial discretion as the classic originalism does. A judicial philosophy that requires judges to establish the 18th or 19th century meanings of vague and moral philosophical concepts like "cruelty" or "equality" or "freedom," and then apply these abstract meanings to today's circumstances, surely involves no less discretion—arguably more—than the non-originalist methodology that prompted the emergence of originalism in the first place.

But by divorcing itself from the cardinal justification of classic originalism—the pretension of an objective fact-based methodology free from the potential influences of judges' political or moral preferences—the new originalism raises with a vengeance the fundamental difficulty of this judicial philosophy: why make the original understanding the only consideration for our constitutional law? Why must constitutional requirements be tethered to the understandings of people who lived in a very different world, and held to some political and moral positions that we find offensive?

IV. Why Originalism? Take II.

Some opponents of originalism make a simple objection. The U.S. Constitution, they say, guarantees the freedom of speech, or equality before the law, and forbids cruel punishments or unreasonable searches and seizures. Read in the most straightforward and natural way, the Constitution guarantees these values—freedom, equality, reasonableness, lack of cruelty—not some archaic and potentially distorted or mistaken versions of them.[21] The prohibition on cruel and unusual punishment forbids punishments that are "cruel and unusual"—not punishments that are "cruel and unusual according to what cruelty and unusualness meant in the 18th century," when flogging, branding, and mutilation—including the cutting of tendons above the knee and the cropping of ears—were in common use, and when the death penalty was imposed for the theft of goods worth 50 dollars (1,200 dollars in today's currency).[22] Similarly, the Fourteenth Amendment guarantees the "equal protection of the laws," not the "equal protection of the laws as equality was understood in the 19th century," when flagrant discrimination against racial minorities and women was considered natural and even necessary. Thus, why regard the understandings of bygone generations as conclusive instead of giving the constitutional text its most natural meaning? In a similar

vein, why not take into account the purposes of constitutional provisions, thus making sure that those purposes are well-served? And
why not allow judges to consider the practical consequences of their
decisions?

The classic originalists had an answer to all this: they purported to offer a method of constitutional interpretation that minimized
judicial value judgments. If judges did not restrict themselves to the
concrete original understanding, said the old originalists, constitutional decisions would be a free-for-all, and judges would become the
de facto constitutional lawgivers in America. That answer, as seen in
the previous chapter, appears to be overly aspirational; but at least
it offered and explanation. The new originalists, by contrast, do not
seem to have any serious response. In fact, some leading new originalists seem to believe that the answer to that important question
is self-explanatory: for them, originalism is simply what textual interpretation consists in; it is what we must do when we do textual
interpretation. Judges must follow the original understanding of the
Constitution because that original understanding embodies the correct meaning of the constitutional text: "[T]he new originalism that
is widely accepted by most originalists today," wrote a leading new
originalist, is "an enterprise in determining what the writing really
means."[23] Another originalist made the same point by analogizing
constitutional interpretation to following an 18th century recipe for
fried chicken: "the meaning of a recipe is . . . the meaning that it
would have to the audience to which the document addresses itself,"
he wrote. And similarly,

> [T]he Constitution's meaning is its original public
> meaning. Other approaches to interpretation are sim-
> ply wrong. Interpreting the Constitution is no more
> difficult, and no different in principle, than interpret-
> ing a late-eighteenth-century recipe for fried chick-
> en.[24]

In other words, the original meaning is simply what the constitutional text "really means": it really means what cruelty meant in 1791, or what equality meant in 1868—not what cruelty and equality mean today.

Needless to say, the idea that texts' "real meaning" is what they meant for their original audiences is highly contested.[25] But putting aside this general objection, the idea that the "real meaning" of the Constitution is its original meaning does nothing to establish originalism as the proper constitutional philosophy. After all, the Constitution is not a recipe for fried chicken; it is, rather, a body of fundamental law, and constitutional interpretation is ultimately a political theory about the proper role of the judiciary in a constitutional democracy. It is possible, of course, that the proper role of the judiciary is to follow the "real meaning" of the Constitution, and also that the "real meaning" of the Constitution is its original meaning. But whether the new originalism is the proper methodology of interpreting the Constitution, or even the better version of originalism, depends on its merit as a judicial philosophy: that is, on its ability to generate good constitutional results, and to ensure properly constrained judicial power. The appeal to "real meaning" does not reach these crucial questions. Moreover, the new originalism does not seem to fare better than classic originalism in these regards. The methodology it describes allows for very limited constraint on judicial power (as the new originalists themselves concede). And at the same time, the results that the new originalism generates derive from potentially harmful and obsolete conceptions that are better fitted for older times.

V. Morality and Truth

The opinion affirming Harmelin's life sentence had an additional argument against a constitutional proportionality requirement: "[T]he proportionality principle becomes an invitation to imposition of subjective values."[26] The proportionality inquiry compares the gravity of an offense to its punishment, but there is no objective measure for the gravity of an offense: it is a moral measure, and a wholly subjective evaluation. Even the seemingly obvious idea that harm to a person is graver than harm to property is belied by our statutes:[27]

> In Louisiana, one who assaults another with a dangerous weapon faces the same maximum prison term as one who removes a shopping basket "from the parking area or grounds of any store . . . without authorization." A battery that results in "protracted and obvious disfigurement" merits imprisonment "for not more than five years," one-half the maximum penalty for theft of livestock or an oilfield seismograph. . . . Congress . . . sanctions "assault by . . . wounding" with up to six months in prison, unauthorized reproduction of the "Smokey Bear" character or name with the same penalty, offering to barter a migratory bird with up to two years in prison, and purloining a "key suited to any lock adopted by the Post Office Department" with a prison term of up to 10 years.[28]

So far as proportionality determinations are concerned, the truth of the matter is that there is no truth to the matter: the application of the doctrine revolves around pure moral judgments and is therefore a matter of mere "subjective values."[29] But the subjective opinions of unelected judges should not trump the subjective opinions of the people's elected representatives, who are responsible for legislating criminal punishments. Constitutional doctrine should therefore abandon the idea that "punishment must be tailored to a defendant's . . . moral guilt."[30]

The idea that moral judgments are mere matters of opinion may be widespread, but the matter is far from settled among those who have thought about it the hardest: moral philosophers have been hotly debating that question, and their debates have important potential ramifications for constitutional law. After all, the Federal Constitution contains a wide variety of moral standards ("cruel," "equal," "impartial," "just," etc.). What judges should do with these standards might depend on whether such standards are indeed matters of mere subjective opinion, or whether their application can be true or false.

The claim that moral judgments can be true or false—and that legal decisions that involve moral judgments can therefore also be true or false—has been forcefully made by Ronald Dworkin, one of the leading legal theorists of our time. The claim was essential for Dworkin's own legal theory, named "law as integrity" (or "interpretivism"). The most ambitious aspect of Dworkin's theory, and arguably its most important contribution, has been its attempt to rehabilitate morality as a legitimate—indeed indispensable—component of legal interpretation (following its falling into relative disrepute, and the collapse of natural law theory).

According to Dworkin, when legal interpreters ascertain the law on a given matter, they must take into account certain moral principles that are relevant to the matter at hand—for example, the principle that a person may not benefit from his own wrong, or that criminal culpability requires some blameworthy state of mind (not only a blameworthy action). Such moral principles, said Dworkin, are part of our law by virtue of their cogent moral content—whether they are or are not explicitly written into a statute, the Constitution, or a binding judicial precedent.[31] Furthermore, their legal authority is not a consequence of their divine origin or their universality (as natural law would have it). Rather, according to Dworkin, some moral principles are part of our law because they already inhere in the law: some moral principles are already respected and expressed in various legal requirements throughout our law. It is the duty of legal interpreters, claimed Dworkin, to tease out and articulate these moral principles, make sure they are mutually consistent, and then take them into account in their legal decisions. This is so, said Dworkin, because the government, through its laws, must speak in a morally coherent voice. The government may not adhere to one moral principle when it regulates some people or some issues, and then turn around and proclaim a contradictory moral principle when it regulates other people or other issues. The government's legitimacy depends on the moral coherence of our laws, and it is the duty of judges (the government officials charged with ascertaining the law) to detect that moral structure and implement it.[32]

Thus, according to Ronald Dworkin, legal determinations always require some moral assessment. For Dworkin and his many followers, judicial reliance on moral values is not only proper: it is necessary. The law consists, in part, of morality.

But while arguing that the law was partly made out of moral principles, Dworkin rejected the idea that the law was therefore made "subjective" or lacking in truth value. To the contrary: Dworkin firmly believed that legal determinations were right or wrong, true or false, just as people (including judges and lawyers) actually assume when they talk about the law. In fact, Dworkin was famous for his claim that practically all legal questions had a right answer.[33] And this meant that Dworkin's ambitious, provocative, and influential legal philosophy depended, at least in part, on the assertion that moral claims themselves had a "truth value"—that they could be true or false, correct or incorrect.

Ronald Dworkin did not shy from the task of defending this deeply philosophical claim.[34] In fact, his engagement with that question—which took him from the realm of legal philosophy to the vast area of moral philosophy—has made him a household name in many philosophy departments.. Dworkin's defense of the truth value of moral propositions is now commonly studied in courses in moral philosophy.

For Dworkin, the truth of a moral claim depended on its coherence with our practices and beliefs, including other moral practices and beliefs. Dworkin's moral truths are therefore not some God-given rules of nature, nor are they universal, nor self-evident: to the contrary, Dworkin's moral truths are a function of a society's practices and beliefs, and they therefore can vary from one society to another. Moreover, getting to the moral truth can take much intellectual labor, and it is impossible to know for certain whether one has actually hit the mark: there is no verification process for moral claims.

When we determine, for example, that punishing the rape of a child with the death penalty is morally disproportionate to the crime (as the Supreme Court has in fact held[35]), there is no validation process for confirming this moral determination—other than the moral argumentation through which we formulated that conclusion in the first place. We must simply do our best: this is our duty as human beings, as citizens of our state and country—and, says Dworkin, it is also the duty of legal interpreters.

Although many of the philosophical arguments employed in the debate about the truth value of moral claims are technical and even arcane, some of the arguments involved are relatively straightforward. Here is a sample.

As an initial matter, the mere fact that many moral judgments are chronically controversial does not mean that they are not true or false. String Theory in theoretical physics is a chronically controversial thesis, but despite the decades-long absence of consensus regarding its veracity, it is generally agreed that it is either true or false.[36] The existence of God is another subject of chronic disagreements, yet, there is a truth to the matter: either there is or there isn't a god. In short, if moral judgments cannot be true or false, it must be due to something beyond mere chronic controversy.

That something, say those who deny that morality has truth value, is the fact that moral claims need not match any objective reality. The truth or falsity of string theory, or of the existence of God, are functions of their correspondence with some objective reality: the claims they raise either fit our universe, or they don't. In fact, string theory is not likely to be controversial forever, since sooner or later dispositive evidence will emerge that would settle the issue. But what's the objective reality against which the truth of a moral claim can be measured?

Dworkin's answer is that the truth of moral claims is measured against the objective reality of our moral beliefs and moral practices. These are the factual benchmarks against which we judge the veracity of moral claims and theories. A moral claim that fails to conform with our beliefs and practices is, by that fact alone, incorrect. It is true, of course, that—unlike claims in the natural sciences, which are proven false by a single contradictory observation—some true moral claims may conflict with some actual practices or beliefs. Slavery may be morally wrong no matter how common it might be, or how many people believe it is morally right. In other words, some of our moral practices and beliefs are wrong. But they cannot all be wrong at the same time: in the end, true morality is a function of our acts and beliefs, and how they all fit together. Slavery is morally wrong because of our other beliefs and practices in regard to human beings: what we think of the value of human beings, how we think people should be treated, what power we allow individuals to have over each other, or how we conduct ourselves vis-à-vis other people. In other words, like theories in the natural sciences, moral theories are also constructed from rich factual data that they must fit and explain: they, too, are measured against some observable reality.

Moreover, while the truth of theories in physics is measured against empirical facts, the link between an empirical fact and the truth of a physical theory is mediated through a complex intellectual structure whose own veracity must be evaluated independently of these empirical facts. That Einstein's theory predicted the existence of black holes does not mean that observation of black holes confirms Einstein's theory. We must first evaluate the way with which Einstein's theory predicted that phenomenon. Witchcraft also makes predictions about physical phenomena; but the occurrence of these phenomena is no proof of the veracity of witchcraft. In other words, whether black holes actually support Einstein's physical theory depends on the intellectual robustness of the theoretical explanation for the existence of black holes. Physical theories are intellectual structures whose rigor must be evaluated before we can determine the significance of empirical observations to the correctness of the theory as a whole. Whether Einstein's theory is confirmed by the presence of black holes depends on the cogency with which his theory arrives at the existence of that phenomenon. And how do we measure the cogency of that intellectual structure? Well, against intellectual standards like rationality, coherence, or clarity—precisely the same intellectual standards against which we measure the accuracy of moral theories.

These are only the opening salvos in the debate over the truth value of moral claims, but they suffice to demonstrate that the issue is a live one. The argument that a moral proportionality requirement has no place in our constitutional law, because its application can be neither right nor wrong, depends on a highly controversial philosophical contention. Many serious philosophers believe that moral determinations—racial discrimination is wrong, the death penalty is right, intentionally causing grievous bodily injury is morally worse than pinching supermarket carts—can be just as right or wrong, and just as accurate or inaccurate, as, say, originalist interpretations (whose truth value the two justices in *Harmelin* did not seem to doubt).

In truth, less philosophical souls may doubt whether this debate even matters. Perhaps the mere fact that people are chronically divided over moral judgments suffices to doom them as legitimate judicial considerations, regardless of their truth value. Perhaps moral judgments—which are so often controversial and divisive, and which often correlate suspiciously with people's self-interest—should be the exclusive prerogative of elected representatives for that fact alone.

But the idea that judges should abstain from relying on controversial and divisive considerations is too sweeping: should originalist judges toss aside their determinations of original understandings that are not universally accepted? That would leave originalists with precious little to work with. Or, should judges ignore the veracity of evolutionary theory or climate change because they are controversial theories? The Supreme Court certainly hasn't.[37] Judicial reliance on morality may make use of controversial considerations, but in that it is no different than many other judicial determinations: judges employ controversial considerations all the time.

117

VI. Civilization and Proportionality

Justice John Paul Stevens (who retired in 2010 and passed away in 2019) was one of the four *Harmelin* dissenters who believed that Harmelin's sentence was unconstitutional because it was disproportionate to his crime. In his 2011 memoir, *Five Chiefs*, the retired Justice opined that *Harmelin* came out as it did, because, in 1991, when the case was decided, the Court had two relatively new justices: Justices Kennedy and Souter replaced Justices Powell and Brennan in 1988 and 1990, respectively.[38] Both Kennedy and Souter sided with the majority in *Harmelin*, and the case was decided on the strength of a single vote.

According to Justice Stevens, both Powell and Brennan would have sided with the dissent, and if the case came before the Court a decade later, Kennedy and Souter would have voted differently as well, because, as Stevens put it, "The views of individual justices become more civilized after 20 years of service on the court."[39]

It is possible, however, that Justice Stevens—relying perhaps on his personal experience—was overly optimistic about the civilizing force of serving on the Court. In reality, a full decade after Harmelin was decided, the Supreme Court continued to uphold sentences that seemed highly disproportionate to their crimes.[40] In 2000, Gary Ewing, a crack addict with a long criminal history, walked into a golf shop in Los Angeles County and soon left limping on account of three golf clubs secreted in his pants.[41] He was arrested in the parking lot, and was subsequently charged with grand theft. Grand theft in California normally carries a maximum sentence of three years in prison, but the prosecutor asked for and received twenty-five years to life based on California's 1994 "three strikes law."[42] In 2003, the Supreme Court upheld Ewing's twenty-five years to life sentence for stealing three golf clubs. On the same day, the Court reversed a decision of the Ninth Circuit Court of Appeals and reinstated a sentence of two consecutive terms of twenty-five years to life (a total of fifty years to life) for the theft of $150 worth of videotapes from two video stores—under the same three strikes law.[43] (Both cases were decided 5 to 4.) Between 1994 and 2004, 7,332 California defendants were sentenced to twenty-five years to life under that law.[44] One of them stole a slice of pizza.[45]

VII. Review

To sum up: classic originalism is chiefly concerned with minimizing judicial value judgments. To achieve that end, classic originalists focus on historical evidence indicating concrete and specific constitutional requirements. The new originalism, by contrast, focuses on the original understanding of often-abstract constitutional terms: constitutional interpreters must seek to comprehend the original meaning of the constitutional text, and must apply that meaning to the constitutional questions before them. Since the constitutional text is often vague and abstract, and even contains some explicitly moral standards, the methodology of the new originalism can hardly minimize judicial value judgments: to the contrary, it affirmatively invites judges to engage in evaluative judgments. Thus, the new originalism disowns the pretense of a constrained and objective methodology. But the theory still tethers constitutional requirements to the Constitution's original understanding. This means that the new originalism, like the old one, may produce results that are obsolete or impractical, and which may derive from long-discredited prejudices or misconceptions.

Unlike the new originalists, many classic originalists reject judicial moral evaluations. One reason for that rejection is their alleged subjectivity, which makes them the proper business of elected representatives rather than unelected and unaccountable judges. Indeed, the idea that legal requirements may depend on individual judges' personal moral preferences appears to conflict with basic principles of the Rule of Law—of a government of laws, not of men. But this conception of moral evaluations has been challenged by some prominent moral and legal philosophers, who argue that moral determinations can be true or false, and are no mere matters of subjective opinion. One such line of reasoning argues that the standards with which we judge and evaluate moral claims are no different than those with which we judge and evaluate scientific claims. And if moral determinations are true or false—claim these theorists—then at least some of the objections to judicial moral determinations are unjustified. Unquestionably, moral determinations are often deeply controversial; but judges regularly rely on allegedly true but controversial considerations. At the very least, they say, there is nothing in the idea of moral judicial deliberations that conflicts with our ideal of the Rule of Law.

It is now time to switch gears and move to a whole new topic: theories of statutory interpretation and their impact on constitutional doctrine. The next three chapters examine some fundamental debates in statutory judicial philosophy, and explain how these theories have shaped our constitutional rights.

CHAPTER 8

Statutory Interpretation, Deviations from Clear Statutory Texts, and Correction of Legislative Mistakes: Exempting Atheists from the Foxholes

The next three chapters are dedicated to theories of statutory interpretation—the process of determining what statutes require in given cases. Statutory interpretation shapes constitutional law in various important ways. One of those includes the "avoidance doctrine," which asks courts to avoid constitutional rulings by interpreting statutes in ways that steer clear of constitutional difficulties. The practice allows courts to leave a host of important constitutional questions unresolved. But when employing the avoidance doctrine, judges are still bound by normal standards of statutory interpretation: the avoidance doctrine is available only in cases where proper statutory interpretation allows for avoidance. Thus, the statutory judicial philosophy that a court employs has a direct impact on the court's ability to use the avoidance doctrine—and hence on the reach and scope of constitutional law.

This chapter begins with some controversial deployments of the avoidance doctrine. In two cases from 1965 and 1970, the Supreme Court avoided deciding a question which remains undecided to this day: namely, whether the government violates the First Amendment when it discriminates in favor of theistic, and against atheistic, beliefs. The cases—which dealt with the very definition of religion—represented a controversial statutory construction that deviated from the clear statutory text. These decisions raised a number of important questions in statutory judicial philosophy, including the limits of textual fidelity, and courts' authority to correct legislative mistakes.

I. Religious Conscientious Exemption

In 1940, as the U.S. was contemplating its entrance into the Second World War, Congress enacted the Selective Training and Service Act.[1] The Act, which introduced the first peacetime conscription in U.S. history, contained an exemption from military service for religious conscientious objectors. Such exemptions have had a long history in the United States, going all the way back to colonial times, but the 1940 statute contained an innovation: it no longer limited the exemption to members of certain religious denominations that opposed war, but extended it to anyone whose opposition to war was based on "religious training and belief."[2] Federal courts soon had to decide what did, and what did not, qualify as religious belief.

Unsurprisingly, distinguishing religious from non-religious beliefs has proven extremely difficult. In 1943, the Second Circuit Court of Appeals came up with a broad definition, which it explained as follows:

> Religious belief arises from a sense of the inadequacy of reason . . . [a sense common to] men in the most primitive and in the most highly civilized societies. It accepts the aid of logic but refuses to be limited by it. It is a belief finding expression in a conscience . . . . A religious obligation forbade Socrates, even in order to escape condemnation, to entreat his judges to acquit him, because he believed that it was their sworn duty to decide questions without favor to anyone and only according to law . . . . [It] moved the Greek poet Menander to write . . . 'Conscience is a God to all mortals' . . . and led Wordsworth to characterize 'Duty' as the 'Stern Daughter of the Voice of God.' . . . [C]all it conscience or God, that is for many persons at the present time the equivalent of what has always been thought a religious impulse.[3]

Taken to its logical conclusion, this definition might classify every conscientious objection to war as a religious belief. That was unacceptable to the Ninth Circuit Court of Appeals, which—three years later—offered a far narrower definition:

> [T]he expression 'by reason of religious training and belief' . . . was written into the statute for the specific purpose of distinguishing between . . . a sincere devotion to a high moralistic philosophy, and one based upon an individual's belief in his responsibility to an authority higher and beyond any worldly one . . . . [P]hilosophy and morals and social policy without the concept of deity cannot be said to be religion in the sense of that term as it is used in the statute.[4]

After the War, Congress undertook a revision of the Selective Training and Service Act, where it made clear that it sided with the Ninth Circuit. The amended statute read:

> Religious training and belief . . . means an individual's belief in a relation to a Supreme Being involving duties superior to those arising from any human relation, but does not include essentially political, sociological, or philosophical views or a merely personal moral code.[5]

That narrow definition, which sought to distinguish objections based on mere moral philosophy from those based on genuine religious belief, was soon challenged in the courts. Conscientious objectors whose exemptions were denied on the ground that they were not based on religious beliefs, claimed that the denial violated the First Amendment's two religious clauses—the Establishment Clause and the Free Exercise Clause, which together read: "Congress shall make no law respecting an establishment of religion, or prohibiting the free exercise thereof . . . ."[6]

II. Secular Conscientious Exemption

In 1957, New York resident Daniel Seeger submitted a Conscientious Objector Form to his local draft board, asking for an exemption from military service. The form, which tracked the language of the federal statute, asked applicants whether their applications were based on a belief in a "Supreme Being." Seeger declined to answer that question, writing instead that "The existence of God cannot be proven or disproven, and the essence of His nature cannot be determined."[7] Where the form asked the applicant to describe "the nature of [his] belief . . . and state whether or not [it is related to a] belief in a Supreme Being," Seeger wrote:

> [S]kepticism or disbelief in the existence of God does not necessarily mean lack of faith in anything whatsoever. . . . Such personages as Plato, Aristotle and Spinoza evolved comprehensive ethical systems of intellectual and moral integrity without belief in God, except in the remotest sense . . . . [I have a] belief in and devotion to goodness and virtue for their own sakes, and a religious faith in a purely ethical creed . . . . It is our moral responsibility to search for a way to maintain the recognition of the dignity and worth of the individual...I cannot participate in actions which betray the cause of freedom and humanity.[8]

The FBI, which prepared a report on Seeger's application, described the 22-year-old—who had an outstanding academic record—as "a truthful, decent young citizen [who was] completely sincere" in his beliefs. The Bureau recommended granting the application. But the Draft Board denied it: although sincere, wrote the Board in its decision, Seeger's beliefs were not in "relation to a Supreme Being," as the statute required. When Seeger refused to submit to the draft, he was prosecuted, tried, and convicted. His appeal went all the way to the Supreme Court.[9]

Seeger's attorneys raised several constitutional challenges to Seeger's conviction. First, they argued that although Seeger's beliefs were not related to a "Supreme Being," they were nevertheless "religious": after all, well-recognized religions like Taoism and (early) Buddhism also lacked a belief in a Supreme Being. They cited a lower federal court decision that read:

> Even the dictionary definitions recognize that religion need have no god. Webster's New International Dictionary, 2nd ed., 1937, defines religion as 'An apprehension, awareness, or conviction of the existence of a supreme being, or more widely, supernatural powers or influences controlling . . . humanity's destiny.'[10]

Thus, although Seeger's beliefs were not related to a Supreme Being (and therefore did not qualify as religious under the statute), their subject matter and his commitment to them qualified them as religious under the U.S. Constitution. Seeger's lawyers argued that refusing to grant Seeger his military exemption would violate the Free Exercise Clause ("Congress shall make no law . . . prohibiting the free exercise thereof"), because it would force Seeger to act in contravention of his religious convictions.

The claim was a long shot. As a general matter, the Free Exercise Clause does not protect people from being forced to act against their religious beliefs—or from being obstructed in their effort to act in accordance with their beliefs—unless courts find that the very purpose of the law in question is to suppress religion. Accordingly, a murder statute can be constitutionally applied to devil worshipers who are religiously obligated to make human sacrifices; a manslaughter statute can be applied to parents who refuse to provide urgent medical care to their children for religious reasons; and statutes criminalizing suicide can be enforced against Hindu brides who wish to immolate themselves on their husbands' funeral pyres. Similarly, the Supreme Court held that the Free Exercise Clause did not grant American Indians the right to use an unlawful hallucinogenic in their religious ceremonies;[11] did not allow Mormons to marry multiple wives (since, per the Court, the prohibition on polygamy was not aimed at suppressing religion);[12] and did not exempt members of the Old Order Amish from the obligation to pay social security taxes, even assuming that such payments violated their religious faith.[13] According to the court, granting religious believers constitutionally mandated exemptions from ordinary laws "would be courting anarchy."[14] And since the purpose of the military draft was not to suppress religion, Seeger was not likely to win on his claim that the Free Exercise Clause required that he be given a conscientious exemption.

But Seeger's attorneys had additional constitutional contentions. They also argued that if Seeger's beliefs were indeed religious, denying him the statutory exemption was a violation of the Establishment Clause ("Congress shall make no law respecting an establishment of religion"). That was a stronger constitutional argument. An "establishment of religion" is the certification of an official religion, such as England's Anglican Church or Iran's Shi'a Islam. But the Establishment Clause forbids much more than the establishment of an official creed: among other things, the Clause also forbids the government to treat some religions more favorably than others. If Seeger's beliefs were religious, and he was denied an exemption from the military draft, whereas applicants whose beliefs involved a "Supreme Being" were granted such exemptions, that could constitute discrimination in violation of the Establishment Clause.

Finally, Seeger's attorneys argued, in the alternative, that if the Court refused to recognize Seeger's beliefs as religious, denying him the exemption would still violate the Establishment Clause because the Clause not only forbids the government to discriminate between different religious beliefs, but also between religious and nonreligious beliefs. Granting conscientious exemptions to those whose objections were based upon religious beliefs, while denying them for those whose objections were based upon sheer moral or ethical beliefs, was also a violation of the Establishment Clause—argued the lawyers.

III. "Religious Belief": A New Definition

The Supreme Court dodged all these constitutional questions by granting Seeger his exemption as a matter of statutory interpretation: Seeger, said the Court, qualified for the exemption under the Selective Training and Service Act. That was a bold move, given that the Selective Training and Service Act explicitly reserved the exemption to those whose beliefs were "in a relation to a Supreme Being." The Court offered two reasons for its ruling. First, it agreed with Seeger's attorneys that true religious beliefs need not involve a Supreme Being:

> Over 250 sects inhabit our land. Some believe in a purely personal God, some in a supernatural deity; others think of religion as a way of life . . . . There are those who think of God as the depth of our being; others, such as the Buddhists, strive for a state of lasting rest through self-denial and inner purification; in Hindu philosophy, the [analogue to a] Supreme Being is the transcendental reality which is truth, knowledge and bliss.[15]

In fact, said the Court, even some Christian theologians were not committed to a belief in a Supreme Being:

> The eminent Protestant theologian, Dr. Paul Tillich [has] written of the . . . power of being, which works through those who have no name for it, not even the name God'. . . . Another eminent cleric, the Bishop of Woolwich, . . . states: 'The Bible speaks of a God 'up there'. . . . (Later) in place of a God who is literally or physically 'up there' we have accepted, as part of our mental furniture, a God who is spiritually or metaphysically 'out there'. . . . But the signs are that we are reaching the point at which the whole conception of a God 'out there' . . . is itself becoming more of

a hindrance than a help . . . . Ever since primordial days, numerous peoples have had a certain perception of that hidden power which hovers over the course of things and over the events that make up the lives of men; some have even come to know of a Supreme Being and Father. Religions in an advanced culture have been able to use more refined concepts and a more developed language in their struggle for an answer to man's religious questions.[16]

Given that religious beliefs need not involve a Supreme Being, the Court offered its second reason: extending the military exemption only to those who believe in a Supreme Being would amount to official discrimination in favor of some religions (those with a Supreme Being) and against others. Such a policy, reasoned the Court, could not have been intended by Congress, given Congress' long-standing position on this matter. Thus, extending the statutory exemption to religious beliefs that did not include a Supreme Being "avoids imputing to Congress an intent to [discriminate among] different religious beliefs . . . and is in accord with the well-established congressional policy of equal treatment for those whose opposition to service is grounded in their religious tenets." In other words, given that Congress could not have intended to discriminate between different religious beliefs, the statutory definition was wrong and had to be replaced with a new one.

The Court therefore replaced the allegedly wrong definition with a new one: belief is "religious" if it "occupies in the life of its possessor a place parallel to that filled by . . . God" [in the life of those who believe in God]." Under this new definition, said the Court, Seeger's beliefs were religious and Seeger was entitled to the military exemption as a matter of statutory interpretation.

Accordingly, the Court avoided the constitutional questions raised by Seeger's attorneys, and did not have to decide whether the Free Exercise Clause or the Establishment Clause were violated by denying Seeger an exemption from the military draft.

IV. The Avoidance Doctrine

Justice William O. Douglas, who joined the Seeger decision, explained his vote in the case in a concurring opinion:

> If I read the statute differently from the Court, I would have difficulties. For then those who embraced one religious faith, rather than another, would be subject to penalties; and that kind of discrimination . . . would violate . . . the First Amendment . . . . The legislative history of this Act leaves much in the dark. But it is, in my opinion, not a tour de force if we construe the words 'Supreme Being' to include the cosmos, as well as an anthropomorphic entity. If it is a tour de force so to hold, it is no more so than other instances where we have gone to extremes to construe an Act of Congress to save it from demise on constitutional grounds . . . . [We have previously] said that the words of a statute may be strained in the candid service of avoiding a serious constitutional doubt.[17]

According to Justice Douglas, the *Seeger* decision was a straightforward application of the avoidance doctrine, which asks courts to interpret statutes so as to avoid potential constitutional difficulties.

But while courts should avoid constitutional difficulties, their interpretations must be legitimate: the avoidance doctrine must be used within the confines of legitimate statutory interpretation and cannot transform an illegitimate statutory interpretation into a legitimate one. As the Supreme Court once put it:[18]

> It must be remembered that although this Court will often strain to construe legislation so as to save it against constitutional attack, it must not and will not carry this to the point of perverting the purpose of a statute or judicially rewriting it. To put the matter

another way, this Court will not consider the abstract question of whether Congress might have enacted a valid statute but instead must ask whether the statute that Congress did enact will permissibly bear a construction rendering it free from constitutional defects.[19]

But did "the statute that Congress did enact" allow the Seeger Court to reach the decision it did? Or was the Seeger decision an illegitimate exercise of statutory interpretation?

V. Deviating from Clear Statutory Texts

One of the most famous rivalries in statutory judicial philosophy is the one between purposivism and textualism—that is, between those who think that legislative purpose is the supreme guide of statutory interpretation, and those who think that the text of a statute must reign supreme. Purposivists believe that judges must deviate from the text of statutes if that's what it takes in order to effectuate the statutory purpose. Courts, say the purposivists, should be concerned with implementing legislative policies—not with blindly following textual precepts. (This discussion employs the concepts of statutory purpose and legislative intent interchangeably, even though, at a higher level of resolution, it is possible to draw a distinction between the two.[20])

The *Seeger* decision employed a purposivist interpretation when it granted Seeger the statutory exemption. The opinion justified its deviation from the clear statutory text by appealing to the alleged Congressional purpose to grant religious exemptions to all religions—not only to some.

But while *Seeger* was a unanimous decision (not one participating justice thought the decision was illegitimate), things soon changed: within a few years, some of the justices had a change of heart.

In 1963—two years before the Supreme Court decided *See-ger*—a young man named Elliot Welsh filed his own application for exemption from the military draft. Where the form asked the applicant to confirm he opposed war by reason of "religious training and belief," Welsh crossed out the words "religious training" (Seeger merely put the term "religious" in quotation marks); Welsh also added that his beliefs were formed through "reading in the fields of history and sociology"—precisely the sort of beliefs that the Selective Training and Service Act contrasted with religious ones. (The statute read: "Religious training and belief . . . does not include essentially political, sociological, or philosophical views or a merely personal moral code."). Like Seeger's, Welsh's application was denied.

The case reached the Supreme Court in 1969—one of the deadliest years of the Vietnam War. As in its *Seeger* decision, the Supreme Court reversed the denial and granted Welsh his exemption. This time, however, despite the case's similarity to *Seeger*, the decision was far from unanimous. Only four justices thought that Welsh was entitled to the exemption as a matter of statutory interpretation: one justice concurred on constitutional grounds; three justices filed a dissenting opinion. (Only eight justices participated in the case.[21])

The four-justice plurality opinion replicated the reasoning in *Seeger*: like Seeger's, Welsh's beliefs qualified as "religious beliefs" under the statute because, like Seeger's, they "occup[ied] . . . a place parallel to that filled by God in traditionally religious persons."[22]

Three justices (two of whom had previously joined the *Seeger* opinion) dissented, arguing that Welsh was not entitled to the statutory exemption: "Whether or not [*Seeger*] accurately reflected the intent of Congress," granting Welsh an exemption did not.[23] Unlike Seeger, wrote the dissenting justices, Welsh explicitly declared his beliefs "represent a purely personal code arising not from religious training and belief as the statute requires but from readings in philosophy, history, and sociology." Thus, whatever doubt could have been entertained about Seeger's beliefs, Welsh's beliefs were clearly not religious, and he was therefore not entitled to a statutory exemption.

Having determined that Welsh was properly denied a statutory exemption, the dissenters had to address the constitutionality of that denial. They quickly concluded that it was perfectly constitutional: while favoring one religion over another was a violation of the Establishment Clause, favoring religion over non-religion, they wrote, was not.

The Court was therefore split 4–3 on the statutory question, and the remaining Justice held the decisive vote: since the Ninth Circuit Court of Appeals denied Welsh the exemption, a 4–4 split on the Supreme Court would have left that denial in place.[24] But Justice John Marshall Harlan II (the grandson of Supreme Court Justice John Marshall Harlan I—connections never hurt) sided with the four-justice plurality: Welsh, he agreed, should get an exemption—but not for the reasons that the plurality gave. Harlan rejected the plurality's opinion, and repudiated his previous vote in Seeger, on the ground that the Welsh plurality and the Seeger majority were improper exercises of statutory interpretation:

> Candor requires me to say that I joined the Court's opinion in *United States v. Seeger* only with the gravest misgivings as to whether it was a legitimate exercise in statutory construction, and today's decision convinces me that, in doing so, I made a mistake which I should now acknowledge.[25]

Justice Harlan was no textualist. In fact, Harlan believed that courts sometimes legitimately deviated from statutory texts. However, he thought that such occasions were limited to "circumstances . . . uncontemplated by the legislature . . . ." As he wrote in his *Welsh* concurrence:

> [I]t is one thing to give words a meaning not necessarily envisioned by Congress so as to adapt them to circumstances also uncontemplated by the legislature in order to achieve the legislative policy . . . it is a wholly

different matter to define words so as to change policy.[26]

Riggs v. Palmer, a New York case from 1889, is a classic example of what Harlan had in mind.[27]

Riggs involved a young man who murdered his grandfather by poisoning him in order to prevent him from amending his will. Notwithstanding the clear text of the New York statute governing wills, the New York Court of Appeals held that the murderous grandson was not entitled to the inheritance. The court explained its decision as follows:

> It was the intention of the law-makers that the donees in a will should have the property given to them. But it never could have been their intention that a donee who murdered the testator to make the will operative should have any benefit under it. If such a case had been present to their minds, and it had been supposed necessary to make some provision of law to meet it, it cannot be doubted that they would have provided for it.[28]

The murderer was denied the estate notwithstanding the clear statutory language.

Unlike textualists, for whom *Riggs v. Palmer* represented an illegitimate statutory construction (two textualist justices filed a dissent in the case[29]), Justice Harlan appeared to agree with the *Riggs* court's refusal to follow the statutory text. But *Seeger* and *Welsh* were different: "Here," wrote Harlan, "the intention of the Congress is revealed too distinctly to permit us to ignore it."[30] For Harlan, far from advancing the legislative purpose, the *Seeger* and *Welsh* opinions positively subverted it. They perpetrated the sort of perversion that the great legal philosopher Lon Fuller—also an avowed purposivist—once decried:

Fidelity to law can become impossible if we do not accept the broader responsibilities . . . that go with a purposive interpretation of law. One can imagine a [purposivist] course of reasoning that might run as follows: This statute says absinthe shall not be sold. What is its purpose? To promote health. Now, as everyone knows, absinthe is a sound, wholesome, and beneficial beverage. Therefore, interpreting the statute in the light of its purpose, I construe it to direct a general sale and consumption of that most healthful of beverages, absinthe.[31]

For Harlan, this farcical example resembled the opinions of *Seeger* and *Welsh*: in these cases, the Court relied on legislative purpose to achieve a result that was the precise opposite of the real legislative purpose (which was to grant military exemptions for religious, but not for non-religious, beliefs).

Since Harlan thought that a proper reading of the Selective Training and Service Act denied Welsh a conscientious exemption, his opinion had to examine the constitutional question raised by that denial. This was avoided by the plurality:

The constitutional question that must be faced in this case is whether a statute that defers to the individual's conscience only when his views emanate from adherence to theistic religious beliefs is within the power of Congress.[32]

Unlike the *Welsh* dissenters, Harlan concluded that the statute did violate the Establishment Clause:

[T]he statute . . . excludes . . . individuals guided by an inner ethical voice that bespeaks secular and not 'religious' reflection. . . .This in my view offends the Establishment Clause . . . [T]he exemption . . . must encompass . . . those whose beliefs emanate from a purely moral, ethical, or philosophical source . . . . Congress . . . can of course decline to exercise its power to conscript to the fullest extent, but it cannot do so without equal regard for men of nonreligious conscience.[33]

Discriminating in favor of religious beliefs and against nonreligious beliefs, Harlan argued, was a violation of the First Amendment.

Although both the dissent and the concurrence addressed this constitutional question, the Supreme Court as a whole never did, thanks to the Court's controversial statutory interpretation. To this day, the issue remains unresolved—a fact that may allow such discrimination to persist. In 2001, for example, the Mississippi Supreme Court held that "the best interest and welfare of the child"—the leading consideration in custody disputes—can include consideration of "religious example," so that a religious parent could be preferred to a nonreligious one.[34] Judicial custody decisions, said the Mississippi Court, could seek to guarantee that "children get regular and systematic spiritual training." Had the Supreme Court reached the constitutional claims raised by Daniel Seeger and Elliot Welsh in a majority opinion, it is likely, given the Court's composition at that time, that the Mississippi decision could not have been made.

VI. Correcting Legislative Errors

Harlan suggested that his disagreement with the *Seeger* and *Welsh* opinions was about their misreading of the legislative purpose behind the Selective Training and Service Act. But Harlan may have misdiagnosed the precise source of the disagreement. After all, the opinions did not disagree that the statutory purpose was to grant conscientious exemptions to those whose opposition to war was based on religious beliefs—and to deny them to those who held to nonreligious objections. But the opinions believed that the statute failed to draw an accurate distinction between religious and nonreligious beliefs. Drawing that distinction by appealing to a "Supreme Being" was a factual and conceptual mistake: some beliefs that were not in relation to a Supreme Being were nevertheless clearly religious. This mistaken definition led to the statute's failure to serve its purpose.[35] The Court was therefore forced to replace the erroneous statutory definition with a new one that would effectuate the purpose of the statute. In other words, the real disagreement between Harlan and the *Seeger* and *Welsh* opinions was whether judges were legitimately empowered—or even obligated—to correct purported legislative mistakes.

Imagine a statute with a provision that reads: "The Zupa virus being an extremely contagious and dangerous disease, individuals afflicted with Zupa shall be barred from practicing medicine on other people." Now suppose that during subsequent litigation it is indisputably established that the Zupa virus is, in fact (in contradiction with the legislature's erroneous belief), *not* contagious. Shouldn't courts applying the statute consider the fact that it is based on a mistake? Shouldn't judges assume that the legislature did not intend to arbitrarily and unjustifiably take away the livelihood of infected doctors or nurses? Shouldn't judges have the authority—nay, the duty—to interpret statutes in ways that prevent arbitrary and unjustified legal requirements? After all, this is arguably what the rule of law is about: making sure that legal requirements are not arbitrary or irrational, and that their applications are reasonably justified.

Broad judicial authority to interpret statutes so as to mitigate arbitrary and unjust results was vigorously defended by Alexander Hamilton in the Federalist Papers. In his discussion of the importance of judicial independence, Hamilton wrote:

> [I]t is not with a view to infractions of the Constitution only, that the independence of the judges may be an essential safeguard against the effects of occasional ill humors in the society. These sometimes extend . . . by unjust and partial laws. Here also the firmness of the judicial magistracy is of vast importance in mit-

igating the severity and confining the operation of such laws. It not only serves to moderate the immediate mischiefs of those which may have been passed, but it operates as a check upon the legislative body in passing them; who, perceiving that obstacles to the success of iniquitous intention are to be expected from the scruples of the courts, are in a manner compelled, by the very motives of the injustice they meditate, to qualify their attempts.[36]

Hamilton thought that courts have a duty to interpret statutes so as to mitigate injustice and iniquity—*even if these were the legislature's very purposes.*

But then again, Hamilton also believed in natural law.

VII. Redefining "Religious Beliefs"

Hamilton's views of proper statutory interpretation go well beyond the conception employed by the *Seeger* and *Welsh* opinions. These opinions had a narrow rationale: they purported to effect the legislative purpose. According to *Seeger* and *Welsh*, congressional drafters failed to define religious beliefs in a way that would give effect to Congress' purpose, which was to grant the military exemption to all religious believers while denying them to those whose objections were not based on religious beliefs. The Court was therefore forced to correct that definitional error.

Seen from this angle, the problem with the *Seeger* and *Welsh* opinions was not their infidelity to the statutory text, but perhaps the overly broad definition with which they replaced the erroneous one: namely, that religious beliefs were those that "occup[ied] . . . a place parallel to that filled by God in traditionally religious persons." It was this broad definition that made Seeger's and Welsh's seemingly nonreligious beliefs eligible for the statutory exemption.

Was there a better definition—one that would have excluded Seeger's and Welsh's allegedly secular beliefs, while including genuine religious beliefs that were unrelated to a Supreme Being? Such a definition would have better accorded with the statutory purpose, and may have even suited Harlan's version of purposivism.

Distinguishing between religious and nonreligious beliefs is no easy feat, but here is a suggestion: the (deeply religious) Danish philosopher Søren Kierkegaard thought that religious beliefs were distinct from nonreligious beliefs in that the former were not susceptible to rational refutation or confirmation.[37] Religious beliefs were grounded in faith—that is, in conviction rather than in rational persuasion. (Think of expressions like "blind faith" or "a leap of faith"). By contrast, political, sociological, or philosophical beliefs stand or fall on their rational merit. This distinction between religious and nonreligious beliefs could have embraced all religious beliefs, whether or not related to a Supreme Being, while excluding all secular ones.

Whether it is sensible for the government to discriminate against rational beliefs in favor of irrational ones—extending conscientious objector exemptions only to those who could not or need not rationally defend their positions—is, of course, an entirely different question.

VIII. Review

To sum up: jurists are divided over whether judges can stray away from statutory texts, and, if they can, under what circumstances. Some think that judges must never deviate from textual prescriptions, while others believe that they may—and that under some circumstances they *must*—deviate from textual prescriptions.[38] But they remain divided over the circumstances that justify or mandate such textual deviations.

Purposivists believe that judges ought to stray from statutory texts whenever necessary in order to effectuate the statutory purpose. Others would limit such deviations to circumstances that could not have been contemplated by the legislature. Some jurists would allow judges to correct factual or even conceptual legislative mistakes. And some proclaim that judges are authorized to ignore clear statutory requirements in order to prevent injustice.[39] These different judicial philosophies can result in widely different applications of the avoidance doctrine, which in turn can determine what constitutional rights are recognized or enforced.

The next chapter delves deeper into the dispute between textualists and purposivists.

CHAPTER 9

Textualism v. Purposivism:
The Fourth Amendment and the
Constitutionality of Pretextual Arrests

The executive branch is responsible for carrying out legislative enactments, and actions by executive officials—be they FBI agents, officials at the EPA, or the President—are usually done in pursuit of some federal statute. In fact, actions that are perfectly constitutional when done in pursuit of a statute may be unconstitutional in the absence of statutory authority. But whether an action falls within the authority of a statute may depend on the judicial philosophy employed in interpreting that statute. This is yet another way with which theories of statutory interpretation impact constitutional law.

This chapter revolves around a 2011 Supreme Court case titled *Ashcroft v. al-Kidd*.[1] The case involved the allegation that the arrest and detention of an individual by the FBI were not authorized by statute and were therefore in violation of the Fourth Amendment to the U.S. Constitution. The case implicated the famous debate between textualism and purposivism, and was resolved in accordance with textualist principles. The Court interpreted a federal statute by following its text and refusing to consider its legislative purpose. It concluded that the actions of the FBI were in fact authorized by a federal statute and were therefore constitutional.

I. The Textualist-Purposivist Debate

Textualists believe that judges must follow the statutory language no matter what the legislative purpose might be, whereas purposivists believe that judges must follow the legislative purpose even if it entails a departure from the statutory language. If the text calls for one resolution and the purpose for another—say the purposivists—judges ought to give effect to the purpose and refuse to follow the text.[2]

One of the main arguments of textualists is that there is no real legislative purpose to which judges can appeal when they deviate from the text. Legislative bodies are comprised of hundreds of individuals: some have one purpose in mind, others have another, and yet others have no legislative purpose at all—they may vote for a bill simply because their party leadership asked them to, or because it is popular, or because they agreed to exchange their votes. Thus statutes can be said to have many purposes, formulated on various levels of specificity or abstraction. In fact (as we saw in Chapter 5), some textualists argue that the legislative process should not be conceived "as if a reasonable person were framing coherent legislative policy"[3] and that "[l]aws promulgated by the Legislative Branch can be inconsistent [or] illogical."[4] And in that case, the search for some rational legislative purpose is unwarranted to begin with.

Purposivists respond that the statutory purpose is not some snapshot of legislators' state of mind, nor is it some combination of their thoughts. It is not an empirical fact about why individual legislators voted for the statute. Rather, the statutory purpose is a judicial construction—a judicial hypothesis—of what the legislature sought to achieve when it enacted the statute. In formulating that hypothesis, judges may make use of empirical facts like legislative history, or the statements of the statute's legislative sponsors, but the statutory purpose is never a mere function of such facts, and is not reducible to them. The legislative purpose is, in the words of the purposivist scholar Lon Fuller, "the intention of the design"—the reason why the statute demands the things that it does.[5] Purposivists maintain that a reasonable policy choice is the necessary working hypothesis of any statutory construction.

But for textualists, the idea that the statutory purpose is some kind of judicial invention or hypothesis is precisely what makes it illegitimate, since this means that judicial appeals to the legislative purpose or intent can quickly devolve into what judges think that purpose or intent *should be*. In other words, appeals to legislative purpose are an illicit back door through which judges can introduce their ideological preferences into the legal decision. As a federal judge once described it, the search for legislative purpose is like "looking over a crowd and picking out your friends."[6] Justice Antonin Scalia, who was a champion of textualism in statutory interpretation,[7] put things this way:

> [U]nder the guise or even the self-delusion of pursuing unexpressed legislative intents, . . . judges . . . in fact pursue their own objectives and desires . . . . When you are told to decide, not on the basis of what the legislature said, but on the basis of what it *meant* . . . your best shot at figuring out what the legislature meant is to ask yourself what a wise and intelligent person *should* have meant; and that will surely bring you to the conclusion that the law means what you think it *ought* to mean . . . .[8]

Appeals to legislative purpose or intent are the mortal enemies of textualists. Indeed, most judicial deviations from statutory texts are justified on the ground that the legislative purpose would be ill-served by following the text. As the familiar judicial refrain has it, "a thing may be within the letter of the statute and yet not within the statute, because not within its spirit, nor within the intention of its makers."[9] It is therefore a fundamental article of the textualist faith that if the statutory text is clear and determinate, legislative purpose has no place in the judicial decision.

As a comprehensive judicial philosophy, textualism is not very useful in the constitutional context, given the vagueness and abstractness of many constitutional terms: "follow the text" provides little guidance to a judge tasked with applying the Fourth Amendment's prohibition on "unreasonable searches and seizures," or the guarantee of the "equal protection of the laws," or the First Amendment's prohibition on "abridging the freedom of speech." But some elements of textualism, including textualist hostility to legislative purpose, have become embedded in a number of constitutional doctrines, including in Fourth Amendment law.

II. The Fourth Amendment: Background and Current State

The Fourth Amendment reads in part:

> The right of the people to be secure in their persons, houses, papers, and effects, against unreasonable searches and seizures, shall not be violated, and no warrants shall issue, but upon probable cause . . . .[10]

The Amendment is a centerpiece of civil liberties in America, and a critical limitation on the power of America's vast police forces. It was designed to prohibit the notorious "general warrants" of the colonial era—those ill-defined authorizations for searches and arrests that were unlimited in scope, were issued with little scrutiny, and had proven a potent tool of oppression at the hands of the British Crown.[11] The newly independent Americans were determined to limit the ability of their own government to conduct such operations. The Fourth Amendment created a legal threshold that the government had to meet before it could arrest someone, or search their premises: the government had to show evidence establishing probable cause to believe that the premises to be searched, or the individual to be detained, were involved in criminal activity.[12]

144

Like many other constitutional rights, the Fourth Amendment came into its own only in the second half of the 20th century. The Amendment became binding on the states (the principal operators of police forces in the U.S.), only in 1949.[13] Prior to that year, the Fourth Amendment was binding only on the federal government. But even after 1949, the Amendment's main enforcement mechanism—the controversial "exclusionary rule," which excludes from criminal trials evidence that was obtained in violation of the defendant's constitutional rights—did not apply to the states for another decade. Before 1961, violations of the Fourth Amendment by state police forces went essentially without a remedy—and were consequently very common.[14] It was only under the liberal Warren Court that the Fourth Amendment began to be earnestly enforced against states' police.

Fourth Amendment doctrine was and remains controversial. Americans are deeply divided over the proper balance between liberty and security: between the right to be free from intrusive police activities, and the power of the police to investigate crime. Recent Supreme Courts presided over ever-shrinking Fourth Amendment rights, as an increasingly conservative Court narrowed Fourth Amendment protections—often in closely divided opinions.[15]

In 2001, the Court held in a 5-4 opinion that police officers who observed a person committing a crime could arrest the offender and place her in jail, no matter how benign the crime may have been.[16] The case before the Court involved a woman who was arrested for a seatbelt violation. According to the record, her two young children were crying inconsolably as she was handcuffed, placed in a police cruiser, and driven to jail. She paid a $50 dollar fine and then sued, claiming that her Fourth Amendment rights were violated by the arrest: the police, she claimed, violate the Fourth Amendment when they arrest individuals for breaking laws whose violations do not carry any jail time, unless there is some compelling need to do so. The Supreme Court rejected the claim: so long as their observations establish probable cause, police officers may arrest for any violation of the criminal code, no matter how petty.[17] Documented cases show

Americans being arrested and jailed for driving with single head-lights, failing to signal a turn, jaywalking, riding a bicycle without an audible bell, and for violating dog leash laws.[18] John Roberts, sitting as a federal Court of Appeals judge before he became Chief Justice of the Supreme Court, wrote an opinion in a case involving the arrest of a twelve-year-old for eating a single French fry at a Washington D.C. Metro station.[19] The girl was searched, handcuffed, then transported in a windowless rear compartment of a police car to a juvenile pro-cessing center, where she was fingerprinted and booked. The terrified girl was sobbing throughout the ordeal. "Given the undisputed ex-istence of probable cause," wrote Roberts for the Court of Appeals, the arrest did not violate the Fourth Amendment's prohibition on "unreasonable seizures."

Other Supreme Court cases authorized the police to thoroughly search every person they arrest—including strip searches, if they were going to be placed with other detainees—irrespective of the crime of arrest. In 2012, the Court upheld the constitutionality of several strip searches conducted on a man who was arrested for an unpaid fine.[20] At the station house, he was told to remove his clothes while an officer scrutinized his head, armpits, nose, mouth, and ears. He was ordered to squat, lift his genitals, and cough while an officer ex-amined his rectum. In his lawsuit claiming a violation of his Fourth Amendment rights, the plaintiff gave a vivid description of his rapid descent from a respectable citizen enjoying a weekend drive with his wife and kid, to a naked and frightened inmate having a crisply uni-formed officer peer into his cavities. The Supreme Court, in another 5–4 opinion, held that the cavity search did not violate the constitu-tional prohibition on "unreasonable searches."

Some of the biggest opponents of strong Fourth Amendment rights are, unsurprisingly, law enforcement officials. Unfortunately, that opposition has assumed a worrying aspect: research shows that police officers frequently lie on the stand when questioned about Fourth Amendment violations, in order to ensure that relevant evi-dence remains available at the trial—often aided by the knowing col-lusion of judges.[21] Such corrupt practices are extremely dangerous in a criminal justice system: police perjuries may begin with resentment at the exclusionary rule—where they end nobody knows.

It was against this background of enfeebled Fourth Amendment protections that Abdullah al-Kidd (born Lavni T. Kidd in Wichita, Kansas) filed his lawsuit alleging a Fourth Amendment violation.

III. Al-Kidd's Material Witness Arrest

Abdullah al-Kidd was a former University of Idaho football player who converted to Islam. He was arrested by FBI agents in March 2003, as he was boarding a plane to Saudi Arabia—where he intended to study Arabic and Islamic law. Al-Kidd had been suspected—erroneously and based on skimpy evidence—of terrorism-related activity. But the FBI could not arrest al-Kidd as a terrorism suspect, due to a lack of evidence showing probable cause. The Bureau therefore decided to arrest al-Kidd under the authority of the federal Material Witness Statute, with the pretext that he was a "material witness."

The Material Witness Statute authorizes the federal government to detain, potentially for an extended period, people who have done nothing wrong.[22] The statute, which has been around since 1789, authorizes the arrest and detention of people who are not themselves accused of any wrongdoing, but whose testimony is required at a criminal trial, if it can be shown that they are not likely to show up for the trial voluntarily. The Statute has been challenged on several occasions as a violation of the Fourth Amendment, but the claim has been repeatedly rejected by federal courts.[23]

The FBI's application for the warrant claimed that al-Kidd was a material witness in the criminal prosecution of one Sami Omar al-Hussayen for visa fraud. The application contained some false allegations (for example, that al-Kidd was flying on a one-way ticket), omitted important information (for example, that al-Kidd was an American-born U.S. citizen), and did not specify what material information al-Kidd possessed. Nevertheless, the warrant was signed, and al-Kidd was arrested.

Following his arrest, al-Kidd was interrogated at length about his relation to Islam. He was then transferred to a high security facility, where he remained for 16 days. The light in his cell was kept lit 24 hours a day; the guards shackled his legs, wrists, and waist whenever he was taken out of his cell; and he was allowed out for only one to two hours every 24-hour period. These were unusually harsh conditions for the detention of an innocent witness. When al-Kidd was finally released, it was on the conditions that he limit his travels, live with his wife at his in-laws, report regularly to a probation officer, and consent to unannounced home visits. These conditions lasted over a year, during which al-Kidd lost his job and separated from his wife (which can easily happen when you live with the in-laws).

Al-Kidd's arrest was not the only such case: following 9/11, several men were detained under the pretext that they were material witnesses—sometimes for lengthy periods, often in similarly harsh conditions. The precise number of such detentions remains unclear: a Department of Justice Inspector General report put the number at 12,[24] while the American NGO Human Rights Watch put it at 70.[25] Like other Muslim men arrested as material witnesses, al-Kidd was never asked to testify in any criminal proceeding, and was evidently arrested on suspicion of terrorist activity in the absence of probable cause. Statements by high federal officials confirmed that the government was using the Material Witness Statute as a pretext to arrest terrorism suspects. Michael Chertoff, the head of the Department of Justice's Criminal Division, stated publicly that the Material Witness Statute was "an important investigative tool in the war on terrorism,"[26] and U.S. Attorney General John Ashcroft announced that the Material Witness Statute was an important tool in "taking suspected terrorists off the street."[27] FBI director Robert Mueller—later the special counsel investigating Russian interference in the 2016 elections—said, when testifying before Congress in 2003, that al-Kidd's arrest as one of five major successes in FBI efforts to dismantle terrorist networks in the United States.[28] (We now know that was complete nonsense: there never was any serious evidence linking al-Kidd to terrorism.)

Al-Kidd's lawsuit, originally filed in 2005, accused Attorney General John Ashcroft of violating al-Kidd's Fourth Amendment rights by implementing a policy authorizing the incarceration of people suspected of ties to terrorism without anything approaching the constitutionally-required probable cause, and under the pretext that they were material witnesses.[29] Two federal courts agreed that the claim was solid. The Ninth Circuit Court of Appeals wrote that:

> To use a material witness statute pretextually, in order to investigate or preemptively detain suspects without probable cause, is to violate the Fourth Amendment.[30]

Such pretextual use of the Material Witness Statute, wrote another federal court,

> gutted the substantive protections of the Fourth Amendment's 'probable cause' requirement [by] giving the state the power to arrest upon the executive's mere suspicion.[31]

If al-Kidd's allegations were true—declared these courts—the federal government made an unconstitutional end-run around the Fourth Amendment's probable cause requirement.

Their decisions were appealed to the Supreme Court. In 2011 the Court issued a 5–4 decision dismissing the lawsuit after holding that al-Kidd's pretextual arrest was authorized by the Material Witness Statute and, consequently, was perfectly constitutional.[32] The Fourth Amendment, said the majority, was not violated when officials arrested individuals on suspicion of criminal activity, in the absence of probable cause, on the pretext that they were material witnesses, even if the officials had no intention of ever using these suspects as witnesses. This startling conclusion was a direct result of the Court's textualist methodology.

IV. The Textualist-Purposivist Debate and the Material Witness Statute

The disagreement between the government and al-Kidd was a variation of the disagreement between textualists and purposivists. Al-Kidd's attorneys argued that the Material Witness Statute, which authorizes the detention of witnesses whose testimony is material but may fail to come and testify on their own volition, did not authorize the detention of individuals who were never intended to be used as witnesses. The purpose of the statute was to enable the government to secure material testimony in criminal trials; the statute did not and could not authorize the detention of people who were not intended to testify—even if, technically speaking, these people could somehow qualify as material witnesses (because they have information that is relevant to some on-going criminal trial, and they would not be amenable to a hypothetical order to testify). If the government had no interest in securing a person's testimony (wrote al-Kidd's attorneys in their brief), the statute simply did not apply. Allowing the government to use the statute in such circumstances would allow the government to evade the Fourth Amendment:

> The material witness statute is designed for a singular purpose—to secure testimony. As a matter of both the Fourth Amendment and statutory construction, the government must therefore adhere to that purpose. Otherwise, the government could circumvent the traditional rule barring custodial investigative arrests in the absence of probable cause of wrongdoing.[33]

The government's brief took the opposite view: "[T]he statute . . . permits a witness to be detained regardless of the prosecutor's motive in seeking detention," claimed the federal government.[34] According to the government's brief, the Material Witness Statute authorized the arrest of people that the government did not intend to use as witnesses.

The claim was a logical extension of textualist principles: if it is irrelevant for the proper application of a statute what the legislature intended the statute to achieve, it is also irrelevant for the proper application of a statute what the Attorney General intended to achieve when enforcing it. The government's brief put the point as follows:

> Respondent . . . contends that [the Material Witness Statute] precludes the use of a material-witness warrant for the subjective purpose of investigation . . . . [But] Respondent arrives at his reading of the statute with little discussion of the statutory language, which contains two requirements: that the testimony be material and that securing the presence of the witness be impracticable. Those are objective criteria, and nothing in the statute calls for an inquiry into the motive or purpose of the prosecutor who seeks the warrant.[35]

What mattered was the statutory text, not the statutory purpose. The brief continued:

> Rather than focus on the text of the statute, respondent attempts to demonstrate that Congress did not intend "to turn the law into a detention and investigation tool." Congress provided an objective standard for obtaining a material-witness warrant, however, and that standard, on its face, does not turn upon the prosecutor's alleged motive. Cf. *Oncale v. Sundowner Offshore Servs., Inc.*, 523 U.S. 75, 79 (1998) ("[I]t is ultimately the provisions of our laws rather than the principal concerns of our legislators by which we are governed.").[36]

Unsurprisingly, *Oncale v. Sundowner Offshore Servs., Inc.*, cited in the government's brief, was a textualist Supreme Court opinion written by the textualist Justice Scalia.

This reading of the statute is absurd!, responded al-Kidd's attorneys: show us the judge who would sign a material witness warrant if the application revealed that the government had no intention to use the arrestee as a witness! But the Supreme Court, in an opinion written by Justice Scalia, agreed with the government: the material witness statute authorized al-Kidd's arrest.[37] The statutory language allowed the arrest, and the fact that the purpose of the statute was to secure testimony was not dispositive for the statute's construction. It was the statutorily text that mattered, not the statutory purpose.

That the statute authorized the arrest did not automatically mean the arrest complied with the Fourth Amendment: after all, the statute, or its specific use in the case, could have been found to violate the Fourth Amendment. But without that statutory authorization, it is hard to see how the arrest could be constitutional, given that the FBI could not establish probable cause. Statutory authorization under the Material Witness Statute was a necessary first finding for the constitutionality of al-Kidd's arrest and detention. Indeed, having found that the Material Witness Statute did authorize al-Kidd's arrest warrant, the Court went on to conclude that the arrest was consistent with the Fourth Amendment: "We hold that [the] arrest and detention of a material witness pursuant to a validly obtained warrant cannot be challenged as unconstitutional on the basis of allegations that the arresting authority had an improper motive."[38] In other words, the allegedly improper purpose of the FBI in arresting al-Kidd—i.e., arresting him for his alleged terrorist activities rather than as a witness—was also not relevant to the constitutionality of the detention. So long as the government could show that al-Kidd's testimony was material to an on-going criminal trial, and that he would be unamenable to a hypothetical order to testify, it did not matter what was the real purpose for his detention—or that there was no intention to use him as a witness.

The al-Kidd decision therefore twice refused to look into the government's purposes or motivations: first by refusing to examine the legislative purpose behind the Material Witness Statute, and second by refusing to examine the executive's purpose in enforcing the statute. And while the refusal to examine the legislative purpose was squarely based on textualist methodology, the refusal to examine the executive's purpose was less clearly so. Still, it is hard to shake the feeling that the two are related: government purpose is government purpose, and if the purpose of the legislature is irrelevant, why should the purpose of the executive matter? In truth, *Al-Kidd v. Ashcroft* is one of those counterintuitive legal conclusions whose convoluted logic is nearly impossible to understand without understanding their relation to judicial philosophy.

V. Statutory and Constitutional Ramifications

The reluctance to inquire into government purposes, be they legislative or executive, has important ramifications for both statutory and constitutional law. From the perspective of statutory law, the refusal to take legislative purposes into account means that statutes might be misapplied to circumstances they were never intended to address. *Al-Kidd* is a good example of that: a statute aimed at securing witness testimony was employed to arrest and detain a wrongly suspected individual. Here is another example: After Oregon authorized physician-assisted suicides for terminally ill patients in the Death with Dignity Act, Attorney General John Ashcroft (the same Ashcroft of *al-Kidd*) issued an executive directive stating that the federal Drug Abuse Prevention and Control Act, whose stated purpose was the prevention of drug abuse and addiction, made it a criminal offense for Oregon doctors to help terminally ill patients die. The text of the federal statute forbade doctors from prescribing certain classified drugs other than for legitimate medical purpose. Following a textual reading of the statute while ignoring the statutory purpose, Ashcroft's directive claimed that helping patients die was not a legitimate medical purpose, and was therefore in violation of the Drug Abuse Prevention and Control Act. Oregon physicians who helped their sick patients die could be convicted of a federal crime, imprisoned, and have their medical licenses revoked. (That time, however, the

Supreme Court declared the directive unlawful. Justice Scalia, joined by two other justices, dissented).[39]

The reluctance to consider the government's purpose in enacting or enforcing the law has significant constitutional ramifications as well—including, as we saw, for the Fourth Amendment. Not only is it not a violation of the Fourth Amendment to arrest material witnesses who are not intended to serve as witnesses, it is also not a violation of the Fourth Amendment to engage in racial profiling. In *Whren v. United States*, another decision authored by the textualist Justice Scalia, the Supreme Court held that police officers did not violate the Fourth Amendment when they used the pretext of a petty traffic violation—the officers claimed that the targeted vehicle failed to signal a turn—in order to stop a vehicle they wanted to examine because its occupiers were African Americans.[40] It did not matter *why* the officers stopped the vehicle, said the Court: the officers' purpose or intent was irrelevant to the constitutionality of their actions.[41] If the officers had probable cause to believe that a traffic offense had been committed, the seizure of the vehicle was constitutional.

The refusal to look into the motivation of police officers may also mean that *vindictive arrests*—arrests whose purpose is to harass or intimidate—may also be constitutional, so long as the officers can point to some probable cause. One year after *al-Kidd* was decided, the Supreme Court accepted review of a lawsuit alleging that Secret Service agents acted unconstitutionally when they arrested a man for his expressed opposition to the Iraq war.[42] Steven Howards happened to be present at a shopping mall in Beaver Creek, Colorado, when Vice President Dick Cheney visited in 2006. A Secret Service agent overheard Howards say on the phone that he intended to ask Cheney how many Iraqi kids he had killed that day. Howards then entered the line to meet Cheney, and when he reached him told Cheney that his "policies in Iraq [were] disgusting." When Cheney turned away from Howards, Howards touched his shoulder in an attempt to keep his attention. That resulted in Howards' arrest and subsequent criminal charge for harassment. After the charges were dismissed, Howards brought suit against the agents who arrested him, claiming that the arrest was vindictive and based on his political views, and that it therefore violated his First Amendment right to free speech and his Fourth Amendment right against unreasonable seizures. The Supreme Court refused to even consider Howards' Fourth Amendment allegation: since intentional but unconsented physical touch—no matter how slight—was a criminal offense, Howards' arrest was perfectly constitutional under the Fourth Amendment even if the arrest was vindictive, since the motivation of the Secret Service agents was irrelevant to the constitutionality of their actions.[43] (The Court granted review to Howards' First Amendment claim—which it then dismissed as well.)

In 2018, the Supreme Court made another decision that refused to inquire into the executive and legislative purposes underlying executive action. During his Presidential campaign, then-candidate Donald Trump pledged that, if elected, he would ban Muslims from entering the United States. When he became president, Trump issued an executive order that banned travelers from many Muslims countries from entering the country. A lawsuit was filed (among others, by Muslim Americans whose family members were barred from entering) claiming that the travel ban was not authorized by the immigration statute it purported to execute, and that it violated the First Amendment's Establishment Clause—which forbids discrimination based on religious belief.[44] Notwithstanding substantial evidence that the travel ban intended to disfavor Muslims, the Supreme Court dismissed the lawsuit after refusing to consider Trump's intent for the travel ban. The Court also rejected the argument that the travel ban was not authorized by the federal immigration statute by refusing to consider the statute's legislative purpose: "plaintiffs' attempts to . . . appeal to the statute's purposes . . . fail to overcome the clear statutory language," said the Court.

The refusal to look into legislative purposes may have a substantial impact on constitutional rights. A number of current constitutional doctrines forbid laws that have nefarious purposes, including an Establishment Clause doctrine that forbids laws whose purpose is to suppress religious beliefs,[45] and an Equal Protection doctrine that forbids laws having a discriminatory purpose against certain specially protected classes (for example, the government cannot demand that police officers be of a certain minimum height if its purpose is to keep women out of police forces, although it may be able to do so if its purpose is different and legitimate).[46] The refusal to inquire into legislative purposes—which is rooted in a textualist philosophy—may put an end to these and other constitutional protections.[47]

VI. Review

To sum up: the leading justification for judicial deviations from statutory texts is the statutory purpose. But textualists claim that the notion of statutory purpose is an illegitimate fabrication: legislators have various and potentially conflicting purposes in mind, and legislative compromises may mean that there is no unified or coherent purpose anyway. According to textualists, there is no singular statutory purpose to which judges can appeal, and which can justify deviations from clear statutory language.

Purposivists respond that a statutory purpose is not some combination of legislators' intentions or expectations, but is, rather, a judicial hypothesis about the policy determinations that underlie statutory requirements. These purposes are judicial constructions of the logical and reasonable bases for statutes' enactments—a logical and reasonable purpose being a necessary presumption of the Rule of Law, and a necessary guide in deciding what statutes actually require.

But for textualists, such judicial hypotheses are a back door through which judges can inject their own policy and moral preferences into legal decisions. For them, deviating from textual strictures in the name of some hypothesized and fictional purpose is, in the final analysis, an abuse of judicial power.

In part, these disagreements reflect different understandings about how best to serve the wishes of the legislature. For textualists, legislative determinations are best served by following the statutorily-enacted text. For the purposivists, legislative determinations are best served by reflecting on what the legislature was trying to achieve. But the disagreement between textualists and purposivists is not only about how best to serve the legislature. It also represents different understandings of separation of powers: different visions of the proper relations between the legislature and the judiciary. These different visions are the subject of the next chapter.

CHAPTER 10

Textualism, Purposivism, and Pragmatism: Judicial Legislation and the Politicization of Judicial Election Campaigns

Unlike federal judges, many state judges are elected for office, and must run judicial election campaigns. The question in *Republican Party of Minnesota v. White* (2002) was whether candidates running for a judicial office have a First Amendment free speech right to make partisan political statements during their campaigns.[1] The answer to that important question depended on whether politicized judicial election campaigns were likely to compromise the professional performance of those judges. If they did, states were allowed to prohibit judges from running political campaigns in order to preserve the professional integrity of their judges. But if politicized election campaigns did not compromise the way elected judges decided cases, judicial candidates were constitutionally entitled to inform voters of their opinions on a host of controversial political issues—including immigration, abortion, gay rights, or guns.

Whether political judicial election campaigns were likely to change the way judges decided their cases depended, in turn, on the judicial philosophy they employed in the first place: whether judicial decisions would be impacted or changed by politicized judicial elections depended on the methodology employed in reaching them. Thus, the decision in the case depended on the judicial philosophies that American judges employed when deciding cases: the Supreme Court had to determine whether the normal judicial methodology would be compromised by judges who get elected on the basis of their potentially controversial political views.

The resulting opinion, written by Justice Antonin Scalia, hewed closely to the textualist creed. This chapter starts by taking a deeper look at textualism, and then examines how textualism shaped this important Supreme Court decision. Purposivism—textualism's biggest philosophical rival—is examined next to see how the decision would have come out with a purposivist understanding of judicial decision-making. The chapter ends with a short discussion of legal pragmatism, the alleged philosophy of some of the justices of the majority—which may have had an indirect but decisive impact on the case.

I. Textualism

Textualists believe that judges must faithfully follow the text of statutes, even if the ensuing result is unfair or unjust or seems to defeat the purpose of the statute. According to textualism, judges who deviate from statutory texts effectively substitute a different text (one of their own choosing) for the text that the legislature enacted. In doing so, they substitute their own policy choices for the policy choices of a democratically elected legislature. But in democracies, policy choices are supposed to be made by the legislature, not by the judiciary.

Textualists recognize that textual fidelity cannot always prevent judges from making policy choices. Many legal rules contain extremely vague or abstract legal standards, such as "reasonable," "negligent," "excessive," "reckless," "material," "fair," etc. Such vague statutory terms are extremely common, and they provide little by way of textualist constraints: what is or is not "fair" or "reasonable" are determinations that leave much to be decided by judges. For example, the Americans with Disabilities Act requires employers to provide employees with disabilities with "reasonable accommodation."[2] Inevitably, judges have a great deal of latitude in deciding what accommodations must be made under the statute. Are employers required to grant employees with disabilities a flexible work schedule? How about acquiring expensive equipment for them? Textual fidelity notwithstanding, such decisions seem to involve substantial policy choices.[3]

Accordingly, textualists draw a clear line between judicial decisions that follow a clear and determinate text and judicial decisions that apply vague and abstract standards. Textualists believe that when judges apply vague and abstract statutory standards, their task is best described as *writing new law*, rather than merely applying pre-existing law: in such cases, say the textualists, judges write in the law's finer details. In other words, in such cases judges legislate from the bench.

In principle, legislating from the bench is not an appropriate judicial action. Writing the law is the proper business of elected representatives. But judges tasked with applying vague and indeterminate statutory texts have no choice: they must make a decision, and making a decision—at least according to how textualists see it—requires that they legislate from the bench. That is why textualists dislike vague and indeterminate statutes. As Justice Scalia put it:

> Statutes that are seen as establishing rules of inadequate clarity or precision are criticized, on that account, as undemocratic . . . because they leave too much to be decided by persons other than the people's representatives.[4]

Put differently, vague and indeterminate statutory terms create "gaps" in the law—gaps that judges must fill. That gap-filling function is, for all intents and purposes, a form of judicial legislation.

Perhaps unsurprisingly, judges are not in the habit of admitting that they are often writing the law. Judges almost always pretend that the statutes they are applying completely determine the outcome of the cases before them. But according to textualists, these pretensions should not be taken too seriously: these are the white lies that judges feel compelled to tell. In truth, whether judges admit it or not, statutory texts are oftentimes too vague to provide solutions to legal questions; and that means that in order to reach a solution, judges must sometimes legislate from the bench.

In short, according to textualists there are two principal modes of judicial decisions: in cases where the legal text is clear and determinate, judges simply follow the text to the required legal conclusion; but in cases where the legal text is vague and indeterminate, judges themselves write the details of the law when they decide how to resolve the case.

This dual conception of the judicial role is crucial for understanding the Supreme Court's opinion in *Republican Party of Minnesota v. White*.

II. Judicial Elections

Under the Federal Constitution, judges of the Supreme Court, the federal courts of appeals, and the federal district courts are nominated by the President and confirmed by the Senate.[5] But things are very different in the states: most of America's state judges, including supreme court justices, obtain their jobs through popular elections.

The plaintiff in *Republican Party of Minnesota v. White* was a lawyer from Minnesota named Gregory Wersal, who decided to run for a seat on the Minnesota Supreme Court. In the course of his election campaign, Wersal made comments about controversial political issues including abortion, welfare, and crime. This resulted in a complaint, filed with the Minnesota Professional Responsibility Board (the body regulating Minnesota's legal profession), which accused Wersal of violating Minnesota's Code of Judicial Conduct. One of the rules in that Code forbade campaigning judicial candidates from announcing their views on "disputed legal or political issues."[6]

Minnesota was not alone in adopting the so-called "announce clause," which sought to keep judicial elections from becoming overly politicized: many other states had similar provisions. In these states, judicial elections were supposed to revolve around issues like candidates' qualifications, their experience, their temperaments, or the professional endorsements they garnered—not around their controversial political views. But Gregory Wersal—and the Republican Party of Minnesota, of which Wersal was a member—wanted things changed. They thought that judicial elections, like other elections, should revolve around the political ideologies and beliefs of the candidates. Thus, Wersal and the Republican Party of Minnesota filed a lawsuit challenging the constitutionality of the "announce clause" on the ground that it violated the First Amendment's freedom of speech. Preventing judicial candidates from disclosing their contested political views during their judicial election campaign was a violation of the constitutional right to free speech, claimed Wersal. A federal district court rejected the claim, the Eighth Circuit Court of Appeals affirmed the rejection, and in 2001 the Supreme Court agreed to hear the case.[7]

Both sides claimed the support of important constitutional interests. Gregory Wersal asserted his right to engage in political speech—the sort of speech that the First Amendment protects with particular rigor. Minnesota, on the other hand, claimed that politicized judicial elections would compromise the impartiality of its judges—and an impartial judge is also a constitutional right.[8] That assertion soon became the central question in the case: was it true that politicized judicial elections were, as Minnesota claimed, a danger to judicial impartiality? In the end, the Supreme Court decided it wasn't. It did so by relying on a textualist understanding of judicial decision-making.

Although textualism remains a controversial judicial philosophy that few judges wholly subscribe to, the theory continues to punch above its weight.[9] *Republican Party of Minnesota v. White* was one more example of textualism's formidable and enduring influence.

III. Textualism and Politicized Judicial Elections

Minnesota made a simple argument: judges who run political election campaigns may feel obligated to decide cases in accordance with the political positions they took during their election campaigns. A judge who campaigned, and then got elected, by proclaiming the constitutionality of gun control, or restricting late-term abortions, or prohibiting hate speech, may feel obligated to rule in accordance with those campaign positions—potentially in violation of the proper judicial decision.

The Supreme Court rejected the argument: according to the Court, politicized judicial elections did not pose the danger to judicial impartiality that Minnesota claimed it did. And indeed, if you look at legal decision-making through the conceptual lens of textualism, there is no real peril in politicized judicial elections.

As discussed above, textualists believe that there is a principled and important distinction between following clear and determinate legal texts and following vague and indeterminate standards: while the former are instances of applying the law, the latter are, for all intents and purposes, instances of judicial legislation. Now take a judge who ran a politicized judicial election campaign and is fully committed to the policy positions that got her elected. If the text of the statute is clear and determinate, that judge's policy positions can have no impact on her legal conclusion: whether she is liberal or conservative, pro-prosecution or pro-defense, a radical progressive or a laissez faire zealot—her judicial decision, and the judicial reasoning toward that decision, would remain the same: namely, she would simply follow the clear and determinate text of the statute. If a legal ordinance reads, "no vehicles in the park," and someone drives his sedan through the park, the textualist legal conclusion is that the statute was violated—no matter what campaign statements the judge may have made about vehicles and parks. Concerns over politicized judicial campaigns have no place if the judge is a textualist and the text is clear and determinate.

On the other hand, if the statutory text is vague or abstract, politicized judicial elections are a positive blessing. After all, in such cases judges essentially "make law." As Justice Scalia's opinion for the Court explained:

> [The] complete separation of the judiciary from the enterprise of 'representative government' might have some truth in those countries where judges [do not] make law themselves . . . . It is not a true picture of the American system . . . . Which is precisely why the election of state judges became popular.[10]

Since judges "make law" whenever they apply vague or abstract statutory language, and since vague and abstract statutory language is a fixture of American law, politicized election campaigns are a positive blessing because they make sure that judges are elected according to their political positions—and therefore that they legislate in accordance with the popular will. After all, this is what representative democracy is about: allowing the public to elect representatives who would implement their policy choices. Since American judges often function as *de facto* legislators, they, too, can—or even should—be elected on the basis of their political beliefs. According to the Court, this is precisely why judicial elections were adopted in the first place—in order to allow the public to influence the policy choices of judges.

In short, if you look at judicial decision-making through the philosophical apparatus of textualism, politicized judicial elections pose no danger to judicial impartiality, and instead offer a significant benefit: when judges apply clear statutory texts, their political campaign statements can play no role in the legal decision; and when judges apply vague and indeterminate statutory texts, they are engaged in policy-making and their political campaign statements allow the public to influence those policies—as democracy requires. And in that case, the "announce clause" subverted the entire purpose of judicial elections, since it prevented citizens from learning the information that was most relevant for their voting choice—namely, candidates' opinions on disputed legal or political issues.

IV. Non-textualism and Politicized Judicial Elections

These conclusions depended on a textualist understanding of judicial decision-making. But if textualism was not how most American judges operated—and in fact it isn't—then the Court's conclusions may have been ill-advised.

In a celebrated article published in 1958, the legal philosopher Lon Fuller explained why he thought that textualism must be wrong.[11] Suppose, he wrote, that a municipal ordinance forbade vehicles from entering a park: "no vehicles in the park," reads the ordinance. And suppose that the park's neighborhood association proposed the creation of a Second World War memorial in the form of a real Second World War truck. A textualist interpretation of that ordinance would appear to forbid the monument. But that interpretation cannot be right (and no judge would make such a ridiculous ruling). Statutory law, said Fuller, is not comprised only of the text of statutes; proper statutory interpretation never blindly follows the text. Judges are always guided by additional considerations—including, most importantly, the purposes of statutes. The proposed monument does not violate the "no vehicles in the park" ordinance because of the ordinance's purpose.

Sure enough, most judicial decisions follow the statutory texts; but that is not because judges unerringly follow the text, but because the statutory purpose points to the same result that the text does—which in most cases would be unsurprising, given that the text was written to serve that purpose. But if the statutory purpose would not be served by blindly following the text, most judges would not hesitate to deviate from that text.[12] Textualism, said Fuller, was an overly simplistic and ultimately wrong conception of judicial practice.

The rejection of textualism also leads to the rejection of the claim that vague or abstract statutory standards must lead to judicial law-making. Judges, say opponents of textualism, always effectuate the political choices of the legislature—not their own—even when those choices are couched in vague and indeterminate language. Judges must ascertain the policies that vague or abstract standards were

166

designed to achieve, and must apply these standards so as to give effect to those legislative goals—not to their own policy preferences. For example, in deciding what is a "reasonable accommodation" under the Americans with Disabilities Act, judges do not consult their own policy choices regarding the rights of employees with disabilities, but rather seek to effectuate the Act's legislative intention, which they may establish by examining the statute's legislative history, or the specific problems that the legislature considered when the statute was enacted. And while that takes some judicial judgment, describing that judgment as "judicial legislation" or as "judicial policy-making" is to misunderstand how that process works.

Now, if judges do not unerringly follow statutory texts, even when they are perfectly clear, but instead follow the purposes of statutes, then politicized judicial elections can actually pose a threat to proper judicial practice. Judges who are elected on the basis of their own policy views may feel empowered—perhaps even justifiably so—to place greater emphasis on their own policy choices than on the policy choices of the legislature. As Minnesota put it, judges who campaign and get elected on the basis of political platforms may feel compelled to decide cases in accordance with the platforms which gave them their jobs. Instead of deferring to the political agenda of the legislature, such elected judges may defer to the political agenda that got them elected: after all, they too were presumably elected in order to implement certain policy choices.

In short, whether political judicial elections are a threat to proper judicial practice depends on how judges decide cases. If the answer is textualism, politicized judicial elections pose little risk and a great benefit; if the answer is purposivism, politicized judicial elections offer no benefit, and create a significant risk. *Republican Party of Minnesota v. White*, an opinion written by the staunchest textualist on the Court, opted—unsurprisingly—for the textualist answer.

V. Regretting the Vote

While *Republican Party of Minnesota v. White* hinged on the Court's understanding of judicial methodology, Justice Scalia's opinion for the Court did not put textualism front and center. Instead, the textualist creed appeared in a subdued and indirect manner—most notably in the claim that American judges often engage in *de facto* legislation. That obliqueness may have been necessary: textualism was and remains a highly controversial judicial philosophy, and two of the justices who joined Scalia's opinion—Anthony Kennedy and Sandra Day O'Connor—were known as no-frills pragmatists with little interest in judicial philosophy, let alone in a philosophy as sharp and polarizing as textualism. Downplaying the opinion's textualist assumptions may have been essential for securing their votes.

The opinion's philosophical opacity may help explain why, soon after she retired from the Supreme Court and merely four years after the decision, Justice O'Connor repudiated her vote in *White*. In 2006, speaking to a gathering of (mostly elected) state judges, O'Connor declared that the case now "gives [her] a pause," and that she came to believe it may endanger proper judicial practice.[13]

It is sheer speculation, but this about-face may have resulted from O'Connor's belated realization that the decision was rooted in a judicial philosophy she did not necessarily share. It may have taken some time for the pragmatic, non-philosophical O'Connor, who was notoriously apathetic to legal philosophy, to realize the philosophical assumptions, and the possible ramifications, of the White decision.[14] If so, that would be unfortunate: *Republican Party of Minnesota v. White* may be a significant detriment to our states' judicial systems—and it was decided on the strength of a single vote.[15]

VI. Pragmatism

Justice O'Connor was one of a number of recent Supreme Court justices who have been described as pragmatists. The list also includes

Justices Anthony Kennedy, Justice Stephen Breyer, and Justice Elena Kagan. Pragmatists are usually contrasted with judicial doctrinaires, who are careful or even pedantic about their judicial methodology. But "pragmatism" is a term that lacks precision, and has been used to denote starkly different forms of methodological flexibility (both statutory and constitutional): from a willingness to engage with extra-textual factors even when the text is clear (which can be said about most American judges), to being particularly attuned to current political winds, or even to carelessness with existing doctrinal structures.

The theorist most commonly identified with American legal pragmatism is Judge Richard Posner. Posner had written extensively about pragmatism; but, unfortunately, his writings fail to bring the theory into sharper focus. Posner's statements about pragmatism have been, so to speak, all over the place. He had described legal pragmatism as everything from a form of modest textualism to full-blown political decision-making. For example, Posner wrote that:

> If judges did not generally interpret . . . statutes in accordance with the ordinary meaning of the sentences appearing in those texts, certainty of legal obligation would be seriously undermined. . . . When the consequences are not catastrophic or absurd, it is usually sensible to go with the plain meaning of a statute. . . . [M]ost . . . cases are decided quickly and easily on the basis of the 'plain meaning' of the relevant text. These are pragmatic decisions . . . .[16]

This suggests that pragmatism is nothing more than textualism plus an emergency exit for catastrophic or absurd textualist results: "Where the pragmatist is likely to differ [from the textualist]," wrote Posner, "is in believing that there should probably be some escape hatch . . . . "[17] In fact, most textualists agree that there should be an escape hatch if following the text would produce an absurd result.[18]

But this version of pragmatism contrasts with much else that Posner says. Here, for example, he describes pragmatism as almost a free-for-all:

> The ultimate criterion of pragmatic adjudication is reasonableness. . . . [T]here isn't too much more to say to the pragmatic judge than make the most reasonable decision you can, all things considered.[19]

Posner had also proclaimed that "Pragmatism may tend to dissolve law into policy analysis,"[20] and that "[T]here is no intrinsic or fundamental difference between how a judge approaches a legal problem and how a businessman [or a politician] approaches a problem . . . ."[21] He wrote that "the judiciary . . . shares lawmaking power with the legislative branch,"[22] and that the law could do with some myth-breaking:

> [That] the judge 'should try to make the decision that is reasonable in the circumstances, all things considered' [is a suggestion that] will horrify many legal professionals. It will strike them as belittlement of legal reasoning and hence an insult to their mystery. But law could do with some demystification.[23]

In short, the writings of the leading expositor of American legal pragmatism fail to provide a coherent conception of that judicial philosophy. What are we to make of that?

Perhaps the most charitable and enlightening way to interpret Posner is to view legal pragmatism as a "no-theory theory": the view that there is no judicial philosophy that can actually guide legal decision-making and, at the same time, adequately capture how judges decide cases. All attempts to reduce judicial decision-making to a judicial philosophy with a finite set of methodological rules are bound to fail. Such philosophies are perforce unfaithful to proper legal practice and, if taken too seriously, can inflict real damage on the quality of legal decisions. Pragmatism can be understood as methodological skepticism—an ideology having a long and illustrious history in American law and in American legal philosophy.

Methodological skepticism can already be seen, for example, in the writings of Justice Oliver Wendell Holmes, the celebrated judge whose career straddled the late 19th and early 20th centuries (and had been described by Posner himself as a pragmatist[24]):

> The life of the law has not been logic, it has been experience. The felt necessities of the time, the prevalent moral and political theories, intuitions of public policy, avowed or unconscious, even the prejudices which judges share with their fellow men, have had a good deal more to do than the syllogism in determining the rules by which men should be governed.[25]

Methodological skepticism is also a staple of American Legal Realism,[26] an influential school of judicial philosophy that was popular in the 1920s and 30s, and of the Critical Legal Studies movement, which flourished in American law schools in the 1980s and 90s.[27] Indeed, a "no-theory theory" is a familiar philosophical idea. It has been long argued by some philosophers that certain human decisions and actions—perhaps lots of them—cannot be properly captured through determinate methodological frameworks, because they constitute a gestalt that cannot be reduced to its constitutive elements.

The French phenomenologist Maurice Merleau-Ponty made such an argument in regard to various human activities, including driving and playing chess.[28] When a person first learns to drive or to play chess, she is given a set of concrete rules to follow (shift to second gear when you reach 10 MPH; signal a turn when 100 feet from the intersection; a pawn is worth one point, a rook is worth five; when you have fewer pieces than your opponent, exchange only pawns.). As she gathers some experience, the instructions become vaguer and more abstract (shift to second gear when you hear the engine exerting itself; signal a turn so as to allow other drivers sufficient time to respond; make sure that your pieces are not over extended on the chessboard). But the decisions and actions of proficient drivers and chess players, and even more so the actions of experts, can no longer be reduced to concrete rules or even to standards. In fact, experts can violate any of the novice's rules and standards in the very process of doing what's best.

Legal interpretation involves a subject matter deeper and more complex than driving or playing chess. Its methodology cannot be reduced to a set of instructional rules if it is to reflect the richness and sophistication that are required for the regulation of human affairs. Legal pragmatism is the realization that, as Posner put it, "there isn't too much more to say" about the proper methodology of legal interpretation than "make the most reasonable decision you can, all things considered."

The "no-theory theory" is a deep and intriguing philosophical question. However, both driving and playing chess have been successfully reduced to sets of algorithms that allow computers to do both expertly. Still, perhaps legal decision-making really cannot be reduced to a neat set of rules that are sufficiently concrete to provide guidance and resolutions to legal interpreters. The question is, of course, of enormous significance: if the legal pragmatists (according to this reading of their theory) are right, well-structured judicial philosophies actually impoverish judicial decision-making and do violence to the law. At the same time, taken to its logical conclusion, such a pragmatic outlook may threaten many of the ideals that make the Rule of Law the cherished institution it is. Consistency, equality before the law, lack of arbitrariness, general standards known and announced in advance, even proper separation of powers—all these may be sheer fantasies if legal resolutions are functions of judges' unconscious *gestalt* intuitions, and the guiding principle of legal decision-making is "make the most reasonable decision you can." But this does not mean, of course, that the "no-theory theory" is wrong.

Still, it is difficult to see why it should be impossible to structure legal interpretation in a way that guides and constrains judicial decisions, while still allowing for wise and enduring results. Notwithstanding Posner's claim to the contrary, judicial decision-making does appear to operate with constraints that are unique to the discipline—including the requirements of consistency, principled and public explanation, and deference to legislative policy choices. These and other requirements can provide substantial guidance and restraint; and in unpacking and articulating these requirements, judicial philosophy ought to say to the judge much more than "just be reasonable."

Be that as it may, one thing is clear: a "no-theory theory" judge, as Justice O'Connor may have been, might easily miss the telltale signs of textualism (such as in the *White* opinion), or even the entire significance of judicial philosophy to that case.

VII. Review

To sum up: textualists believe that judges engage in one of two very different tasks when they interpret statutes: if the statutory text is clear and determinate, judges merely apply the law; but if the text is vague and indeterminate, judges actually write it—by filling in the law's finer details. That is why textualists favor legislation that employs clear and determinate language: such statutes, they say, keep the judiciary within its proper institutional role—i.e., applying, rather than writing, the law. Of course, judges like to pretend that they always apply the law, and that the legal resolution is always determined by the pre-existing rules and statutes. But when the law is vague and indeterminate, that pretension is untrue. In such cases, the law does not dictate any specific resolution, and it is the judge who gets to decide what the resolution should be.

Non-texualists dispute all that: judges, they say, never really legislate, even when they apply vague and indeterminate language. That is so because the text is never the sole or even the most important determinant in legal interpretation. Judges are always guided by other considerations—including the famed statutory purpose—whether the statutory text is clear and determinate, or unclear and vague. And this means that there is a correct legal resolution even when the text is too vague to determine that resolution on its own. Proper judicial decisions are never a form of legislation: they are always determined by existing law, never by judges' own policy preferences.

As for pragmatists, they may care little for this debate. Their outlook may best be described as the negation of theory—that is, as the thesis that the proper methodology of legal interpretation cannot be reduced to a set of methodological instructions, be they textualist or purposivist.

CHAPTER 11

Conclusion: Judicial Philosophies and Political Ideologies

> When [courts] are said to exercise a discretion, it is a mere legal discretion, a discretion to be exercised in discerning the course prescribed by law . . . Judicial power is never exercised for the purpose of giving effect to the will of the judge, always for the purpose of giving effect . . . to the will of the law.
>
> *Osborn v. Bank of the United States*, 22 U.S. 9 Wheat. 738 (1824) (Chief Justice John Marshall)

No discussion of judicial philosophies and their impact on constitutional law would be complete without an inquiry into the relation between judicial philosophy and political ideology. We have seen again and again in the previous chapters a clear ideological divide between liberals and conservatives in the choice of judicial philosophies. Some judicial philosophies appear to attract conservatives, others appear to attract liberals, and it is important to ask why there is this distinction.

The answer to that question has much to do with judicial discretion, and the different viewpoints of conservatives and liberals in regard to it—viewpoints with deep intellectual roots in American conservatism and liberalism.

I. Judicial Discretion

In 2008, New York University held a symposium in honor of Ronald Dworkin's receipt of Norway's prestigious Holberg Prize.[1] According to the Prize's academic committee, Dworkin won the award for his "original and highly influential legal theory grounding law in morality."[2] One of the speakers at that symposium was Cass Sunstein, known for his advocacy of Judicial Minimalism—a constitutional judicial philosophy that, in direct contradiction to Dworkin's own theory, condemns the use of moral principles in legal interpretation. According to minimalism, judges should rely on relatively concrete considerations, and steer clear of abstract moral tenets when they make constitutional decisions. Judges—wrote Sunstein—are not especially good at deep moral or philosophical theorizing, so a minimalist approach would reduce judicial errors and produce more adaptable constitutional precedents.[3]

Speaking of minimalism at that 2008 conference, Dworkin said it reminded him of an exchange he once overheard at a barber shop: "How would you like your hair cut?" asked the barber, "Not too short," answered the customer. The minimalist mantra "not too deep," said Dworkin, sounds equally unhelpful. Judges are in the business of making justified decisions: their opinions must explain their conclusions and justify them. How morally deep or morally shallow these opinions should be depends entirely on the case at hand. Sometimes—perhaps oftentimes when it comes to important constitutional questions—there is no way to avoid deep and abstract moral questions. The constitutionality of criminalizing abortions cannot be properly decided without asking deep moral questions about women's autonomy; the constitutionality of affirmative action depends on deep moral judgments regarding racial equality. "Not too deep" sounds like reasonable judicial advice, but it offers little assistance to a profession committed to justified decision-making.[4]

Ironically, given minimalism's position on the capacity of judges for deep theoretical reasoning, the very question of whether judges should follow minimalism or Dworkin's philosophy is a question necessitating deep theoretical reasoning about democracy and the nature of constitutional separation of powers.[5] Settling on a judicial philosophy requires deep theoretical thinking. In part, that is why judges are so divided over the choice of judicial philosophy: what philosophy best captures the proper judicial role is a complicated question of political theory that is likely to produce many reasonable disagreements.

But disagreements over the choice of judicial philosophy are not only a function of the decision's complexity and theoretical depth. There is a strong ideological component to the choice of judicial philosophy: some judicial philosophies—like textualism or classic originalism—are greatly favored by conservatives, whereas others—like purposivism or a moral reading of the Constitution—primarily enjoy the support of liberal jurists. There is something deeply ideological in the choice of judicial philosophy—and it seems to involve the issue of judicial discretion.

Disagreements over broad or narrow judicial discretion play an outsized role in the debate over the proper judicial philosophy: the impulse for narrow judicial discretion is central to the philosophies of textualism and originalism, underlies the emphasis on history and tradition, and explains the objections to moral judicial considerations and to unenumerated constitutional rights. By contrast, acquiescence or even endorsement of broad judicial discretion underlies purposivism, judicial appeals to morality and justice, the idea of the "living constitution," or the view that the Constitution protects our most cherished political values (whether or not it does so explicitly).

The preoccupation with judicial discretion is a modern concern: for many centuries it was simply assumed that judicial decisions involved judgments over matters of justice or public policy, and that this was both necessary and desirable. But then again, for many centuries it was also assumed that justice was fixed, universal, and knowable: a code ordained by an omniscient god (or gods). With the onset of modernity, that assumption began to give way. Modern times brought different religious and moral sensibilities, and an increasing acceptance of moral and religious pluralism. They also brought increasing regard for the ideals of the Rule of Law, including the knowability and predictability of legal requirements; and increasing demand for democracy, with its insistence that political choices be made by elected representatives. These developments produced profound reevaluations of the role of judges and their interpretive methodologies.

Today, it is a matter of near-universal acceptance (a few self-declared pragmatists aside) that a proper judicial methodology must impose substantial limitations on judicial discretion. Indeed, the entire idea of the Rule of Law—of "a government of laws, not of men"—depends on such limitations, as do principles of democracy and separation of powers. However, how much restraint is appropriate remains a hotly debated question. When do judges operate with insufficient guidance and insufficient control—or, by contrast, at what point do guidance and control become too stultifying to allow for good judicial decisions? The differing answers to these pivotal questions are leading factors in the disagreements over the choice of judicial philosophy, and the fault lines appear to be ideological. American liberals gravitate toward judicial philosophies that afford judges broad deliberative discretion, whereas American conservatives favor philosophies that seek to minimize and greatly constrain the considerations that judges can employ. This is a broad generalization, and exceptions can be found, but as a generalization, it is sound. And so the question arises: why this ideological divide? How does the choice between broad or narrow judicial discretion relate to liberalism and conservatism? Scholars proposed several answers to this interesting question.[6]

One common answer traces the conservative rejection of broad judicial discretion to the liberal Warren Court of the 1950s and 60s—which, among other things, greatly expanded constitutional protections to criminal defendants, recognized a right to procure an abortion, strengthened protections against gender discrimination, and even extended constitutional protections to welfare payments.[7] Conservative jurists abhorred many of the decisions of the Warren Court, and they attacked these decisions by denouncing not only their substance, but also the judicial philosophy that produced them.

178

Conservatives charged that the judicial philosophy of the Warren Court allowed the justices to impose their own (liberal) ideology on constitutional doctrine.[8] For these conservative critics, broad judicial discretion meant policy-making by politically unaccountable, and mostly liberal, judges. The solution resided in judicial philosophies that minimized the potential influence of political preferences and other value judgments.

This popular explanation sees the conservative rejection of broad judicial discretion as a historical fluke: the result of a period of strong liberal domination of the Supreme Court. But while the Warren Court surely produced conservative resentment at broad judicial discretion, that is unlikely the whole story: after all, even today—after decades of conservative domination of the Supreme Court—most liberals continue to accept broad judicial discretion, and most conservatives continue to denounce it.[9] Something deeper than a reaction to a series of historical decisions appears to be at work, and it seems to concern the relation between rationality and morality.

II. Conservatives, Liberals, and Rationality

Many of the conservatives who oppose broad judicial discretion believe that value judgments are too subjective and too indeterminate to constitute valid judicial considerations. They claim that judicial deliberations over morality or public policy usurp the powers of the legislature, violate separation of powers, and reduce the predictability of legal and constitutional decisions.[10] By contrast, liberal proponents of broad judicial discretion argue that judicial value judgments only improve the quality and even the determinacy of judicial decisions: morality, political values like freedom or equality, and good public policy are essential for establishing legal requirements.[11]

This disagreement between conservatives and liberals springs from a dispute about the relation between value judgments and rationality. Conservatives and liberals disagree about the legitimacy of judicial judgments on matters of justice and policy because they disagree about the objective rationality of such judgments. Simply put, if you think that moral judgments are ultimately a matter of faith, or matters of cultural conditioning, or self-interest, or mere matters of sentiment, you might understandably conclude that legal decisions should not be based on such judgments. Conservatives reject broad judicial discretion because they are skeptical about the objectivity and the rational standards governing judgment of justice or politics. By contrast, liberals endorse broad discretion because they have confidence in reason's ability to guide and correct our judgment in these domains.

These respective positions have deep roots in the intellectual traditions of the two political movements. Edmund Burke, the 18th century conservative icon, articulated the conservative creed as follows:

> We know that we have made no discoveries; and we think that no discoveries are to be made, in morality; nor many in the great principles of government, nor in the ideas of liberty, which were understood long before we were born . . . We are afraid to put men to live and trade each on his own private stock of reason; because we suspect that this stock in each man is small, and that the individuals would do better to avail themselves of the general bank and capital of nations, and of ages.[12]

Conservatives favor the practices of yore—and despise so-called "social engineering" (which they often attributed to the Warren Court)—because they doubt humanity's ability to employ reason to gain new insights into matters of "morality [and] the great principles of government . . . ."[13] For conservatives, tradition represents the accumulated wisdom of millennia, and reason often lacks the potency to even grasp it, let alone to improve on its hard-won lessons.[14]

These fundamental insights continue to animate conservatism to this day. Michael Oakeshott, a central figure in contemporary conservative thought, writing almost two centuries after Burke, echoes Burke's sentiments in his book *Rationalism in Politics*, which criticized the excessive reliance on rationalism in politics:[15]

> [A]lmost all politics today have become Rationalist or near-Rationalist. . . . The general character of the Rationalist . . . is at once skeptical and optimistic: skeptical, because there is no opinion, no habit, no belief, nothing so firmly rooted or so widely held that he hesitates to question it and to judge it by what he calls his 'reason'; optimistic, because the Rationalist never doubts the power of his 'reason' (when properly applied) to determine the worth of a thing, the truth of an opinion or the propriety of an action. . . . He has no sense of cumulation of experience . . . .[16]

In the legal context, this skepticism of reason leads to judicial philosophies that reject judicial value judgments as legitimate judicial considerations. To repeat, if you doubt the possibility of objective rational conclusions in regard to justice or public policy, you may well conclude that judges should abstain from basing legal conclusions on such value judgments.[17]

Liberals, by contrast, seem to believe that reasoning and deliberations over morality or public policy can produce objectively accurate and desirable results. Such judicial value judgments are not the self-evident truths of natural law theory, or, for that matter, the moral judgments of the traditional Islamic judge, who—as recounted in Max Weber's classic description—*intuits* the requirements of Islamic justice in reaching his verdict.[18] Rather, judicial value judgments are fully deliberative, and they follow the normal constraints of the judicial process: they must appear in the form of general principles, properly articulated and uniformly applied, and must be reconciled with the authoritative value judgment of the elected branches of government. Like any other judicial consideration, they are structured by the rationality of our legal discourse; and that rationality assures their legitimacy.

As with conservative skepticism, the idea that value judgments are amenable to rational deliberations has its own deep roots in the liberal intellectual tradition. The belief in the power of reason to guide humanity into better understandings of morality and politics stands at the center of the Western Enlightenment—the philosophical revolution that brought us the modern age. Edmund Burke accused the Western Enlightenment of causing the bloodshed of the French Revolution; but the Western Enlightenment also ushered in the liberty and democracy that lie at the heart of the United States' political creed.

In fact, some see the Enlightenment's faith in the power of reason as an essential assumption of democracy. In *The Open Society and Its Enemies* (1945), the (liberal) philosopher Karl Popper argued that belief in the ability of reason to provide accurate social, moral, and political insights lies at the heart of the democratic political structure.[19] Popper contrasted "open societies," which evidence faith in reason, with "closed societies," which evidence skepticism of reason and—according to Popper—carry the hallmarks of authoritarianism.[20] For Popper, a society's belief in the power of reason is a measure of its democratic character.

In fact, some see the belief in the power of reason not only an assumption of democracy, but also an assumption of American legal culture. It is no coincidence, they say, that the political ideal of the Rule of Law takes off at the Age of Enlightenment—the age marking humanity's turn toward reason and rationality in the management of its affairs. Reasoning, argumentation, and deliberation lie at the heart of our legal process—where judges are made to listen to litigants' arguments, to read their often lengthy briefs, and to respond by articulating the reasons for their legal conclusions. The American legal system is all about the rational justifiability of legal requirements—it is all about the power of reasoning.

Liberals and conservatives draw from deep intellectual wells in their respective positions on broad judicial discretion—and, by extension, on the proper judicial philosophy. But we should hasten to add that these respective positions are not set in stone: there is nothing necessary in these ideological affiliations. They are both unique to the American context and are, by nature, temporal. Indeed, political ideologies are themselves in constant flux. As a matter of fact, some recent commentaries purport to detect a growing conservative openness to morally-engaged constitutional interpretation.[21] Moreover, different political circumstances may call for different reactions to broad judicial discretion. Healthy and robust democracies may afford to constrain judicial judgments in ways that are ill-advised for less wholesome politics. In short, present judicial philosophies have their clear political affiliations, and these affiliations do have deep historical and intellectual roots; but the present situation is a snapshot of an ever-changing reality.

III. Our Current Constitution

The question of the proper judicial philosophy—of what sort of considerations judges can or must employ when interpreting statutes or constitutional provisions—is a fundamental question for legal practice. It is a question about the nature of law, and what it is made of (text, purposes, legislative intents, justice, fairness, history, political values, expected consequences, etc.). The answers, as seen in these chapters, are varied, but they all obey one inescapable rule: the more limited the judicial considerations that judges employ, the more limited the potential justifiability of the ensuing results. Preclude judges from considering legislative purposes, and you will get more legal requirements that serve no sensible aim;[22] forbid judges from engaging in moral deliberations, and you will get more unjust results;[23] bar judges from considering the consequences of their decisions, and you will see more decisions with harmful consequences.[24] Reduction in judicial discretion may advance some aspects of democracy and the Rule of Law; but it may equally harm democracy and the Rule of Law, for it means less reasoned and less justified judicial results.

This simple and inescapable fact accounts for the broad judicial discretion underlying most of our constitutional law: the awesome responsibility and the great stakes involved in many constitutional decisions have pushed judges to take a broad view of their responsibilities and their interpretive role. Notwithstanding some of the trends we examined above, when surveyed through the wide lens of history, broad judicial discretion has been the dominant mode of American constitutional interpretation.

Almost two and a half centuries after it was first adopted, the U.S. Constitution still governs the most important aspects of our social and political lives. Some of the credit for this long-lasting and often salutary influence surely goes to the constitutional drafters, who had the foresight to write such an enduring document. But much of the credit belongs to the judges and lawyers who have interpreted the Constitution after it was ratified: they are the ones whose work has kept the document relevant and incisive. If you examine their most important and most cherished constitutional decisions, you can see that they rarely shied from bold engagement with public policies, morality and justice, political realities, and concern for the practicalities of everyday life. Had these judges limited themselves to the original understanding of the Constitution or to its literal text, or had they refused to consider justice or the expected consequences, it is doubtful that the Constitution would have remained the revered document it still is today.

Notes

Chapter 1.
Introduction: The U.S. Constitution and Constitutional Interpretation

1   In the end, Congress did not condemn the breach of the Article of Confederation, but neither did it officially adopt the new document before sending it to the states for ratification. *See* COMMENTARIES ON THE CONSTITUTION, Vol. XIII, no. 1, reprinted in THE DOCUMENTARY HISTORY OF THE RATIFICATION OF THE CONSTITUTION DIGITAL EDITION, (John P. Kaminski et al. eds., U. Va. Press 2009).

2   Rhode Island at first voted against ratification, and ratification was won belatedly and narrowly in both Virginia and New York.

3   Some early drafts of the Bill of Rights sought to limit the power of state governments as well, but they were rejected. For example, James Madison's proposed First Amendment read: "No State shall violate the equal rights of conscience, or the freedom of the press, or the trial by jury in criminal cases." 1 Annals of Cong. 434–36, 440–43 (1789). But the proposal was not adopted, and the final version of the First Amendment begins by stating: "Congress shall make no law . . . ." .

4   *See, e.g.,* Mass. Const. art. II, III. *See also* Paul Finkelman, *School Vouchers, Thomas Jefferson, Roger Williams, and Protecting the Faithful: Warnings from the Eighteenth Century and the Seventeenth Century on the Danger of Establishments to Religious Communities,* 2008 B.Y.U. L. REV. 525, 545–6 (2008).

5   *See, e.g., Barron v. Baltimore,* 32 U.S. 243 (1833).

6   In *Timbs v. Indiana,* 586 U.S. 139 S. Ct. 682 (2019), the U.S. Supreme Court held, for the first time, that the excessive fines clause of the Eighth Amendment was also binding on the states.

7   The most notable exception to this general principle is the Thirteenth Amendment's abolition of slavery and involuntary servitude, which is also binding on private individuals. Another caveat to this broad statement is that constitutional rights control government regulations of the relations between private individuals—and can therefore influence the legal relations between individuals indirectly. *See generally,* Stephen Gardbaum, *The 'Horizontal Effect' of Constitutional Rights,* 102 MICH. L. REV. 387 (2003).

8   *Fisher v. University of Texas at Austin,* 645 F. Supp. 2d 587 (W.D. Tex. 2009).

9   U.S. Const. amend. XIV, § 1.

10 The U.S. Supreme Court explained the vagueness of many constitutional provisions as follows:

> A Constitution, to contain an accurate detail of all [that it does], would partake of the prolixity of a legal code, and could scarcely be embraced by the human mind. . . . Its nature, therefore, requires that only its great outlines should be marked, its important objects designated, and the minor ingredients which compose those objects be deduced from the nature of the objects themselves.

McCulloch v. Maryland, 17 U.S. 316, 407 (1819).

11 Alternatively, a constitutional amendment can be proposed by a special convention called for by two thirds of state legislatures, and ratified by three quarters of special conventions convened in each state. *See* U.S. Const. art. V.

12 *See, e.g.*, DONALD S. LUTZ, PRINCIPLES OF CONSTITUTIONAL DESIGN 171 (Cambridge U. Press 2006) (ranking the U.S. Constitution as the second most difficult constitution to amend among the constitutions of the world).

13 Encyclopedia Britannica describes Marshall as "perhaps the Supreme Court's most influential chief justice," https://www.britannica.com/biography/John-Marshall.

14 *McCulloch* 17 U.S. at 325.

15 *McCulloch*, 407.

16 *National Mut. Ins. Co. v. Tidewater Transfer Co.*, 337 U.S. 582, 647 (1949) (Justice Frankfurter, dissenting).

17 *See, e.g.*, Antonin Scalia, *Originalism: The Lesser Evil*, 57 U. CIN. L. REV. 849 (1989) ("The purpose of constitutional guarantees is . . . to prevent the law from reflecting certain changes in original values that the society adopting the Constitution thinks fundamentally undesirable.").

18 In a 2011 interview with California Lawyer, Justice Scalia explained that "In 1868, when the 39th Congress was debating and ultimately proposing the 14th Amendment, I don't think anybody would have thought that equal protection applied to sex discrimination, or certainly not to sexual orientation. So does that mean that we've gone off in error by applying the 14th Amendment to both? Yes, yes. Sorry, to tell you that." CALIFORNIA LAWYER, Sept. 2011, http://legacy.callawyer.com/2016/02/antonin-scalia-2/.

19 *See e.g.*, Ronald Dworkin's articulation of that position in *The Moral Reading of the Constitution*, N.Y. REV. BOOKS, March 21, 1996 at 46, https://www.nybooks.com/articles/1996/03/21/the-moral-reading-of-the-constitution/. Dworkin himself is no textualist.

20 Some scholars believe that constitutional interpretation and statutory interpretation are intrinsically different—mostly because of the difficulty of amending the constitution as compared with the relative ease of amending statutes. *See generally* Richard Primus, Kevin M. Stack, Christopher Serkin, and Nelson Tebbe, *Debate*, 102 CORNELL L. REV. 1649 (2017).

21 RONALD DWORKIN, LAW'S EMPIRE 90 (Belknap Press of Harv. U. Press 1986). Not all judicial philosophies are equally ambitious. Constitutional originalism, for example, is a comprehensive judicial philosophy that purports to apply, in principle, to all constitutional cases. But other judicial philosophies are localized and limited in scope. They tackle questions like: should judges deliberate on the meaning of "cruelty" when they apply the Eighth Amendment's prohibition on "cruel and unusual punishment"? Or: should judges follow American history when deciding whether a certain category of speech is excluded from First Amendment protections? These are important questions of judicial philosophy, but (unlike originalism) they apply only to a small number of cases.

22 *See* Jeffrey Rosen, *Supreme Leader: On the Arrogance of Anthony Kennedy*, New Republic, June 16, 2007, https://newrepublic.com/article/60925/supreme-leader-the-arrogance-anthony-kennedy; Sarah Krakoff, *Undoing Indian Law One Case at a Time: Judicial Minimalism and Tribal Sovereignty*, 50 AM. U. L. REV. 1177, 1189 (2001); Thomas R. Hensley, Christopher E. Smith, and Joyce A. Baugh, *The Changing Supreme Court: Constitutional Rights and Liberties 75* (West Publications 1997); Stephen E. Gottlieb, *Three Justices in Search of a Character: The Moral Agendas of Justices O'Connor, Scalia and Kennedy*, 49 RUTGERS L. REV. 219, 238 (1996); Michael Comiskey, *The Real and Imagined Consequences of Senatorial Consent to Silent Supreme Court Nominees,* 11 J.L. & POL. 41, 50 (1995); Robert F. Nagel, *Liberals and Balancing*, 63 U. COLO. L. REV. 319, 323 (1992). *See also* Interview by Judy Woodruff with Sandra Day O'Connor, Retired Justice, U.S. Supreme Court (April 4, 2014), https://www.pbs.org/newshour/politics/sandra-day-oconnor-a-look-at-the-history-of-the-supreme-court-in-out-of-order ("As for her own 'judicial philosophy' O'Connor says: 'I'm not on the court anymore so no use looking for my philosophy. If somebody's waiting for that, they can wait for another justice.'").

23 RICHARD POSNER, THE PROBLEMATICS OF MORAL AND LEGAL THEORY (Belknap Press of Harv. U. Press 1999).

24 *See, e.g.*, RONALD DWORKIN, LAW'S EMPIRE 378 (Belknap Press of Harv. U. Press 1986).

25 *See, e.g.*, Jeremy Waldron, *The Core of the Case against Judicial Review*, 115 YALE L.J. 1346 (2006).

26 U.S. Const. art. III, § 2, cl. 1 does state that, "The judicial power shall extend to all cases, in law and equity, arising under this Constitution, the laws of the United States, and treaties made, or which shall be made, under their authority"; and the Supremacy Clause of Article VI adds that "This Constitution, and the Laws of the United States which shall be made in Pursuance thereof; and all Treaties made, or which shall be made, under the authority of the United States, shall be the supreme Law of the land; and the judges in every state shall be bound thereby, anything in the Constitution or laws of any State to the contrary notwithstanding."

27 The Dutch Constitution, for example, explicitly denies the power of judicial review from Dutch courts. Switzerland employs a mixed system where federal statutes are not subjected to judicial review but cantonal laws are. And many countries that do have the institution of judicial review impose severe restrictions on its exercise—from confining that power to specialized constitutional courts or to certain subject matters, to allowing the legislature to override judicial review by a parliamentary vote. No such restrictions exist in the U.S., where practically all courts (federal, state, county, or tiny village courts) can exercise judicial review—and regularly do so in regard to all sorts of legal disputes, from lawsuits involving international wars to cases about traffic tickets.

28 ERWIN CHEMERINSKY, THE CASE AGAINST THE SUPREME COURT 5 (Penguin Press 2015).

29 *See, e.g.*, Mark Tushnet, *Against Judicial Review*, (Harvard Public Law Working Paper No. 09-20, 2009), https://papers.ssrn.com/sol3/papers.cfm?abstract_id=1368857.

30 Lawrence Sirovich, *A Pattern Analysis of the Second Rehnquist Court*, 100 PROC. OF THE NAT'L ACAD. OF SCI. 7432 (2003).

31 *See* Mark Sherman, *Roberts, Trump spar in extraordinary scrap over judges*, Associated Press, November 21, 2018, https://www.apnews.com/c4b34f9639e141069c08cf1e3deb6b84.

32 The accusation that legal reasoning is a mere after-the-fact justification for political decisions has an impressive pedigree in American legal history. Most influentially, that charge was made in the first half of the 20th century by some Legal Realists, who claimed that American courts were purporting to rely on vacuous and indeterminate judicial philosophies that allowed them to do as they pleased—which was to favor the rich and powerful. *See, e.g.*, Felix S. Cohen, "Transcendental Nonsense and the Functional Approach," 35 COLUM. L. REV. 809 (1935); Robert Hale, "Bargaining, Duress, and Economic Liberty," 43 COLUM. L. REV. 603 (1943). In more recent times, a somewhat similar claim was made by the Critical Legal Studies movement, which had its heyday during the 1980s and 90s. *See, e.g.*, the writings of Duncan

Kennedy, Roberto Unger, Gary Peller, Robert Gordon, or Clare Dalton.

33 *See generally* Jeffrey A. Segal & Harold J. Spaeth, The Supreme Court and the Attitudinal Model (Cambridge U. Press 1993).

34 *National Federation of Independent Business v. Sebelius*, 567 U.S. 519 (2012); *McCullen v. Coakley*, 573 U.S. 464 (2014). *See also, e.g.*, David Cole, *Keeping Up Appearances*, N.Y. Rev. Books, August 15, 2019, https://www.nybooks.com/articles/2019/08/15/john-roberts-supreme-court-keeping-up-appearances/ ("Since Kagan replaced Stevens in 2010, the justices' ideologies for the first time in history have aligned precisely with the party of the president who appointed them. Yet even in this period, the Court's results cannot be explained on simple partisan grounds. During the eight terms between 2010 and 2017, Democrat-appointed justices were more often in the majority than Republican appointees in three terms, Republicans were in the majority more often in four terms, and one term was a tie.").

35 Judicial review is an important component of our checks and balances. It provides an independent—and hence a more accurate—appraisal of constitutional compliance. The alternative would be to simply allow the legislature and the executive to determine for themselves the constitutionality of their actions. Since federal judges are appointed for life and are not elected for office, they may be better positioned to enforce the Constitution because, unlike elected representatives, they are less amenable to popular pressures to violate it. Elected officials may be tempted to violate the Constitution whenever it is popular to do so. For example, California's prisons had been in open violation of the Eighth Amendment's prohibition on cruel and unusual punishment since the 1990s—a result of operating these prisons at twice their capacity, and of failing to provide prisoners with adequate medical care. These well-documented violations could have continued even longer if not for judicial intervention. Jerry Brown, a liberal governor, has refused to comply with the Constitution and remedy the situation because, like his predecessors, he was unwilling to spend the required funds, and equally reluctant to release prisoners. Judicial review has been crucial for assuring compliance with constitutional requirements. *See Brown v. Plata*, 563 U.S. 493 (2011). Finally, judicial decisions must be explained and justified, must show consistency with standing constitutional doctrine, and must be published and be available for public scrutiny. By contrast, the decisions of elected officials have no such restrictions of rationality or transparency: politicians have no obligation to explain the logic their decisions; no obligation that their decisions be consistent with standing constitutional law; and no requirement that their rationales be available for scrutiny and criticism.

Chapter 2.
The Rise and Fall of Natural Law:
The Controversy Surrounding Incorporation
Doctrine, and The Right to a Trial By Jury

1 *Thus passes the glory of the world.*

2 *See Barron v. City of Baltimore,* 32 U.S. 243 (1833).

3 *The Slaughter-House Cases,* 83 U.S. 36 (1873).

4 *See Timbs v. Indiana,* 139 S. Ct. 682 (2019) (holding that the Eighth Amendment's prohibition on excessive fines is binding on the states).

5 *Brown v. Mississippi,* 297 U.S. 278 (1936).

6 A Supreme Court decision from 1897 recognized that the states were bound by the Fifth Amendment's prohibition against taking private property for public use without just compensation (*Chicago, B. & Q.R. Co. v. City of Chicago,* 166 U.S. 226 [1897]), and a 1925 opinion implied that the states may be bound by the First Amendment (*Gitlow v. New York,* 268 U.S. 652 [1925]). But that was the extent of the applicability of the Bill of Rights to the states in 1936.

7 The Court ended up reversing the convictions for failing to abide by the minimal procedural standards for criminal trials required by the Fourteenth Amendment.

8 *See, e.g., Twining v. State of N.J.,* 211 U.S. 78, 96 (1908).

9 *Palko v. Connecticut,* 302 U.S. 319, 328 (1937).

10 *See Palko,* 325.

11 U.S. Const. amend. V.

12 *Adamson v. California,* 332 U.S. 46, 70 (1947) (Justice Black, joined by Justice Douglas, dissenting).

13 I Cicero, De Re Publica 270 (Francis Barham trans., Edmund Spettigue 1841). Roman lawyers used to divide the laws of their vast empire into natural laws, which applied throughout, and local laws, which were allowed to vary from one locality to another. Local laws were valid unless they came into conflict with natural law, in which case they were null and void.

14 Augustine, On Free Choice of the Will 395 (Thomas Williams trans., Hackett 1993)Thomas Aquinas, Summa Theologiae, I–II, Q.95, A.II, (Thomas Gilby ed., Cambridge U. Press 2006).

15 I–II Thomas Aquinas, Summa Theologiae (Thomas Gilby ed., Cambridge U. Press 2006).

16 William Blackstone, Commentaries on the Laws of England (Oxford: Clarendon Press, 1765–69).

17 The Declaration of Independence para. 1 (U.S. 1776).

18 *See, e.g.,* John Finnis, Natural Laws and Natural Rights 30 (Oxford U. Press 2011).

19 *See, e.g., Jones v. Jones*, 2 Tenn. 2 (Tenn. Super. L. & Eq. 1804); *Kilham v. Ward*, 2 Mass. 236 (1806); *Cook v. Corn*, 1 Tenn. 340 (Tenn. Super. L. & Eq. 1808); *Dash v. Van Kleeck*, 7 Johns. 477 (N.Y. Sup. Ct. 1811); *Simmons v. Commonwealth*, 5 Binn. 617 (Pa. 1813); *Gardner v. Trustees of Newburgh*, 2 Johns Ch. 161 (N.Y. 1816); *State Bank v. Seghers*, 6 Mart.(o.s.) 724 (La. 1819); *Astor v. Winter*, 8 Mart.(o.s.) 171 (La. 1820); *Bourke v. Granberry*, 21 Va. 16 (1820); *Heath v. White*, 5 Conn. 228 (1824); *Crenshaw v. Slate River Co.*, 27 Va. 245 (1828). *See generally* R. H. Helmholz, *The Law of Nature and the Early History of Unenumerated Rights in the United States*, 9 U. Pa. J. Const. L. 401 (2007).

20 *Calder v. Bull*, 3 U.S. 386, 387–88 (1798).

21 *Calder*, 398 (Justice Iredell, Concurring).

22 II Jeremy Bentham, *Anarchical Fallacies; Being an Examination of the Declarations of Rights Issued During the French Revolution – an Examination of the Rights of Man and The Citizen Decreed by the Constituent Assembly in France* in The Works of Jeremy Bentham, 523 (John Bowring ed., William Tait 1843).

23 John Austin, The Province of Jurisprudence Determined 279 (John Murray 1832).

24 Austin, 72–73.

25 Austin, 78.

26 *Adamson v. California*, 332 U.S. 46, 75 (1947) (Justice Black, joined by Justice Douglas, dissenting).

27 Leo Strauss, Studies in Platonic Political Philosophy 137 (U. Chi. Press, 1983).

28 *See, e.g.*, Laurence H. Tribe, *Clarence Thomas and 'Natural Law'*, N.Y. Times, July 15, 1991, https://www.nytimes.com/1991/07/15/opinion/clarence-thomas-and-natural-law.html.

29 *Nomination of Clarence Thomas to Be Associate Justice of the Supreme Court of the United States: Hearings Before the S. Comm. on the Judiciary*, 102nd Cong. 112 (1991), https://www.loc.gov/law/find/nominations/thomas/hearing-pt1.pdf.

30 *See, e.g.*, Allen Mendenhall, *Gorsuch and natural law: He's not another SCOTUS faux-philosopher*, The Hill, February 7, 2017, http://thehill.com/blogs/pundits-blog/the-judiciary/318299-gorsuch-and-natural-law-hes-not-another-scotus-faux.

31 Stephanie Mencimer, *Does Donald Trump's Supreme Court Nominee Believe the Constitution Is God's Law?*, Mother Jones, February 21, 2017, https://www.motherjones.com/politics/2017/02/supreme-court-nominee-neil-gorsuch-was-student-natural-law/.

32 Much of Justice Gorsuch's confirmation hearings revolved around his allegedly stolen seat, following the Republican-dominated Senate's refusal to hold confirmation hearings for President Obama's Supreme

Court nominee, Judge Merrick Garland.

33 *See The Slaughter-House Cases*, 83 U.S. 36 (1873).

34 *See* U.S. Const. amend. XIV, § 1 ("No State shall make or enforce any law which shall abridge the privileges or immunities of citizens of the United States . . . .").

35 *Duncan v. Louisiana*, 391 U.S. 145, 149 n. 38 (1968) (emphasis added). The Supreme Court's reorientation of incorporation doctrine—from a pure question of morality and justice into a more historical inquiry—reached its peak in *McDonald v. City of Chicago*, 561 U.S. 742 (2010), which incorporated the Second Amendment into the Due Process Clause. In *McDonald*, Justice Alito's opinion for the Court alleged that in fact no question of morality or justice was necessary *at all* when determining whether a Bill of Rights provision is applicable to the states: the question of incorporation can be reduced to whether the right in question "is deeply rooted in this Nation's history and tradition." With that, the Supreme Court appeared to complete the transformation of incorporation doctrine: what began as a question of justice and then turned into a question of justice and history, was finally transformed into a question of history alone. But the position immediately faced stiff opposition from the dissenting justices: "A rigid historical test is inappropriate . . . . [T]he liberty safeguarded by the Fourteenth Amendment . . . . is a dynamic concept," wrote Justice Paul Stevens; and Justice Stephen Breyer added: "Under this Court's precedents . . . the majority must show that the right is . . . 'fundamental to the American scheme of justice.' . . . The majority . . . relies almost exclusively upon history to make the necessary showing. But to do so for incorporation purposes is both wrong and dangerous. As Justice Stevens points out, our society has historically made mistakes . . . ." *McDonald* (Justice Breyer, joined by Justices Ginsburg and Sotomayor, dissenting). The Supreme Court retracted from Justice Alito's position nine years later, in *Timbs v. Indiana*, 586 U.S. ___ (2019), where—incorporating the Eighth Amendment's Excessive Fines Clause into the Fourteenth Amendment's Due Process Clause—the Court considered both the question of justice and the question of history.

36 *Griswold v. Connecticut*, 381 U.S. 479, 493 (1965) (quotations omitted). *Griswold* dealt with a related doctrine under the Due Process Clause that employed a similar test to the one used in incorporation.

37 *See, e.g., Gideon v. Wainwright*, 372 U.S. 335 (1963) (holding the right to counsel applicable to the states), and *Malloy v. Hogan*, 378 U.S. 1 (1964) (holding the right against self-incrimination applicable to the states). Needless to say, not everyone was happy with this result. In 1985, almost two decades after the methodological switch, President Reagan's Attorney General Edwin Meese—speaking for many conservative jurists and advocates of states' power—offered harsh criticism

of the application of the Bill of Rights to the states.

38 *Palko v. Connecticut*, 302 U.S. 319, 325 (1937).

39 *Duncan v. Louisiana*, 391 U.S. 145, 149 n. 14 (emphasis added).

40 *See Bushell's Case*, 124 Eng. Rep. 1006 (C.P. 1670).

41 *Id.*

42 *See, e.g.*, *United States v. Kleinman*, 880 F.3d 1020 (9th Cir. 2017).

43 *See, e.g.*, *Turney v. Pugh*, 400 F.3d 1197 (9th Cir. 2005).

44 *See* Jack B. Weinstein & Ian Dewsbury, *Comment on the meaning of 'proof beyond a reasonable doubt,'* 5 Law, Probability and Risk 167, 172 (2006), https://doi.org/10.1093/lpr/mgl016.

45 Nor was it shared by the framers of a number of state constitutions. The constitutions of Maryland, Indiana, Oregon, and Georgia all gave jurors the explicit right to determine the *law* in criminal cases, not only the facts. Article 23 of Maryland's Constitution states: "In the trial of all criminal cases, the Jury shall be the Judges of Law, as well as of fact, except that the Court may pass upon the sufficiency of the evidence to sustain a conviction." Article 1, Section 19, of Indiana's Constitution says: "In all criminal cases whatever, the jury shall have the right to determine the law and the facts." Article 1, Section 16 of the Oregon's Constitution states: "In all criminal cases whatever, the jury shall have the right to determine the law, and the facts under the direction of the Court as to the law . . . ." Article 1, Section 1 of Georgia's Constitution says: "[T]he jury shall be judges of the law and the facts."

46 John Adams, The Works of John Adams, Second President of the United States 254–55 (Little & Brown 1850).

47 *See, e.g.*, Fed. R. Cr. P. 29 (Motion for a Judgment of Acquittal).

48 *See Tanner v. United States*, 483 U.S. 107 (1987).

49 *See Andres v. United States*, 333 U.S. 740 (1948) (requiring jury unanimity under the Sixth Amendment). A hung jury often results in a new trial.

50 *Tanner*, 483 U.S. at 115.

51 *Tanner,* 136 (Justice Marshall, with whom Justices Brennan, Blackmun, and Stevens joined, concurring in part and dissenting in part).

52 *United States v. Dioguardi*, 492 F.2d 70, 84 (2d Cir. 1974).

53 *Id.* (Judge Feinberg, dissenting).

Chapter 3.
The Debate Over Unenumerated Constitutional Rights:
The Ninth Amendment, Substantive Due Process, and
The Right to Not Be Executed If Innocent

1   The two clauses are essentially identical in the protections they afford—except that the Due Process Clause of the Fourteenth Amendment is the vehicle for the application of the Bill of Rights to the states, and the Due Process Clause of the Fifth Amendment is the vehicle for the application of the Equal Protection Clause to the federal government—a form of reverse incorporation. The Equal Protection Clause appears in the Fourteenth Amendment, which restricts the powers of the states, not the federal government. Still, the Supreme Court found it unreasonable that this important constitutional guarantee did not apply to the most powerful government in the land, and it held that the federal government must also abide by the requirements of equal protection.

2   *See, e.g., U.S. v. Carlton*, 512 U.S. 26, 39 (1994) (Justice Scalia, joined by Justice Thomas, concurring).

3   *See, e.g.,* James W. Ely, Jr., *The Oxymoron Reconsidered: Myth and Reality in the Origins of Substantive Due Process*, 16 CONST. COMMENT. 315 (1999).

4   One deplorable case that relied on substantive due process was the infamous *Dred Scott v. Sanford*, 60 U.S. (19 How.) 393 (1857).

5   *Poe v. Ullman*, 367 U.S. 497 (1961) (Justice Harlan, dissenting).

6   Textually speaking, it may have been more appropriate to locate such substantive rights in, say, the Ninth Amendment (which reads: "The enumeration in the Constitution, of certain rights, shall not be construed to deny or disparage others retained by the people"), or in the Fourteenth Amendment's Privileges or Immunities Clause (which reads: "No state shall make or enforce any law which shall abridge the privileges or immunities of citizens of the United States . . ."). But these more textually-fitting clauses were ruled out as possible sources for such substantive rights by long standing precedents.

7   In THE REPUBLIC, Plato envisioned a polity governed by an austere elite of philosopher-kings he called "guardians."

8   *Meyer v. Nebraska*, 262 U.S. 390, 401–02 (1923).

9   *Rochin v. California*, 342 U.S. 165 (1952).

10   *See Cruzan v. Dir., Missouri Dep't of Health*, 497 U.S. 261 (1990).

11   *Griswold v. Connecticut*, 381 U.S. 479 (1965).

12   *Moore v. City of East Cleveland*, 431 U.S. 494 (1977).

13   *Roe v. Wade*, 410 U.S. 113 (1973).

14   *Lawrence v. Texas*, 539 U.S. 558 (2003).

15 *Obergefell v. Hodges*, 135 S. Ct. 2584 (2015).

16 *Washington v. Glucksberg*, 521 U.S. 702, 720 (1997).

17 *Obergefell*, 135 S. Ct. 2631 (2015) (Justice Thomas, joined by Justice Scalia, dissenting) (internal quotations omitted).

18 In this they were famously influenced by the writings of John Locke, the celebrated 17th Century English philosopher and expositor of natural rights theory. *See, e.g.*, Michael W. McConnell, *Natural Rights and the Ninth Amendment: How Does Lockean Legal Theory Assist in Interpretation?* 5 N.Y.U. J. OF LAW & LIBERTY 1 (2010).

19 II JEREMY BENTHAM, *Anarchical Fallacies; Being an Examination of the Declarations of Rights Issued During the French Revolution – an Examination of the Rights of Man and The Citizen Decreed by the Constituent Assembly in France* in THE WORKS OF JEREMY BENTHAM 501 (John Bowring ed., William Tait 1843).

20 *See, e.g., Schowengerdt v. United States*, 944 F.2d 483, 490 (9th Cir. 1991) ("[The Ninth Amendment] has not been interpreted as independently securing any constitutional rights for purposes of making out a constitutional violation."), cert. denied, 503 U.S. 951 (1992).

21 Some have argued that the Amendment did not come to secure the protection of any unenumerated individual rights, but to underline the limited powers of the federal government. *See, e.g.*, Kurt T. Lash, *The Lost Jurisprudence of the Ninth Amendment*, 83 TEX. L. REV. 597 (2005). *See also Griswold v. Connecticut*, 381 U.S. 479, 529 (1965) (Justice Stewart, dissenting) ("The Ninth Amendment . . . states but a truism . . . that the adoption of the Bill of Rights did not alter the plan that the Federal Government was to be a government of express and limited powers . . . .") (internal quotations omitted). Others have claimed that the Amendment says not a thing about these unenumerated rights being *constitutional*. As one federal district court opinion put it: "[T]he Ninth Amendment does not specify any rights of the people . . . [and] does not raise those unmentioned rights to constitutional stature; it simply takes cognizance of their general existence . . . although they were never intended to be rights of constitutional magnitude. . . . [T]here are no constitutional rights secured by that Amendment." *Charles v. Brown*, 495 F. Supp. 862, 863–64 (N.D. Ala. 1980). *See also, Troxel v. Granville*, 530 U.S. 57, 92 (2000) (Justice Scalia, dissenting) ("[T]he Constitution's refusal to 'deny or disparage' other rights is far removed from affirming any one of them, and even farther removed from authorizing judges to identify what they might be . . . .).

22 *See Nomination of Robert H. Bork to Be Associate Justice of the Supreme Court of the United States: Hearings before the S. Comm. on the Judiciary*, 100th Cong. 249 (1989).

23 The Ninth Amendment is not the only constitutional provision pres-

ently considered unenforceable. Another such example is Article 4 Section 4: "The United States shall guarantee to every State in this Union a Republican Form of Government . . . ." In 1849, the Supreme Court was faced with the claim that Rhode Island's denial of the right to vote to its poorer residents—through the imposition of property qualifications for the franchise—was a violation of that constitutional provision, which appears to guarantee some form of democratic self-rule in state governments. But the Court refused to enforce this potentially significant guarantee, stating instead that "Under this article of the Constitution it rests with Congress to decide . . . what government . . . is republican or not"—essentially turning that constitutional clause into a dead letter. *Luther v. Borden*, 48 U.S. 1 (1849).

24   *See, e.g., H.P. Hood & Sons v. Du Mond*, 336 U.S. 525 (1949) (enforcing the dormant commerce clause doctrine); *Alden v. Maine*, 527 U.S. 706 (1999) (holding that states enjoy sovereign immunity in state courts); *United States v. Nixon*, 418 U.S. 683 (1974) (holding that the president has a constitutional qualified immunity from subpoenas in criminal proceedings).

25   *United States v. Fry*, 787 F.2d 903 (1986).

26   Jason C. Glahn, *I Teach You the Superman: Why Congress Cannot Constitutionally Prohibit Genetic Modification*, 25 WHITTIER L. REV. 409 (2003).

27   *Juliana v. United States*, No. 6:15-CV-1517-TC, 2016 WL 1442435 (D. Or. Apr. 8, 2016).

28   *See, e.g., Richmond Newspapers, Inc. v. Virginia*, 448 U.S. 555, 579 (1980) (plurality opinion) (invoking the Ninth Amendment in support of the right of a public school pupil to grow his hair); *Olff v. E. Side Union High Sch. Dist.*, 404 U.S. 1042 (1972) (Justice Douglas, dissenting from a denial of certiorari) (invoking the Ninth Amendment in support of the right of the public to attend criminal trials); *Palmer v. Thompson*, 403 U.S. 217, 231 (1971) (Justice Douglas, dissenting) (invoking the Ninth Amendment in support of an alleged right to public education and public recreation).

29   *See Roe v. Wade*, 314 F. Supp. 1217 (N.D. Tex. 1970).

30   *See Roe v. Wade*, 410 U.S. 113 (1973).

31   *Roe*, 152–53 (1973). *See also Planned Parenthood of Cent. Missouri v. Danforth*, 428 U.S. 52, 61 (1976); *Planned Parenthood of Se. Pennsylvania v. Casey*, 505 U.S. 833, 999–1000 (1992).

32   *Griswold*, 381 U.S. at 486–89 (Justice Goldberg, joined by Chief Justice Warren and Justice Brennan, concurring).

33   *Michael H. v. Gerald D.*, 491 U.S. 110 (1989) (plurality opinion).

34   It was later contended that the first murdered officer was involved in drug trafficking. The note found on Herrera at the time of his arrest read: "I am terribly sorry for those [to whom] I have brought grief

. . . . What happened to [the officer] was for a certain reason . . . [H] e violated some of [the] laws [of my drug business] and suffered the penalty, like the one you have for me when the time comes . . . . The other officer [Carrisalez] . . . had not[hing] to do [with] this. He was out to do what he had to do, protect, but that's life . . . . [I]f this is read word for word over the media, I will turn myself in."

35 *Herrera v. Collins*, 506 U.S. 390 (1993).

36 U.S. Const. amend. VI ("In all criminal prosecutions, the accused shall enjoy the right to a . . . public trial, by an impartial jury . . . .").

37 *Gideon v. Wainwright*, 372 U.S. 335 (1963).

38 U.S. Const. amend. V ("No person . . . shall be compelled in any criminal case to be a witness against himself . . .").

39 U.S. Const. amend. VI ("In all criminal prosecutions, the accused shall enjoy the right . . . to be informed of the nature and cause of the accusation; to be confronted with the witnesses against him; to have compulsory process for obtaining witnesses in his favor . . . .").

40 *In re Winship*, 397 U.S. 358, 361 (1970).

41 *See Brady v. Maryland*, 373 U.S. 83 (1963).

42 *Herrera v. Collins*, 506 U.S. 390, 397 (1963).

43 *Herrera*, 430–31 (Justice Blackmun, joined by Justices Stevens and Souter, dissenting).

44 *Id.* (quoting *Poe v. Ullman*, 367 U.S. 497, 543 (1961) (Justice Harlan, dissenting).

45 *Herrera*, 428 (Justice Scalia, joined by Justice Thomas, concurring).

46 *Herrera*, 417.

47 Not all the justices of the majority were happy with the refusal to decide whether the Due Process Clause protected a right not be executed if innocent. Justices Antonin Scalia and Clarence Thomas, staunch opponents of substantive due process rights, wrote in a separate concurrence that such a constitutional right simply did not exist. *See Herrera*, 427.

48 *Id.* (Justice O'Connor, joined by Justice Kennedy, concurring).

49 *Herrera*, 446 (Justice Blackmun, dissenting).

50 *Death Row Information*, TEX. DEP'T CRIM. JUST., https://www.tdcj. texas.gov/death_row/dr_info/hererraleonellast.html. (last visited, Aug. 1, 2019).

51 *DNA Exonerations in the United States: Fast Facts*, https://www.innocenceproject.org/dna-exonerations-in-the-united-states/.

52 *United States v. Quinones*, 205 F. Supp. 2d 256, 265 (S.D.N.Y. 2002).

53 *Executions Overview*, DEATH PENALTY INFO. CTR., https://deathpenalty info.org/executions/executions-overview.

54 *United States v. Quinones*, 205 F. Supp. 2d 256, 265 (S.D.N.Y. 2002).

55 *United States v. Quinones*, 313 F.3d 49, 63 (2d Cir. 2002).

56 *See Nomination of Samuel Alito to Be Associate Justice of the Su-*

preme Court of the United States: Hearing before the S. Comm. on the Judiciary, 109th Cong. 773 (2006).

57 January 12, 2006, Samuel Alito confirmation hearing:

> **ALITO:** The person would first have to avail himself or herself of the procedures that Congress has specified for challenging convictions after they've become final.
>
> If this individual has been convicted and has gone through the whole process of direct appeal, either in the state system or in the federal system, then there are procedures. States have procedures for collateral attacks and there are procedures under federal statutes for collateral attacks on federal conventions and on state convictions. And the person would have to go through the procedures that are set out in the statute.
>
> And the system is designed to prevent a person from being executed if the person is innocent. And actual innocence figures very importantly even in these sometimes complex procedures that have to be followed in these collateral attacks.
>
> For example, usually, there's this doctrine of procedural default, which is not something that ordinary people are familiar with, but it means that if a state prisoner is challenging a state conviction, the state prisoner has to take advantage of the procedures that are available under state law. And if the state prisoner doesn't do that . . . .
>
> **FEINGOLD:** My question assumes that all that's been done and the process went through and there's no legal or constitutional or procedural problems, but evidence suddenly proves that the person convicted was unquestionably innocent.
>
> The question is: Does that person in that posture have a constitutional right not to be executed?
>
> **ALITO:** Well, then the person would have to, as I said, file a petition. And if it was an initial petition, it would fall into one category. If it was a second or a successive petition, it would fall into another category and the person would have to satisfy the requirements the Congress has set out for filing a second or successive petition.

FEINGOLD: You can't say that the person has a constitutional right not to be executed?

ALITO: Well, I have to know the specific facts of the case and the way it works its way through the legal system.

58 152 Cong. Rec. 184 (2006).

59 *House v. Bell*, 547 U.S. 518 (2006) ("[The Petitioner] urges the Court to answer the question left open in *Herrera* and hold not only that freestanding innocence claims are possible but also that he has established one. We decline to resolve this issue.") The newly appointed Alito did not participate in the decision.

60 Various modern judicial philosophers defend the use of morality in judicial deliberations. Perhaps the most significant of these modern philosophers is Ronald Dworkin, who argued that judges must consider the moral principles that are manifested in our legal system. *See* RONALD DWORKIN, LAW'S EMPIRE (Belknap Press of Harv. U. Press 1986). Predictably, Dworkin's theory had been accused (falsely, in my opinion) of being a modern reincarnation of natural law. *See, e.g.*, Ronald Dworkin, "Natural" Law Revisited, 34 U. Fla. L. Rev. 165 (1982) (examining the criticism that his legal theory is a version of natural law). *See also* Chapter 7 ("V. Dworkin on Morality and Truth"). Be that as it may, the continuing controversy surrounding Dworkin's legal theory is a testament to the continuing struggle over the place of morality and justice in judicial deliberations.

Chapter 4.
The Role of History in Constitutional Interpretation: The First Amendment and Unprotected Speech

1 *United States v. Stevens*, 559 U.S. 460 (2010).

2 *Michael H. v. Gerald D.*, 491 U.S. 110, 122 (1989) (Justice Scalia, joined by Chief Justice Rehnquist and Justices O'Connor and Kennedy).

3 *Michael H.*, 141 (Justice Brennan, joined by Justices Marshall and Blackmun, dissenting).

4 *Michael H.*, 137.

5 JOHN STUART MILL, ON LIBERTY 63, (Elizabeth Rappaport ed., Hackett, 1978).

6 *Shenck v. United States*, 249 U.S. 47, 52 (1919).

7 *Brandenburg v. Ohio*, 395 U.S. 444, 447 (1969). The definition is the Supreme Court's modern iteration of the famous "clear and present danger" test, which removes First Amendment protections from

speech that creates a clear and present danger of unlawful action.

8   Since 9/11 there have been various calls for revising this doctrine so as to make it easier to punish the advocacy of terrorism. *See, e.g.*, Eric Posner, *ISIS Gives Us No Choice but to Consider Limits on Speech*, SLATE, December 15, 2016, http://www.slate.com/articles/news_and_politics/view_from_chicago/2015/12/isis_s_online_radicalization_efforts_present_an_unprecedented_danger.html. *See also* David Post's opposing view, *Protecting the First Amendment in the Internet Age*, WASHINGTON POST, December 21, 2015, https://www.washington-post.com/news/volokh-conspiracy/wp/2015/12/21/protecting-the-first-amendment-in-the-internet-age/.

9   *New York v. Ferber*, 458 U.S. 747 (1982).

10   *Ashcroft v. Free Speech Coalition*, 535 U.S. 234 (2002).

11   *Cohen v. California*, 403 U.S. 15, 20 (1971).

12   According to the Supreme Court, obscene materials enjoy no First Amendment protections because they are offensive to the community's sense of propriety. *See, e.g., Paris Adult Theatre I v. Slaton*, 413 U.S. 49 (1973). It is worth noting that Justice William Brennan, who authored the first Supreme Court opinion recognizing obscenity as an unprotected category, *Roth v. United States*, 354 U.S. 476 (1957), ended up regretting that opinion: "[We] have been unable to . . . separate obscenity from other sexually oriented but constitutionally protected speech," he lamented sixteen years later in *Paris Adult Theatre I v. Slaton*, 413 U.S. 49, 79 (1973) (Justice Brennan, dissenting).

13   *United States v. Stevens*, 559 U.S. 460, 491 (2010) (Justice Alito, dissenting).

14   18 U.S.C. § 48 (2019) ("Depictions of Animal Cruelty. Whoever knowingly creates, sells, or possesses a depiction of animal cruelty with the intention of placing that depiction in interstate or foreign commerce for commercial gain, shall be fined under this title or imprisoned not more than 5 years, or both. (b) EXCEPTION—Subsection (a) does not apply to any depiction that has serious religious, political, scientific, educational, journalistic, historical, or artistic value. (c) DEFINITIONS—In this section— (1) the term 'depiction of animal cruelty' means any visual or auditory depiction . . . in which a living animal is intentionally maimed, mutilated, tortured, wounded, or killed, if such conduct is illegal under Federal law or the law of the State in which the creation, sale, or possession takes place").

15   *Stevens* 559 U.S. at 470.

16   *Id.*

17   The introduction of a historical test was a break from Supreme Court precedent: "Categories of speech may be exempted from the First Amendment's protection without any long-settled tradition . . . .,"

wrote the lawyers defending the statute. *Stevens*, 469 (quoting Brief for Petitioner at 12 n.8, *United States v. Stevens*, 559 U.S. 460 (2010) (No. 08-769)). They gave the example of the Court's 1982 decision, *New York v. Ferber*, 458 U.S. 747 (1982), which held that child pornography was unprotected speech, even though legal prohibitions on child pornography emerged only in the 1970s.

18   Animal Crush Video Prohibition Act of 2010, 111 P.L. 294, 124 Stat. 3177.

19   18 U.S.C. § 704(b), (c) (2019).

20   *United States v. Alvarez*, 567 U.S. 709 (2012).

21   Another demonstration of the controversial nature of the historical test can be seen in *Stevens* itself—in the majority opinion's controversial claim that child pornography was a historically unprotected category of speech (and was therefore not a counter-example to the historical test).

22   *Alvarez*, 567 U.S. at 711.

23   *Alvarez*, 733.

24   *Alvarez*, 711.

25   *United States v. Alvarez*, 638 F.3d. 666, 674–75 (9th Cir. 2011) (Chief Judge Kozinski, concurring).

26   *Alvarez*, 675.

27   *Alvarez*, 567 U.S. at 737–38 (2012) (Justice Breyer, joined by Justice Kagan, concurring).

28   18 U.S.C. § 704 (2019).

Chapter 5.
The Rationality of History and Tradition:
The Equal Protection Clause and
The Right to Same-Sex Marriage

1   Strong justifications are also required when the challenged law regulates the all-important issues of voting or access to the courts. *See Harper v. Virginia State Board of Elections*, 383 U.S. 663 (1966); *M.L.B. v. S.L.J.*, 519 U.S. 102 (1996).

2   *Lawrence v. Texas*, 539 U.S. 558 (2003). *See also United States v. Windsor*, 570 U.S. 744 (2013) (invalidating part of the Defense of Marriage Act that limited federal recognition to marriages between a man and a woman); *Romer v. Evans*, 517 U.S. 620 (1996) (invalidating a Colorado constitutional provision that withdrew anti-discrimination protections for homosexuals).

3   *Obergefell v. Hodges*, 135 S. Ct. 2584 (2015).

4   *Obergefell*, 2594.

5   *See, e.g., Perry v. Schwarzenegger*, 704 F. Supp. 2d 921 (N.D. Cal. 2010), *aff'd sub nom. Perry v. Brown*, 671 F.3d 1052 (9th Cir. 2012); *Bostic v. Rainey*, 970 F. Supp. 2d. 456 (E.D. Va. 2014), *aff'd sub nom. Bostic v. Schaefer*, 760 F.3d 352 (4th Cir. 2014).

6   *Obergefell,* 2624 (Chief Justice Roberts, joined by Justices Scalia and Thomas, dissenting).

7   *Obergefell,* 2626, 2630 n.22. (Justice Scalia, joined by Justice Thomas, dissenting).

8   *Obergefell,* 2638 (Justice Thomas, joined by Justice Scalia, dissenting).

9   *Obergefell,* 2643 (Justice Alito, joined by Justices Scalia and Thomas, dissenting).

10   *Lawrence v. Texas*, 539 U.S. 558 (2003). *See also, United States v. Windsor,* 570 U.S. 744 (2013) (invalidating part of the federal Defense of Marriage Act that limited federal recognition to marriages between a man and a woman).

11   *Baskin v. Bolan*, 766 F.3d 648 (7th Cir. 2014).

12   *Baskin,* 661.

13   *DeBoer v. Snyder*, 772 F.3d 388, 406 (6th Cir. 2014).

14   *Baskin,* 766 F.3d at 667.

15   *Baskin,* 666–67.

16   Oliver Wendell Holmes, Jr., *The Path of the Law*, 10 HARV. L. REV. 457 (1897).

17   *Obergefell v. Hodges*, 135 S. Ct. at 2642 (Justice Alito, joined by Justices Scalia and Thomas, dissenting).

18   *Id.* (Chief Justice Roberts, joined by Justices Scalia and Thomas, dissenting).

19   *See, e.g.*, Frank H. Easterbrook, *Statutes' Domains*, 50 U. CHI. L. REV. 533, 547 (1983) ("Because legislatures comprise many, they do not have 'intents' or 'designs,' hidden yet discoverable. Each member may or may not have a design. The body as a whole, however, has only outcomes. . . . This follows from the discoveries of public choice theory. Although legislators have individual lists of desires, priorities, and preferences, it turns out to be difficult, sometimes impossible, to aggregate these lists into a coherent collective choice").

20   *See, e.g.*, DENNIS C. MUELLER, PUBLIC CHOICE, (Phyllis Deane and Mark Perlman eds., Cambridge U. Press 1979); KENNETH J. ARROW, SOCIAL CHOICE AND INDIVIDUAL VALUES, (2nd ed., Murray Printing Co. 1973); DUNCAN BLACK, THE THEORY OF COMMITTEES AND ELECTIONS (Cambridge U. Press 1958). Some public choice theorists dispute this orthodoxy, and have focused on institutional mechanisms that help produce coherent policies, notwithstanding the problems plaguing the combination of voting preferences. *See generally* MAXWELL L. STEARNS & TODD J. ZYWICKI, PUBLIC CHOICE CONCEPTS AND

APPLICATIONS IN LAW (West 2009); Daniel A. Farber, *Public Choice Theory and Legal Institutions*, U. CALIF. BERKELEY, Feb. 14, 2014, at SSRN, Pub. Law Res. Paper No. 2396056, http://papers.ssrn.com/sol3/papers.cfm?abstract_id=2396056. *See also,* BRYAN CAPLAN, THE MYTH OF THE RATIONAL VOTER: WHY DEMOCRACIES CHOOSE BAD POLICIES (Princeton U. Press 2007) (arguing that democracy produces irrational policies because voters' choices are themselves irrational).

21 Changing the sequence by which different versions of the same legislative proposals are voted on may change the ensuing statute even as legislators' policy preferences remain fixed. *See, e.g.,* JEREMY WALDRON, LAW AND DISAGREEMENT (Oxford U. Press 1999), "Legislators' Intentions and Unintentional Legislation" ("It is perfectly possible [that a statute] does not reflect the purposes or intentions of any of the legislators who together enacted it. . . . Accordingly, when the Statute is read for the first time . . . [we are] not entitled to say that the aim of the reading must be to determine what somebody meant").

22 John F. Manning, *What Divides Textualists from Purposivists?*, 106 COLUM. L. REV. 70, 113 (2006).

23 *Vieth v. Jubelirer*, 541 U.S. 267, 278 (2004) (Justice Scalia, plurality opinion).

24 The Honorable Antonin Scalia & John F. Manning, *A Dialogue on Statutory and Constitutional Interpretation*, 80 GEO. WASHINGTON L. REV. 1610, 1614–15 (2012).

25 Justice Scalia has written that the rationality requirement should be used only in regard to those constitutional rights whose explicit language presumes a requirement of rationality, but not otherwise. *See D.C. v. Heller*, 554 U.S. 570, 628 n.27 (2008) ("Rational-basis scrutiny is a mode of analysis we have used when evaluating laws under constitutional commands that are themselves prohibitions on irrational laws. In those cases, 'rational basis' is not just the standard of scrutiny, but the very substance of the constitutional guarantee. Obviously, the same test could not be used to evaluate the extent to which a legislature may regulate a specific, enumerated right, be it the freedom of speech, the guarantee against double jeopardy, the right to counsel, or the right to keep and bear arms"). Of course, in many of the latter cases a more demanding scrutiny than rational basis review might apply.

26 *See, e.g.,* Hans A. Linde, *Due Process of Lawmaking*, 55 NEB. L. REV. 197 (1976); Michael Perry, *Modern Equal Protection: A Conceptualization and Appraisal*, 79 COLUM. L. REV. 1023 (1979); Gary C. Leedes, *The Rationality Requirement of the Equal Protection Clause*, 42 OHIO ST. L. J. 639 (1981).

27 Felix Cohen, *Transcendental Nonsense and the Functional Approach*, 35 COLUM. L. REV. 808, 819 (1935).

28 *See* H. Jefferson Powell, *Reasoning About the Irrational: The Rob-*

erts Court and the Future of Constitutional Law, 86 WASH. L. REV. 217, 229 (2011) ("Rational basis scrutiny, as traditionally understood, flows from [the] presupposition [that] in its dealings with persons, the American government is under a constitutional obligation to act rationally. Rationality in turn requires . . . that public actions make sense . . . [But arguments made by Justice Scalia and Chief Justice Roberts] rests on a presupposition that . . . [w]hat makes good sense . . . belongs to the world of politics.").

29 Constitutional rationality requirements are found not only under the Equal Protection Clause, but in many other constitutional doctrines— including, among other places, in measuring the extent of congressional regulative powers, *see, e.g., Katzenbach v. McClung*, 379 U.S. 294 (1964), or under the Due Process Clause, *see, e.g., Washington v. Glucksberg*, 521 U.S. 702 (1997) (refusing to recognize a Due Process right of the terminally ill for physician-assisted suicide), *Abigail Alliance v. Eschenbach*, 495 F.3d 695 (D.C. Cir. 2007) (upholding an FDA policy denying terminally ill patients access to not-yet-approved experimental drugs as rational).

Chapter 6.
Classic Originalism: The Second Amendment, 18th Century Dictionaries, and Semiautomatic Glocks

1 *See District of Columbia v. Heller*, 554 U.S. 570, 574 (2008).
2 One successful test case, *Fisher v. Univ. of Texas at Austin*, 570 U.S. 297 (2013), was mentioned in the Introduction. Other famous constitutional test cases included *Griswold v. Connecticut*, 381 U.S. 479 (1965) (reviving Substantive Due Process doctrine and declaring a right to privacy that forbade the government to criminalize the use of contraceptives); *Roe v. Wade*, 410 U.S. 113 (1973) (recognizing a constitutional right to obtain an abortion); *Riley v. California*, 573 U.S. 373 (2014) (requiring a warrant for the search of cell phones seized in the course of arrests). This is a small sample of the many test cases that have shaped our constitutional law. Needless to say, not all test cases succeed: one famous test case that misfired spectacularly was *Plessy v. Ferguson*, 163 U.S. 537 (1896), which sought racial equality and led, instead, to the "separate but equal" doctrine under the Equal Protection Clause. *Plessy* was overruled by another famous test case, *Brown v. Bd. of Ed. of Topeka*, Shawnee Cty., Kan., 347 U.S. 483, 495 (1954), which declared that, "separate educational facilities are inherently unequal," and forced public schools to desegregate.
3 *Heller*, 554 U.S. at 599.

4   *Heller,* 634.

5   I say "most" because the "new originalists"—discussed below—are different.

6   This inquiry illustrates the tension between legitimate methodology and good results discussed in the Introduction. *See Chapter 1: The Silent Prologue: How Judicial Philosophy Shapes Our Constitutional Rights,* text accompanying fn. 24–26.

7   1 Stat. 596, 5 Cong. Ch. 74.

8   *See* Gregory E. Maggs, *A Concise Guide to the Records of the Federal Constitutional Convention of 1787 As A Source of the Original Meaning of the U.S. Constitution,* 80 GEO. WASH. L. REV. 1707 (2012).

9   THE RECORDS OF THE FEDERAL CONVENTION OF 1787 (Max Farrand ed., Yale U. Press 1911).

10   Bret Boyce, *Originalism and the Fourteenth Amendment,* 33 WAKE FOREST L. REV. 909 (1998).

11   *See, e.g.,* Cass R. Sunstein, *Originalism for Liberals,* NEW REPUBLIC, September 28, 1998, https://newrepublic.com/article/64084/originalism-liberals.

12   *District of Columbia v. Heller,* 554 U.S. 570, 603 (2008).

13   Jack Rakove, *Thoughts on Heller from a 'Real Historian',* BALKINIZATION (June 27, 2008) https://balkin.blogspot.com/2008/06/thoughts-on-heller-from-real-historian.html.

14   U.S. Const. art. I, § 8.

15   *Stare decisis,* an abbreviation of *stare decisis et non quieta movere,* is Latin for 'standing by made decisions and not disturbing matters that are settled.'

16   Antonin Scalia, *Originalism: The Lesser Evil,* 57 U. CIN. L. REV. 849, 861 (1989).

17   As to be expected, most originalists are anxious to reject the claim that originalism deems racially segregated public schools not to violate the Equal Protection Clause. *See, e.g.,* Michael W. McConnell, *Originalism and the Desegregation Decisions,* 81 VA. L. REV. 947 (1995) (arguing that the school desegregation decisions are consistent with the original understanding of the Equal Protection Clause).

18   Scalia, 864.

19   *See* H. Jefferson Powell, *The Original Understanding of Original Intent,* 98 HARV. L. REV. 885 (1985).

20   *Heller,* 554 U.S. 570, 722 (2008) (Justice Breyer, dissenting).

21   *Id.*

22   *See generally* Bret Boyce, *Originalism and the Fourteenth Amendment,* 33 WAKE FOREST L. REV. 909, 946 (1998).

23   *Brown v. Entm't Merchants Ass'n,* 564 U.S. 786 (2011).

24   Transcript of Oral Argument at 15–16, *Brown v. Entm't Merchants Ass'n,* 564 U.S. 786 (2011) (No. 08-1448).

25 *Brown* Transcript, 16–17.
26 *United States v. Jones*, 565 U.S. 400 (2012).
27 *Jones*, 420 n.3 (Justice Alito, joined by Justices Ginsburg, Breyer, and Kagan, concurring).

Chapter 7.
New Originalism and Moral Truths:
The Cruel and Unusual Punishment Clause,
and Ear Cropping for Overtime Parking

1   The originalism of these originalists was not identical. Bork and Meese, for example, thought originalism to revolve around the original intent of the constitutional framers, whereas Justice Scalia preferred to speak of the original meaning of the constitutional text. *See* Thomas Colby, *The Sacrifice of the New Originalism*, 99 GEO. L.J. 713 (2011). But the interpretive methodology these originalists employed was very similar—and was aimed, first and foremost, at reducing judicial discretion.

2   Michigan repealed this mandatory sentencing law in 1998. By then, those opposing the law included many prosecutors, as well as former Michigan Governor William G. Milliken, who had declared that signing the law had been "the worst mistake of my career."

3   *See Weems v. United States*, 217 U.S. 349, 366–367, 371 (1910), quoting *O'Neil v. Vermont*, 144 U.S. 323, 339–340 (1892) (Justice Field, dissenting). ("Such penalties for such offenses amaze those who . . . believe that it is a precept of justice that punishment for crime should be graduated and proportioned to [the] offense.) [T]he inhibition [of the cruel and unusual punishments clause] was directed, not only against punishments which inflict torture, 'but against all punishments which by their excessive length or severity are greatly disproportioned to the offenses charged.'"

4   *Coker v. Georgia*, 433 U.S. 584, 592 (1977).

5   *Solem v. Helm*, 463 U.S. 277 (1983).

6   *Harmelin v. Michigan*, 501 U.S. 957 (1991). Justice Scalia announced the judgment of the Court and delivered the opinion of the Court with respect to Part IV, in which Chief Justice Rehnquist and Justices O'Connor, Kennedy, and Souter, joined, and an opinion with respect to Parts I, II, and III, in which Chief Justice Rehnquist, joined. Justice Kennedy, filed an opinion concurring in part and concurring in the judgment, in which Justices O'Connor and Souter, joined. Justice White filed a dissenting opinion, in which Justices Blackmun and Stevens joined. Justice Marshall filed a dissenting opinion. Justice Stevens

filed a dissenting opinion, in which Justice Blackmun joined.

7   *Harmelin,* 1009 (Justice White, joined by Justices Blackmun and Stevens, dissenting).

8   *Harmelin,* 1002 (Justice Kennedy, joined by Justices O'Connor and Souter, concurring in part and concurring in the judgment).

9   *Id.*

10 *Harmelin,* 987 n. 11.

11 *Harmelin,* 975.

12 *Harmelin,* 979.

13 *See generally* JACK M. BALKIN, LIVING ORIGINALISM (Harv. U. Press 2011); Lawrence B. Solum, *Originalism and Constitutional Construction,* 82 FORDHAM L. REV. 453 (2013); Thomas B. Colby & Peter J. Smith, *Living Originalism,* 59 DUKE L.J. 239 (2009).

14 *See generally* Lawrence Solum, *The Interpretation-Construction Distinction,* 27 CONST. COMMENT 95 (2010).

15 *See* Jack M. Balkin, *Abortion and Original Meaning,* 24 CONST. COMMENT 291, 296 (2007) for a new originalist's critique of the classical originalism's approach to the Cruel and Unusual Punishment Clause.

16 Randy E. Barnett, *The Golden Mean Between Kurt & Dan: A Moderate Reading of the Ninth Amendment,* 56 DRAKE L. REV. 897 (2008).

17 *Marsh v. Chambers,* 463 U.S. 783 (1983). *See also Town of Greece, N.Y. v. Galloway,* 572 U.S. 565, 602 (2014) ("This Court has often noted that actions taken by the First Congress are presumptively consistent with the Bill of Rights, and this principle has special force when it comes to the interpretation of the Establishment Clause").

18 *See Marsh v. Chambers,* 463 U.S. 783 (1983) (Justice Brennan, joined by Justice Marshall, dissenting) ("James Madison, writing subsequent to his own Presidency on essentially the very issue we face today, stated:

> Is the appointment of Chaplains to the two Houses of Congress consistent with the Constitution, and with the pure principle of religious freedom?

> In strictness, the answer on both points must be in the negative. The Constitution of the U.S. forbids everything like an establishment of a national religion. The law appointing Chaplains establishes a religious worship for the national representatives, to be performed by Ministers of religion, elected by a majority of them; and these are to be paid out of the national taxes. Does not this involve the principle of a national establishment, applicable to a provision for a religious worship for the Constituent as well as of the representative Body, approved by the majority, and conducted by Ministers of religion paid by the entire nation.

Fleet, *Madison's "Detached Memoranda,"* 3 WM. & MARY QUARTERLY 534, 558 (1946).

19 *See, e.g.*, EARL M. MALTZ, CIVIL RIGHTS, THE CONSTITUTION, AND CONGRESS, 1863–69 109–13, 118–20 (U. Press of Kan. 1990) (explaining why the Originalist understanding of the Equal Protection Clause did not require school desegregation).

20 *See, e.g.*, Steven G. Calabresi & Julia T. Rickert, *Originalism and Sex Discrimination*, 90 TEXAS L. REV. 1 (2011).

21 The principal Supreme Court precedents on the Eighth Amendment agree with Dworkin. The Court has repeatedly said that "the words of the [Eighth] Amendment are not precise, and . . . their scope is not static. The Amendment must draw its meaning from the evolving standards of decency that mark the progress of a maturing society." *Trop v. Dulles*, 356 U.S. 86, 101 (1958) (plurality opinion). *See also Coker v. Georgia*, 433 U.S. 584 (1977); *Roper v. Simmons*, 543 U.S. 551 (2005).

22 *See* the Crimes Act of 1790 1 Stat. 114, 1 Cong. Ch. 9 ([I]f any captain or mariner of any ship or other vessel, shall piratically and feloniously run away with such ship or vessel, or any goods or merchandize, to the value of fifty dollars, or yield up such ship or vessel voluntarily to any pirate; . . . every such offender shall be deemed, taken, and adjudged to be, a pirate and felon, and being thereof convicted, shall suffer death).

23 Randy E. Barnett, *The Golden Mean Between Kurt & Dan: A Moderate Reading of the Ninth Amendment*, 56 DRAKE L. REV. 897, 909 (2008).

24 Gary Lawson, *On Reading Recipes . . . and Constitutions*, 85 GEO. L.J. 1823, 1826, 1834 (1997).

25 *See* STEVEN D. SMITH, LAW'S QUANDARY (Harv. U. Press 2004).

26 *Harmelin v. Michigan*, 501 U.S. 957, 986 (1991) (Justice Scalia, joined in this part of the opinion only by Chief Justice Rehnquist).

27 *Harmelin*, 989. The opinion also pointed out that the legislature may want to impose a heavy penalty for reasons other than the purported gravity of an offense: "For example, since deterrent effect depends not only upon the amount of the penalty, but upon its certainty, crimes that are less grave but significantly more difficult to detect may warrant substantially higher penalties." If insider trading is difficult to detect, it may be justified to impose a stiff penalty on those who caught doing it, even if that penalty is not proportionate to the severity of the offense.

28 *Harmelin*, 988.

29 *See id.*

30 *Harmelin*, 1023 (Justice White, with whom Justices Blackmun and Stevens joined, dissenting).

31 *See* Ronald Dworkin, The Model of Rules, 35 U. Chi. L. Rev. 14

(1967).

32   *See generally* Dworkin, Law's Empire (Belknap Press of Harv. U. Press 1986).

33   *See* Ronald Dworkin, '*No Right Answer?*', 53 N.Y.U. L. Rev. 1 (1978).

34   *See generally*, Ronald Dworkin, Justice for Hedgehogs (Belknap Press of Harv. U. Press 2011); Ronald Dworkin, '*Objectivity and Truth: You'd Better Believe It*', 25 Phil. & Pub. Aff. 87 (1996); Ronald Dworkin, Law's Empire (Belknap Press of Harv. U. Press 1986).

35   *Kennedy v. Louisiana*, 554 U.S. 407 (2008)

36   *But see* John Horgan, *Why String Theory Is Still Not Even Wrong*, Scientific American: Cross-Check *(April 27, 2017), https://blogs. scientificamerican.com/cross-check/why-string-theory-is-still-not-even-wrong/.*

37   *See, e.g., Epperson v. State of Ark.*, 393 U.S. 97 (1968) (invalidating an Arkansas statute making it a crime to teach evolutionary theory in public schools, on the ground that the statute violated the Establishment Clause); *Edwards v. Aguillard*, 482 U.S. 578 (1987) (invalidating Louisiana's Creationism Act that forbade the teaching of the theory of evolution in public elementary and secondary schools unless accompanied by instruction in the theory of creation science); *Massachusetts v. E.P.A.*, 549 U.S. 497 (2007) (relying on man-made global warming in allowing a lawsuit against the Environmental Protection Agency to proceed for meeting the constitutional standing requirement).

38   John Paul Stevens, Five Chiefs: A Supreme Court Memoir (Little, Brown and Company 2011).

39   *Id.*

40   However, the call for the complete elimination of the proportionality requirement never achieved a majority on the Court. The requirement thus retains some limited vitality—especially in regard to the death penalty. In recent years, the Supreme Court held that the death penalty was a disproportionate punishment (and therefore unconstitutional) for the mentally disabled, for minors, and for non-homicide offenses (including the rape of a child), and that a life sentence without the possibility of parole was a disproportionately excessive punishment for juvenile non-homicide offenders. *See Atkins v. Virginia*, 536 U.S. 304 (2002); *Roper v. Simmons*, 543 U.S. 551 (2005); *Kennedy v. Louisiana*, 554 U.S. 407 (2008); *Graham v. Florida*, 560 U.S. 48, 81 (2010).

41   *Ewing v. California*, 538 U.S. 11 (2003). Ewing's previous convictions included petty theft, theft, grand theft, possession of drug paraphernalia, appropriation of lost property, possession of a firearm, battery, burglary, and a robbery in which he brandished a knife.

42   A defendant had to have two previous serious or violent felony offenses to qualify for the law, but the triggering offense could be neither. In 2012, California voters approved some major modifications to the

law, including abolishing life sentences for nonviolent offenders. The changes have also led to the release of more than 1,000 inmates.

43   *Lockyer v. Andrade*, 538 U.S. 63 (2003) (reinstating the conviction under the federal habeas corpus statute, and refusing to reach the defendant's claim that his sentence was in violation of the Eighth Amendment).

44   *See Prosecutors' Perspective on California's Three Strikes Law: A 10-Year Retrospective* 3, 17 (Cal. Dist. Att'ys Ass'n. 2004).

45   *See* Jack Leonard, *'Pizza Thief' Walks the Line*, L.A. Times, Feb. 10, 2010, http://articles.latimes.com/2010/feb/10/local/la-me-pizza-thief10-2010feb10. Several years later, Jerry DeWayne Williams' sentence was reduced to six years imprisonment—for reasons unrelated to the Cruel and Unusual Punishment Clause.

Chapter 8.
Statutory Interpretation, Deviations From Clear Statutory Texts, and Correction of Legislative Mistakes: Exempting Atheists From the Foxholes

1   Selective Training and Service Act of 1940, Pub. L. No. 76-783, 54 Stat. 885.

2   That predecessor, The Draft Act of 1917, exempted religious objectors only, but the Secretary of War instructed that, "personal scruples against war" be included as well. Selective Service System Monograph No. 11, Conscientious Objection at 54–55 (1950).

3   *United States v. Kauten*, 133 F.2d 703, 708 (2d Cir. 1943).

4   *Berman v. United States*, 156 F.2d 377, 380–81 (9th Cir. 1946).

5   Selective Service Act of 1948, Pub. L. No. 80-759, 62 Stat. 604.

6   U.S. Const. amend. I.

7   *United States v. Seeger*, 326 F.2d 846, 849 (2d Cir. 1964).

8   *Seeger*, 848.

9   *United States v. Seeger*, 380 U.S. 163 (1965).

10   *Berman*, 156 F.2d at 384 (Judge Denman, dissenting).

11   *Emp't Div., Dept. of Human Res. of Oregon v. Smith*, 494 U.S. 872 (1990).

12   *Reynolds v. United States*, 98 U.S. 145 (1878).

13   *United States v. Lee*, 455 U.S. 252 (1982).

14   *Smith*, 494 U.S. at 888.

15   *United States v. Seeger*, 380 U.S. 163, 174–75.

16   *Seeger*, 181–82.

17   *Seeger*, 188 (Justice Douglas, concurring). Douglas's use of the French expression *"tour de force"* is rather peculiar, since he uses it in a nega-

tive sense whereas the usual connotations of the expression are, in fact, *absolument positif.*

18 *See, e.g., United States v. Stevens,* 559 U.S. 460 (2010) ("Nor can we rely upon the canon of construction that . . . statutory language should be construed to avoid serious constitutional doubts. This Court may impose a limiting construction on a statute only if it is readily susceptible to such a construction. We will not rewrite a law to conform it to constitutional requirements . . . ." (internal quotations and alterations omitted)).

19 *Aptheker v. Secretary of State,* 378 U.S. 500, 515 (1964) (internal quotation omitted).

20 Some scholars distinguish between legislative purpose and legislative intent. *See, e.g.,* William N. Eskridge & Philip J. Frickey, *Statutory Interpretation as Practical Reasoning,* 42 STAN L. REV. 321, 324–35 (1990). Legislative intent is understood as the psychological intention of legislators, whereas legislative purpose is an objective construct about the goals that a statute seek to achieve. But since courts use the two terms interchangeably, and since the discussion in the next chapter will examine these different ideas, I will avoid that unnecessary complication.

21 Justice Blackmun, who joined the Court a mere month before the decision was issued, did not participate in the case.

22 *Welsh v. United States,* 398 U.S. 333, 340 (1970) (plurality opinion).

23 *Welsh,* 367 (Justice White, dissenting).

24 *Welsh v. United States,* 404 F.2d 1078 (9th Cir. 1968).

25 *Welsh,* 398 U.S. at 344 (Justice Harlan, concurring).

26 *Welsh,* 347 (Justice Harlan, concurring).

27 *Riggs v. Palmer,* 115 N.Y. 506 (1989).

28 *Riggs,* 509.

29 The dissent argued that the murderous grandchild was entitled to the fruit of his evil deed because "[w]e are bound by the rigid rules of law, which have been established by the legislature, and within the limits of which the determination of this question is confined." *Riggs,* 515 (Judge Gray, dissenting).

30 *Welsh,* 398 U.S. at 355 (1970) (Justice Harlan, concurring).

31 Lon Fuller, *Positivism and Fidelity to Law—A Reply to Professor Hart,* 71 HARV. L. REV. 630 (1958).

32 *Welsh,* 398 U.S. at 356 (Justice Harlan, concurring).

33 *Welsh,* 360 n.12 (Justice Harlan, concurring).

34 *Blevins v. Bardwell,* 784 So. 2d 166, 175 (Miss. 2001).

35 *United States v. Seeger,* 380 U.S. 163, 176 ("This construction avoids imputing to Congress an intent to classify different religious beliefs, exempting some and excluding others, and is in accord with the well-established congressional policy of equal treatment for those

whose opposition to service is grounded in their religious tenets").

36 THE FEDERALIST NO. 78 (Alexander Hamilton).

37 *See* SØREN KIERKEGAARD, FEAR AND TREMBLING (1843).

38 Many textualists believe that judges can legitimately deviate from statutory texts in some extreme circumstances—namely, where the textually produced result is patently absurd and harmful. This is a highly limited exception that applies only to what is universally and non-controversially recognized as absurd. *See generally* John F. Manning, *The Absurdity Doctrine*, 116 HARV. L. REV. 2387 (2003).

39 *See, e.g., Devillers v. Auto Club Ins Assn*, 702 N.W.2d 539 (2005) (Cavanagh, J., Dissenting) ("[T]he majority's ardent devotion to the strict language of the statute is admirable, but really quite misplaced. . . . [E]quitable remedies are . . . entirely within the sanctioned parameters of the judiciary's powers. . . . [T]he judiciary is not a mere robotic cog in the wheel of our three-branch system of government. Rather, the judiciary has the ability—indeed, the responsibility—to do equity where equity is required").

Chapter 9.
Textualism v. Purposivism: The Fourth Amendment and The Constitutionality of Pretextual Arrests

1 *Ashcroft v. al-Kidd*, 563 U.S. 731 (2011).

2 *See* Chapters 4, 7. Probably the most famous debate over the matter is the Hart-Fuller exchange in the Harvard Law Review. *Compare* H.L.A. Hart, *Positivism and the Separation of Law and Morals*, 71 HARV. L. REV. 593 (1958) *with* Lon Fuller, *Positivism and Fidelity to Law – A Reply to Professor Hart*, 71 HARV. L. REV. 630 (1958).

3 John F. Manning, *What Divides Textualists from Purposivists?*, 106 COLUM. L. REV. 70 102, 77 (2006).

4 *Vieth v. Jubelirer*, 541 U.S. 267, 278 (2004) (Justice Scalia, plurality opinion).

5 Fuller, 86.

6 The terms "purpose" and "intent" are used interchangeably here. See Chapter 8, endnote 20. Attributed to Federal Judge Harold Leventhal. *See* Abner J. Mikva, *Statutory Interpretation: Getting the Law to be Less Common*, 50 OHIO ST. L.J. 979, 982 (1989).

7 A number of scholars alleged that Justice Antonin Scalia's textualism was incompatible with his originalism. As a textualist, Scalia wrote that: "[I]t is simply incompatible with democratic government, or indeed, even with fair government, to have the meaning of the law determined by what the lawgiver meant, rather than by what the lawgiver

promulgated . . . . It is the *law* that governs, not the intent of the lawgiver." (ANTONIN SCALIA, A MATTER OF INTERPRETATION (Princeton U. Press 1997). But originalism seems to require the opposite: in *Harmelin*—which we examined in Chapter 7—Justice Scalia rejected the proportionality requirement by stating that "what evidence exists from debates at the state ratifying conventions . . . as well as the floor debates in the First Congress which proposed it, confirms the view that the cruel and unusual punishments clause was directed at prohibiting certain *methods* of punishment." *Harmelin v. Michigan*, 501 U.S. 957, 979 (1991) (emphasis in original) (internal quotation and alteration omitted). This is precisely the sort of claim—and the sort of evidence— that textualists think judges should never use when interpreting statutes.

Ronald Dworkin was one of the critics pointing to Scalia's alleged inconsistency: if Scalia were faithful to his textualism, wrote Dworkin, he would have insisted that the Eighth Amendment's Cruel and Unusual Punishment Clause required what the meaning of its text required. *See* SCALIA, 119 (Ronald Dworkin Comment). Instead, Scalia habitually interpreted the Cruel and Unusual Punishment Clause in accordance with what its framers and ratifiers *expected* the Clause to require.

Scalia responded to the criticism by claiming that he is a textualist in both the statutory and the constitutional contexts: the meaning of the constitutional text was what mattered—not the expectations of the drafters. However, according to Scalia, the expectations of the drafters were crucial for establishing the meaning of the constitutional text. The drafters' expectations were often conclusive evidence of the original meaning. The expectations of the framers and ratifiers of the Eighth Amendment do not *govern* the matter, but these expectations were indicative as to the original meaning of the Amendment's text. Thus, there was no contradiction—wrote Justice Scalia—between his statutory textualism and his constitutional originalism.

8   SCALIA, A MATTER OF INTERPRETATION, 17–18.
9   *Holy Trinity Church v. United States*, 143 U.S. 457 (1892).
10 U.S. Const. amend. IV.
11 According to the widely cited National Law Enforcement Officers Memorial Fund, "There are more than 900,000 sworn law enforcement officers now serving in the United States." Available at http://www. nleomf.org/facts/enforcement/.
12 Also, warrants had to specify who was to be searched or detained, what were the precise premises to be searched, and what precisely was to be searched for ("particularly describing the place to be searched, and the persons or things to be seized").
13 *Wolf v. People of the State of Colo.*, 338 U.S. 25 (1949).

14 *Mapp v. Ohio*, 367 U.S. 643 (1961).

15 For example, if the police obtained evidence through an unconstitutional search, that evidence could still be admitted at the trial if it could be shown that the police would have discovered that evidence even without the unconstitutional search. Additionally, evidence seized in violation of a defendant's Fourth Amendment rights may still be admissible in many judicial proceedings other than a criminal trial (*habeas corpus*, grand jury, deportation, civil tax proceedings, etc.), and may be admitted even into a criminal trial under an ever-growing list of exceptions (e.g., if used only to impeach defense testimony, if the violation resulted from mere clerical error, if the result of mere isolated negligence attenuated from the violation, etc.). *See, e.g., Arizona v. Evans*, 514 U.S. 1 (1995); *Herring v. United States*, 555 U.S. 135 (2009).

16 *Atwater v. Lago Vista*, 532 U.S. 318 (2001).

17 That holds true even if state law does not authorize an arrest for such violations.

18 *See, e.g., Florence v. Burlington*, 566 U.S. 318 (2012) (Justice Breyer, with whom Justices Ginsburg, Sotomayor, and Kagan join, dissenting).

19 *Hedgepeth v. Washington Metro. Area Transit Auth.*, 386 F.3d 1148 (D.C. Cir. 2004).

20 *See Florence*, 566 U.S. 318.

21 Studies based on extensive anonymous surveys reveal that judges routinely feign belief and accept police misrepresentations in order to allow in all relevant evidence. *See, e.g.,* Myron W. Orfield, Jr., *Deterrence, Perjury, and the Heater Factor: An Exclusionary Rule in the Chicago Criminal Courts*, 63 U. COLO. L. REV. 75 (1992).

22 The statute authorizes the arrest of witnesses if the testimony is "material in a criminal proceeding" and if it may "become impracticable to secure the presence of the [witness] by subpoena." Release or detention of a material witness, 18 U.S.C. § 3144.

23 The Supreme Court never addressed the issue directly, but has implied that the statute is constitutional. *See Stein v. New York*, 346 U.S. 156 (1953); *Barry v. United States ex. rel. Cunningham*, 279 U.S. 597 (1929). *See also Ashcroft v. al-Kidd*, 563 U.S. 731, 743 (2011) ("It might be argued, perhaps, that when, in response to the English abuses, the Fourth Amendment said that warrants could only issue 'on probable cause,' it meant only probable cause to suspect a violation of law, and not probable cause to believe that the individual named in the warrant was a material witness. But that would make all arrests pursuant to material-witness warrants unconstitutional, whether pretextual or not—and that is not the position taken by al-Kidd in this case").

24 The report by the U.S. Department of Justice claimed there were only 12 'questionable' cases of pretextual arrests—and then concluded that all were in fact proper. *See* OFFICE OF THE INSPECTOR GEN., U.S. DEP'T

OF JUSTICE, A REVIEW OF THE DEPARTMENT'S USE OF THE MATERI-
AL WITNESS STATUTE WITH A FOCUS ON SELECT NATIONAL SECURI-
TY MATTERS (2014), available at https://oig.justice.gov/reports/2014/
s1409r.pdf. Lawyers representing the arrested men called the DOJ report "a whitewash."

25   Anjana Malhotra, *Witness to Abuse: Human Rights Abuses under the
     Material Witness Law since September 11*, 17 HUMAN RIGHTS WATCH
     1 (June 2005), https://www.hrw.org/report/2005/06/26/witness-abuse/
     human-rights-abuses-under-material-witness-law-september-11.

26   Steve Fainaru & Margot Williams, *Material Witness Law Has Many
     in Limbo*, WASH. POST, Nov. 24, 2002, https://www.washington-
     post.com/archive/politics/2002/11/24/material-witness-law-has-
     many-in-limbo/a89486fb-be3b-469d-ba64-8b67cf6037ee/?utm_
     term=.da87dd8cf2be.

27   Jess Bravin & Gary Fields, *U.S.'s Zero-Tolerance Approach to Terror-
     ism Suspects is Tested*, WALL STREET J., Oct. 8, 2002, https://www.wsj.
     com/articles/SB1034028193943544280.

28   Adam Liptak, *Threats and Responses: The Detainees: For Post-9/11
     Material Witness, It Is a Terror of a Different Kind*, N.Y. TIMES, Aug.
     19, 2004, https://www.nytimes.com/2004/08/19/us/threats-responses-
     detainees-for-post-9-11-material-witness-it-terror-different.html.

29   John Ashcroft, by the way, had a history of pretextual, off-label use of
     statutes. In 2001, Ashcroft issued a directive claiming that the federal
     Drug Abuse Prevention and Control Act, whose stated purpose was
     the prevention of drug abuse and addiction, made it a criminal offense
     for Oregon doctors to help terminally ill patients die in accordance
     with Oregon's Death with Dignity Act. That directive was declared
     unlawful by the Supreme Court in 2006. *See Gonzales v. Oregon*, 546
     U.S. 243, 253–54 (2006).

30   *Al-Kidd v. Ashcroft*, 580 F.3d 949, 970 (9th Cir. 2009).

31   *Al-Kidd*, 972.

32   *See Ashcroft v. al-Kidd*, 563 U.S. 731 (2011). Other parts of the opin-
     ion received the unanimous support of all justices.

33   Brief for Respondent at 42–43, *Ashcroft v. al-Kidd*, 563 U.S. 731 (No.
     10-98).

34   Reply Brief for Petitioner at 16, *Ashcroft v. al-Kidd*, 563 U.S. 731 (No.
     10-98).

35   Petitioner, 15.

36   *Id* (brackets added).

37   For an in-depth look at this convoluted Supreme Court opinion, *see*
     Ofer Raban, *Judicial Fundamentalism, the Fourth Amendment, and
     Ashcroft v. al-Kidd*, 1 VA. J. CRIM. L. 446 (2013).

38   *al-Kidd*, 563 U.S. at 744.

39   *See Gonzales v. Oregon*, 546 U.S. 243 (2006).

40 *Whren v. United States*, 517 U.S. 806 (1996).

41 The Court did say that racial profiling may violate another constitutional provision: the Equal Protection Clause ("[T]he Constitution
prohibits selective enforcement of the law based on considerations
such as race. But the constitutional basis for objecting to intentionally
discriminatory application of laws is the Equal Protection Clause, not
the Fourth Amendment"). However, violations of the Equal Protection
Clause do not seem to implicate the exclusionary rule—the most effective mechanism for deterring abusive police practices. *See, e.g., United
States v. Nichols*, 512 F.3d 789, 791 (6th Cir. 2008) ("[T]here does
not appear to be any case in which a court has ever actually applied
suppression as a remedy [for Equal Protection violation], at least in the
absence of a concomitant Fourth Amendment violation").

42 *See Reichle v. Howards*, 566 U.S. 658 (2012).

43 In 2018, the Court again decided a case claiming a retaliatory arrest
due to the arrestee's speech. Fane Lozman dared criticize his city council during a council meeting open to the public, and was arrested on the
orders of city council members. *See Lozman v. City of Riviera Beach*,
138 S. Ct. 1945 (2018). But while the Supreme Court agreed to decide
"whether the existence of probable cause defeats a First Amendment
claim for retaliatory arrest," it ended up ducking the principal issue,
opting, instead, for a very narrow decision: the presence of probable
cause, said the Court, should not defeat a "unique class of retaliatory
arrest claims." To fall within that unique class, the plaintiff must present "objective evidence" of an official municipal policy of retaliation,
formed well before the arrest, in response to highly protected speech,
that has little relation to the offense of arrest.

44 *Trump v. Hawaii*, 138 S. Ct. 2392 (2018) at 2434. "When the government acts with the ostensible and predominant purpose of disfavoring
a particular religion," protested the dissenters, "it violates that central
Establishment Clause value of official religious neutrality, there being
no neutrality when the government's ostensible object is to take sides."
(Justice Sotomayor, joined by Justice Ginsburg, dissenting) (quotation
marks omitted).

45 *See, e.g., Church of the Lukumi Babalu Aye v. City of Hialeah*, 508
U.S. 520 (1993) ("In our Establishment Clause cases we have often
stated the principle that the First Amendment forbids an official pur-
pose to disapprove of a particular religion or of religion in general.
See, *e.g., Grand Rapids School Dist. v. Ball*, 473 U.S. 373, 389 (1985);
Wallace v. Jaffree, 472 U.S. 38, 56 (1985); *Epperson v. Arkansas*, 393
U.S. 97, 106–107 (1968); *School Dist. of Abington v. Schempp*, 374
U.S. 203, 225 (1963); *Everson v. Board of Ed. of Ewing*, 330 U.S. 1,
15–16 (1947)."). *See also Batson v. Kentucky*, 476 U.S. 79 (1986);
Minnesota v. Clover Leaf Creamery, 449 U.S. 456, 471 n.15 (1981).

46   *See, e.g., Batson,* 476 U.S. 79, (1986), *United States v. Virginia,* 518 U.S. 515 (1996).

47   *See, e.g., Clover Leaf Creamery,* 449 U.S. at 471 n.15. *See generally McCreary County, Ky. v. American Civil Liberties Union of Ky.,* 545 U.S. 844, 861 (2005) ("[G]overnmental purpose is a key element of a good deal of constitutional doctrine . . . .").

Chapter 10.
Textualism, Purposivism, and Pragmatism: Judicial Legislation and The Politicization of Judicial Election Campaigns

1   *Republican Party of Minn. v. White,* 563 U.S. 765 (2002).

2   Americans with Disabilities Act, 42 U.S.C § 12101 (2019).

3   One reason why textualism is not a popular method of constitutional interpretation is that it does not constrain judicial discretion in regard to vague and abstract legal standards—and the U.S. Constitution is replete with vague and abstract constitutional terms.

4   Antonin Scalia, *The Rule of Law as a Law of Rules,* 56 U. CHI. L.REV. 1175, 1176 (1989).

5   U.S. Const. art. II, § 2, cl. 2.

6   Minn. Code of Judicial Conduct, Canon 5A(3)(d)(i) (2000).

7   *Republican Party of Minn. v. Kelly,* 63 F. Supp. 2d 967 (D. Minn. 1999) *aff'd,* 247 F.3d 854 (8th Cir. 2001) *rev'd sub nom, Republican Party of Minn. v. White,* 563 U.S. 765 (2002).

8   *See, e.g., Caperton v. A. T. Massey Coal Co.,* 556 U.S. 868 (2009).

9   *See, e.g.,* Abbe R. Gluck & Richard A. Posner, *Statutory Interpretation on the Bench: A Survey of Forty-Two Judges on the Federal Courts of Appeals,* 131 HARV. L. REV. 1298 (2018) ("This Article reports the results of a survey of a diverse group of forty-two federal appellate judges concerning their approaches to statutory interpretation. . . .None of the judges we interviewed was willing to associate himself or herself with "textualism" without qualification").

10   *Republican Party of Minn. v. White,* 536 U.S. 765, 784 (2002).

11   Lon Fuller, *Positivism and Fidelity to Law – A Reply to Professor Hart,* 71 HARV. L. REV. 630 (1958).

12   *See, e.g., United States v. Kirby,* 74 U.S. 482 (1868) (holding, in direct contradiction with the clear statutory language, that a federal statute making it a crime to knowingly delay the delivery of U.S. mail, was not violated by a sheriff who arrested a U.S. mail carrier on suspicion of murder and thereby knowingly delayed the delivery of U.S. mail);

Hamilton v. Lanning, 560 U.S. 505 (2010) (holding that the clear statutory formula for calculating debtors' future earnings under the Bankruptcy Act should not be followed if it produced unrealistic estimates; *Bond v. United States*, 572 U.S. 844 (2014) (holding that a statute implementing the Chemical Weapons Convention was inapplicable to a domestic marital dispute, notwithstanding its clear text).

13 Bob Egelko, *Former Justice Warns of Threat to Judiciary*, S.F. CHRON., November 4, 2006, http://www.sfgate.com/bayarea/article/SAN-FRANCISCO-Former-justice-warns-of-threat-to-2467339.php).

14 That fact was lore even among political commentators. *See, e.g.*, Charles Krauthammer, *Philosophy for a Judge*, WASH. POST, July 8, 2005 ("Unlike a principled conservative such as Antonin Scalia, or a principled liberal such as Ruth Bader Ginsburg, O'Connor had no stable ideas about constitutional interpretation . . . . Such elasticity earned O'Connor the title of "pragmatist," a coveted virtue in Washington . . . . The problem with ad hoc pragmatism, however, is that it turns the Supreme Court not only into a super-legislature but also into a continuously sitting one . . . . Democrats are demanding that O'Connor be the model for the next Supreme Court appointment. 'I urge the President and the Senate,' says Sen. Barbara Boxer, 'to ensure that her replacement reflects Justice O'Connor's judicial philosophy—mainstream, prochoice, and independent.' But that's not a judicial philosophy. That's political positioning embedded in a social agenda. What we need is a nominee who has a judicial philosophy—grounded in constitutional principles that provide legal guidelines that politicians and citizens can understand and live by. I happen to prefer conservative ('originalist') to liberal constitutional principles. But either is preferable to none."). *See also Chapter 1: The Silent Prologue: How Judicial Philosophy Shapes Our Constitutional Rights*, n. 23.

15 In 2015, the Supreme Court retracted a little from the alleged equivalence between political and judicial elections, and held that while forbidding political candidates from personally soliciting funds for their election campaigns was a violation of the First Amendment, forbidding judicial candidates from doing so was not. *See Williams-Yulee v. Fla. Bar*, 135 S. Ct. 1656 (2015). Justice Scalia dissented.

16 RICHARD POSNER, LAW, PRAGMATISM, AND DEMOCRACY (2003).

17 *Id.*

18 This is a highly limited exception that applies only to what is universally and non-controversially recognized as absurd. *See generally* John F. Manning, *The Absurdity Doctrine*, 116 HARV. L.R. 2387 (2003).

19 RICHARD POSNER, THE PROBLEMATICS OF MORAL AND LEGAL THEORY (Belknap Press of Harv. U. Press 1999).

20 RICHARD POSNER, LAW, PRAGMATISM, AND DEMOCRACY (Harv. U. Press 2003).

21   POSNER, 73.

22   RICHARD POSNER, LAW, PRAGMATISM, AND DEMOCRACY (Harv. U. Press 2003).

23   *Id.*

24   *See, e.g.*, Richard A. Posner, *What Has Pragmatism to Offer Law?*, 63 S. CAL. L.R. 1653 (1990).

25   From the first of twelve Lowell Lectures delivered by Oliver Wendell Holmes, Jr. on November 23, 1880.

26   The literature on legal realism is enormous. *See generally* AMERICAN LEGAL REALISM (William W. Fisher et al. eds., Oxford U. Press 1993).

27   *See e.g.*, Duncan Kennedy, *The Critique of Rights in Critical Legal Studies*, *in* LEFT LEGALISM/LEFT CRITIQUE 178 (Wendy Brown & Janet Halley eds., 2002); ROBERTO MANGABEIRA UNGER, KNOWLEDGE AND POLITICS (1975).

28   *See generally* Hubert L. Dreyfus, *The Current Relevance of Merleau-Ponty's Phenomenology of Embodiment*, J. ANALYTIC PHIL. (1998).

Chapter 11.
Conclusion: Judicial Philosophies and Political Ideologies

1   Awarded by the government of Norway, this is one of the most prestigious awards for work in the social sciences.

2   *Holberg Prize Laureates:* Ronald Dworkin, HOLBERG PRIZE, http://www.holbergprisen.no/en/ronald-dworkin.html (last visited Aug. 7, 2019).

3   *See e.g.*, Cass R. Sunstein, *Neutrality in Constitutional Law* (with Special Reference to Pornography, Abortion, and Surrogacy), 92 COLUM. L. REV. 1 (1992). *See generally* Cass R. Sunstein, *Foreword: Leaving Things Undecided*, 110 HARV. L. REV. 4 (1996).

4   *See generally* Ronald Dworkin, *Looking for Cass Sunstein*, N.Y. REV. BOOKS 56, no. 7 (2009), reviewing CASS R. SUNSTEIN, A CONSTITUTION OF MANY MINDS: WHY THE FOUNDING DOCUMENT DOESN'T MEAN WHAT IT MEANT BEFORE (2009).

5   *See id.* ("In the end, moreover, the justices must inevitably make difficult and essentially controversial judgments for themselves. . . . They cannot decide whether a series of narrow decisions is more likely to reveal the correct answer . . . without deciding philosophical issues . . . that are at least as difficult as the questions minimalists say they are not competent to answer.").

6   *See generally* Ofer Raban, *Between Formalism and Conservatism: On*

the Resurgent Legal Formalism of the Roberts Court, 8 N.Y.U. J. L. & LIBERTY 342 (2014).

7   *See, e.g., Rochin v. California*, 342 U.S. 165, 174 (1952), *Griffin v. Illinois*, 351 U.S. 12 (1956), *Mapp v. Ohio*, 367 U.S. 643 (1961), *Gideon v. Wainwright*, 372 U.S. 335 (1963), *Griswold v. Connecticut*, 381 U.S. 479 (1965), *Miranda v. Arizona*, 384 U.S. 436 (1966), *Goldberg v. Kelly*, 397 U.S. 254 (1970), *Roe v. Wade*, 410 U.S. 113 (1973), *Frontiero v. Richardson*, 411 U.S. 677, 690 (1973).

8   *See generally, e.g.,* RAOUL BERGER, GOVERNMENT BY JUDICIARY: THE TRANSFORMATION OF THE FOURTEENTH AMENDMENT (1977); ROBERT H. BORK, SLOUCHING TOWARD GOMORRAH: MODERN LIBERALISM AND AMERICAN DECLINE (1996); ANTONIN SCALIA, A MATTER OF INTERPRETATION: FEDERAL COURTS AND THE LAW (1998); MARK I. SUTHERLAND, EDWIN MEESE, ET AL., JUDICIAL TYRANNY: THE NEW KINGS OF AMERICA? (2005). *See generally* Andrew C. Spiropoulos, *Rights Done Right: A Critique of Liberation Originalism*, 78 UMKC L.R. 661 (2010): 661 ("Bork and Scalia, after all, turned to originalism in response to what they believed was the Court's illegitimate use of judicial power in the Warren and post-Warren Court era. They believed the Court imposed its own moral opinions on the Constitution and the people, replacing the rule of law with its own moral ukases. They sought an alternative to an interpretive method too reliant on the subjective opinions of judges and, thus, corrosive of the foundations of the rule of law").

9   *See, e.g.,* Robert F. Nagel, *Conservatives and the Court*, 36 NAT'L AFF. (2018), ("During the campaign, candidate Donald Trump promised to select conservatives who would practice 'judicial restraint.' This continues the pattern set by Republican presidents.") Practically all recent conservative appointments to the Supreme Court voiced admiration for textualism and originalism.

10   For an evaluation of some of these claims, *see* Ofer Raban, *Is Textualism Required by Constitutional Separation of Powers?*, 49 LOY. L.A. L. REV. 421 (2016); Ofer Raban, *The Rationalization of Policy: On the Relation Between Democracy and the Rule of Law*, 18 N.Y.U. J. LEGIS. & PUBLIC POL'Y 45 (2015).

11   *See generally* Ofer Raban, *The Fallacy of Legal Certainty: Why Vague Legal Standards May Be Better for Capitalism and Liberalism*, 19 BOSTON UNIVERSITY PUBLIC INTEREST LAW JOURNAL 175 (2010).

12   EDMUND BURKE, REFLECTIONS ON THE REVOLUTION IN FRANCE: AND ON THE PROCEEDINGS IN CERTAIN SOCIETIES IN LONDON RELATIVE TO THAT EVENT 114–129 (J. Dodsley 1790) (Burke continues: "Thanks to our sullen resistance to innovation, thanks to the cold sluggishness of our national character, we still bear the stamp of our forefathers. We have not (as I conceive) lost the generosity and dignity of thinking of

the fourteenth century; nor as yet have we subtilized ourselves into savages. We are not the converts of Rousseau; we are not the disciples of Voltaire; Helvetius has made no progress amongst us"). BURKE, 127.

13 See KARL POPPER, CONJECTURES AND REFUTATIONS 7 (1968) ("[W]e can interpret traditionalism as the belief that, in the absence of an objective and discernable truth, we are faced with the choice between accepting the authority of tradition, and chaos . . . . Rationalism [by contrast] has . . . always claimed the right of reason . . . to criticize, and to reject, any tradition and any authority, as being based on sheer unreason or prejudice or accident").

14 See generally, M. MORTON AUERBACH, THE CONSERVATIVE ILLUSION (Colum. U. Press 1959).

15 The rejection of reason can arguably be seen in today's conservative hostility to theories like evolution, or climate change. See, e.g., Karl W. Giberson & Randall J. Stephens, The Evangelical Rejection of Reason, N.Y. TIMES, October 11, 2011, http://www.nytimes.com/2011/10/18/ opinion/the-evangelical-rejection-of-reason.html (describing the anti-intellectualism and the rejection of science by Republican presidential candidates); Luke Brinker, Evolution and the GOP's 2016 candidates: A complete guide, SALON, February 11, 2015, http://www. salon.com/2015/02/11/evolution_and_the_gops_2016_candidates_a_ complet_guide/ (From climate change to vaccines to the theory of evolution, much of the Republican Party has made clear that it's not exactly enamored of modern science).

16 MICHAEL OAKESHOTT, RATIONALISM IN POLITICS AND OTHER ESSAYS, (Timothy Fuller ed., 2nd ed. 1991). See generally, Timothy Fuller, The Work of Michael Oakeshott, 19 POL. THEORY 3 (1991).

17 The rejection of broad judicial discretion is not a necessary consequence of this skepticism of reason. Some in legal academia have aligned themselves with such skepticism without also rejecting broad judicial discretion. Scholars associated with the Critical Legal Studies movement (CLS) have long denied the objective rationality of legal reasoning (with book titles like Pierre Schlag's The Enchantment Of Reason [1998]); but they never came to endorse the elimination of judicial discretion as a possible way out of that difficulty. To the contrary: CLS scholars usually attack this solution as untenable. See, e.g., Pierre Schlag, Formalism and Realism in Ruins (Mapping the Logics of Collapse, 95 IOWA L. REV. 195, 215 (2009) ("So, as a working theory of law, comprehensive formalism is impossible. Too much of what we consider to be 'law,' and likely would wish to retain as integral to what we call law, would have to be jettisoned or declared errant, spurious, or otherwise pathological. For a judge to be a comprehensive formalist would render him antediluvian. For a lawyer to be a com-

prehensive formalist would be malpractice"). But CLS has no solution to the problem raised by the alleged failure of reason, and in fact CLS scholars are admittedly not concerned with finding one: CLS is a critical school of thought with no interest in redeeming legal practice from the charge of illegitimate policy-making. CLS scholars generally do not believe that this is at all possible: for them the law is irredeemably political. But for those who are interested in a positive proposal—like the conservative opponents of the liberal Warren Court—the rejection of broad judicial discretion is a natural corollary of their skepticism. If there are no objectively rational solutions to questions of public policy and morality, so that any such deliberations are irremediably a matter of mere ideology, eliminating broad judicial discretion is the way to go.

18   MAX WEBER, ECONOMY AND SOCIETY 813 (Guenther Roth & Claus Wittich eds., 1968) (originally published posthumously in 1922).

19   *See generally* KARL POPPER, THE OPEN SOCIETY AND ITS ENEMIES (5th ed. 1966). Liberal business magnate George Soros named his "Open Society Foundations" after Popper's book.

20   *See* POPPER, n. 186–87 and accompanying text. This idea also underlies the modern political philosophy of "deliberative democracy." *See, e.g.*, JÜRGEN HABERMAS, BETWEEN FACTS AND NORMS (William Rehg trans., 1996).

21   *See, e.g.*, Linda Greenhouse, *A Conservative Plan to Weaponize the Federal Courts*, N.Y. TIMES, May 23, 2017; Randy E. Barnett, *Judicial Conservatism v. A Principled Judicial Activism: Foreword to the 'Symposium on Law and Philosophy,'* 10 HARV. J. L. & PUB. POL'Y 273 (1987).

22   *See, e.g.*, *Cameron v. Auto Club Ins Assn*, 476 Mich. 55 (2006) (holding that Michigan law allows people to file a lawsuit against insurance companies that fail to pay benefits due under insurance policies, but that they are barred from recovering any damages for their loss); *Devillers v. Auto Club Ins Assn*, 473 Mich. 562 (2005) (holding that a plaintiff was precluded from recovering unpaid medical bills from his insurance company because the suit was filed too late, although the lawsuit was filed within weeks of the insurance company's notification of denial of coverage).

23   *See, e.g.*, *Bowles v. Russell*, 551 U.S. 205, 215 (2007) (holding that a man lost his right to appeal a murder conviction after his lawyer followed the erroneous instruction of a federal judge regarding the deadline for submitting the notice of appeal).

24   *See, e.g.*, *People v. Chavis*, 468 Mich. 84 (2003) (holding that a man who complained of a violent robbery but, for obvious reasons, omitted to disclose that he was buying drugs at the time, could be convicted of a felony for intentionally making a false report of the commission

of a crime). The decision, which employed a textualist methodology that refused to consider the consequences of the decision, essentially removed police protection from individuals engaged in criminal activities unless they were willing to confess to committing crimes.

Review Questions

Chapter 1.
Introduction: The U.S. Constitution and Constitutional Interpretation

1. Why was the Bill of Rights originally binding only on the federal government?
2. Why are judicial decisions so central to American constitutional law?
3. What are some of the methodological questions that judges face when they make constitutional decisions?
4. Why is judicial philosophy a *prologue* to all legal decisions?
5. Why is judicial philosophy usually a *silent* prologue?
6. What are the main criteria for evaluating judicial philosophies?
7. In what ways do these criteria pull in opposite directions?
8. What is the power of judicial review?
9. What are the arguments for judicial review?
10. What are the arguments against judicial review?
11. Why does the legitimacy of judicial review depend upon the judicial philosophies that judges use?

Chapter 2.
The Rise and Fall of Natural Law: The Controversy Surrounding Incorporation Doctrine, and The Right to a Trial By Jury

1. What are the basic tenets of natural law theory?
2. What are the reasons for the decline of natural law theory?
3. Why did the decline of natural law theory bring the delegitimization of the use of morality in legal interpretation? Do you agree with that delegitimization?

4. Why was the Supreme Court reluctant to make the Bill of Rights binding on the states?
5. Why did the Supreme Court eventually change its decision on this matter?
6. What is the process called "incorporation" and what explains its name?
7. In what way did incorporation doctrine resemble natural law theory?
8. How did incorporation doctrine change in response to that criticism, and what were the consequences of that change?
9. Why is jury nullification an alleged offense to democracy?
10. What are the justifications for jury nullification?
11. Do you think that lawyers should be allowed to argue for jury nullification to juries? Why?
12. Why can courts overrule jury convictions but not jury acquittals?
13. Should convicted defendants be able to challenge jury verdicts by relying on the mental incompetence of jurors?

Chapter 3.
The Debate Over Unenumerated Constitutional Rights: The Ninth Amendment, Substantive Due Process, and The Right to Not Be Executed If Innocent

1. Why are substantive due process rights controversial?
2. How do unenumerated constitutional rights relate to natural law theory?
3. What are the objections to unenumerated constitutional rights?
4. What are the justifications for unenumerated constitutional rights?
5. What was the purpose of the Ninth Amendment?
6. Why do courts hold that the Ninth Amendment is unenforceable?
7. How did the Supreme Court avoid the constitutional question presented in *Herrera v. Collins*, 506 U.S. 390 (1993)?

8. What are the two conflicting visions of constitutional interpretation in the debate between the majority and the dissent in *Herrera v. Collins*, 506 U.S. 390 (1993)?

9. Explain how the *Herrera* decision prevented the constitutional invalidation of the death penalty on the theory advanced in *United States v. Quinones*, 205 F. Supp. 2d 256 (S.D.N.Y. 2002).

Chapter 4.
The Role of History in Constitutional Interpretation: The First Amendment and Unprotected Speech

1. Explain the difference between comprehensive judicial philosophies and localized judicial philosophies.

2. What are the advantages of historical constitutional tests?

3. What is the critique of historical constitutional tests?

4. Name some unprotected categories of speech.

5. What was the constitutional test adopted by *United States v. Stevens*, 559 U.S. 460 (2010) for distinguishing between protected and unprotected categories of speech?

6. How was that test different than the test proposed by the government?

7. Which test do you think is better? Why? Do the facts involved in *United States v. Stevens*, 559 U.S. 460 (2010) influence your conclusion?

8. What are the reasons for providing constitutional protections for factual lies?

9. Can you explain why the majority and the dissent in *United States v. Alvarez*, 567 U.S. 709 (2012) reached different conclusions under the historical test?

10. What are the values or policy judgments that led the two concurring justices in *United States v. Alvarez*, 567 U.S. 709 (2012) to conclude that the Stolen Valor Act was unconstitutional?

11. Do you think that the plurality and the dissent also considered values or policy judgments in reaching their respective conclusions? What were they, in your opinion?

Chapter 5.
The Rationality of History and Tradition:
The Equal Protection Clause and
The Right to Same-Sex Marriage

1. Can you articulate the basic requirement of the Equal Protection Clause?
2. What is the precise constitutional argument alleging that prohibiting same-sex marriage is in violation of the Equal Protection Clause?
3. Why was it so important that the Supreme Court, in *Lawrence v. Texas*, 539 U.S. 558 (2003), removed moral disapproval as a valid constitutional basis for discriminating against homosexuals?
4. What were the justifications advanced by the states for the prohibition on same-sex marriage? Do you find the justifications rational?
5. Do you think that rationality should be a constitutional requirement? Why?
6. Do you think that traditions should receive special constitutional solicitude? Why?
7. Why do conservatives venerate traditions?
8. How does public choice theory support the claim that judges should not invalidate statutes for being irrational?
9. Assuming that the democratic process can produce irrational statutes, do you think that judges should have the authority to declare such statutes unconstitutional? Explain.

Chapter 6.
Classic Originalism: The Second Amendment, 18th Century Dictionaries, and Semiautomatic Glocks

1. What is the principal justification for classic originalism?
2. What role does the purpose of constitutional provisions play in originalist interpretation? Why?
3. What are the reasons, according to the critics of originalism, for the theory's failure to constrain judicial discretion? Name a few.
4. What are the two dimensions with which we can evaluate the merit of originalism as a judicial philosophy?
5. Assuming that the critics of originalism are correct, and originalism fails to constrain judicial discretion to the degree that it claims: How do you think originalism fares as a judicial philosophy? Why?
6. Explain the claim that originalism is less transparent than other judicial philosophies. Do you agree?
7. What is the doctrine of *stare decisis*? Do you agree with its requirements? How does it increase judicial discretion under originalist methodology?
8. Why should judges adhere to one judicial philosophy?

Chapter 7.
New Originalism and Moral Truths: The Cruel and Unusual Punishment Clause, and Ear Cropping for Overtime Parking

1. Do you think that the prohibition on Cruel and Unusual Punishment also prohibits punishments that are disproportionate to the crime? What is the basis for your belief?
2. Why does an originalist interpretation of the Eighth Amendment's Cruel and Unusual Punishment Clause allegedly negate a constitutional proportionality requirement?

3. Does such an interpretation follow the classic originalism, or the new originalism?
4. On what points do the classic originalists and the new originalists agree?
5. On what points do the classic originalists and the new originalists disagree?
6. Which do you think is the more proper originalism, and why?
7. How would a classic originalist determine whether Cruel and Unusual Punishment prohibits ear cropping? How would a new originalist make that determination?
8. How do the new originalists justify the originalist methodology?
9. Why might it matter for constitutional doctrine if moral positions can be true or false? Do you think it matters?

Chapter 8.
Statutory Interpretation, Deviations From Clear Statutory Texts, and Correction of Legislative Mistakes: Exempting Atheists From the Foxholes

1. What is the principal interest protected by the Free Exercise Clause?
2. What is the principal interest protected by the Establishment Clause?
3. What is the argument for the claim that Seeger was entitled to declare a conscientious objection under the Free Exercise Clause, and why is it a weak constitutional argument?
4. Why does the Free Exercise Clause forbid laws that *intentionally* stifle religious practice, but not laws that stifle religious practices unintentionally?
5. What is the argument for the claim that Seeger was entitled to declare his conscientious objection under the Free Establishment Clause?
6. What is the "avoidance doctrine"?

7. Why is the reach of the avoidance doctrine dependent on the judicial philosophy that a judge employs?
8. What is the principal thesis of textualism?
9. What is the principal thesis of purposivism?
10. Why were the *Seeger* and *Welsh* opinions mistaken from a textualist perspective?
11. Do you think that judges should be authorized, or even required, to correct legislative mistakes?
12. What are the dangers of such broad judicial authority?
13. In what way was Alexander Hamilton's view of judicial power broader than purposivism?

Chapter 9.
Textualism v. Purposivism: The Fourth Amendment and The Constitutionality of Pretextual Arrests

1. What are the main arguments against judges relying on legislative purpose or intent when interpreting statutes?
2. What was the historical purpose of the Fourth Amendment?
3. Why is Fourth Amendment doctrine so controversial? What are the opposing interests implicated in Fourth Amendment decisions?
4. In what way did the Supreme Court rely on textualist principles in *Ashcroft v. al-Kidd*, 563 U.S. 731 (2011)?
5. Do you think that the Court correctly applied the Material Witness Statute in *Ashcroft v. al-Kidd*, 563 U.S. 731 (2011)? Why?
6. Why is it that, even if the Material Witness Statute authorized the arrest and detention of Abdullah al-Kidd, it was still possible that al-Kidd's arrest and detention were unconstitutional?
7. Explain how John Ashcroft's directive, claiming that the Drug Abuse Prevention and Control Act prevented doctors from complying with Oregon's Death with Dignity Act, derived from textualist principles.

8. Explain how the Supreme Court's refusal to invalidate Donald Trump's travel ban derived from textualist principles.

9. What are some of the constitutional protections that might be impacted if the courts refuse to examine legislative purposes?

Chapter 10.
Textualism, Purposivism, and Pragmatism: Judicial Legislation and The Politicization of Judicial Election Campaigns

1. What do you think is the purpose of electing judges? Is it a good idea?

2. What was the purpose of Minnesota's announce clause?

3. Why, according to textualists, are there gaps in the law? What creates those gaps?

4. What, according to textualists, are the two modes of judicial decision-making?

5. Why do you think judges might be reluctant to admit that they make law?

6. What were the opposing constitutional interests that clashed in *Republican Party of Minnesota v. White*, 536 U.S. 765 (2002)?

7. Why do politicized election campaigns pose no danger to textualist judicial decision-making?

8. Why do politicized election campaigns pose a danger to non-textualist judicial decision-making?

9. What is the democratic advantage of politicized judicial election campaigns according to textualism?

10. Why are there no democratic advantages to politicized judicial election campaigns according to non-textualists?

11. Articulate the fundamental position of legal pragmatism that is presented in the chapter. Do you find it convincing?

12. What are the possible ramifications for our understanding of law and legal practice if this understanding of legal pragmatism is correct?

Chapter 11.
Conclusion: Judicial Philosophies and Political Ideologies

1. What is the historical explanation for the correlation between political *ideologies* and judicial *philosophies*?
2. Why is broad judicial discretion a matter of particular concern in modern times, as opposed to earlier times?
3. Why does conservatism accord special deference to traditions?
4. In what way does Western Enlightenment dispute this conservative deference?
5. Explain how conservative principles might lead jurists to adopt judicial philosophies like textualism or originalism.
6. What are the dangers of broad judicial discretion?
7. What are the benefits of broad judicial discretion?
8. What are the benefits of narrow judicial discretion?
9. What are the dangers of narrow judicial discretion?

Table of Cases

Grand Rapids Sch. Dist. v. Ball, 473 U.S. 373 (1985), 218

Griffin v. Illinois, 351 U.S. 12 (1956), 222

Griswold v. Connecticut, 381 U.S. 479 (1965), 194, 196–198, 206, 222

H.P. Hood & Sons v. Du Mond, 336 U.S. 525 (1949), 198

Hamilton v. Lanning, 560 U.S. 505 (2010), 219

Harmelin v. Michigan, 501 U.S. 957 (1991), 117–118, 208–210, 215

Harper v. Virginia State Bd. of Elections, 383 U.S. 663 (1966), 203

Heath v. White, 5 Conn. 228 (1824), 193

Hedgepeth v. Wash. Metro. Area Transit Auth., 386 F.3d 1148 (D.C. Cir. 2004), 216

Herrera v. Collins, 506 U.S. 390 (1993), 49–53, 199, 201

Herring v. United States, 555 U.S. 135 (2009), 216

Holy Trinity Church v. United States, 143 U.S. 457 (1892), 215

House v. Bell, 547 U.S. 518 (2006), 201

In re Winship, 397 U.S. 358 (1970), 201

Jones v. Jones, 2 Tenn. 2 (Tenn. Super. L. & Eq. 1804), 193

Jones, United States v., 565 U.S. 400 (2012), 99, 208

Juliana v. United States, 217 F. Supp. 3d 1224, 1238 (D. Or. 2016), 198

Katzenbach v. McClung, 379 U.S. 294 (1964), 206

Kauten, United States v., 133 F.2d 203 (2d. Cir. 1943), 212

Kennedy v. Louisiana, 554 U.S. 407 (2008), 211

Kilham v. Ward, 2 Mass. 236 (1806), 193

Kirby, United States v., 74 U.S. 482 (1868), 219

Kleinman, United States v., 880 F.3d 1020 (9th Cir. 2017), 195

Lawrence v. Texas, 539 U.S. 558 (2003), 75, 196, 203–204

Lee, United States v., 455 U.S 252 (1982), 212

Lockyer v. Andrade, 538 U.S. 63 (2003), 212

Loving v. Virginia, 388 U.S. 1 (1967), 80

Lozman v. City of Riviera Beach, 138 S.Ct. 1945 (2018), 218

Luther v. Borden, 48 U.S. 1 (1849), 198

M.L.B. v. S.L.J., 519 U.S. 102 (1996), 203

Malloy v. Hogan, 378 U.S. 1 (1964), 194

Mapp v. Ohio, 367 U.S. 643 (1961), 215, 222

Marsh v. Chambers, 463 U.S. 783 (1983), 209

Massachusetts v. E.P.A., 549 U.S. 497 (2007), 211

McCreary County, Ky. v. American Civil Liberties Union of Ky., 545 U.S. 844 (2005). 219

McCullen v. Coakley, 573 U.S. 464 (2014), 191

Index